Postcard History Series

The South Bay

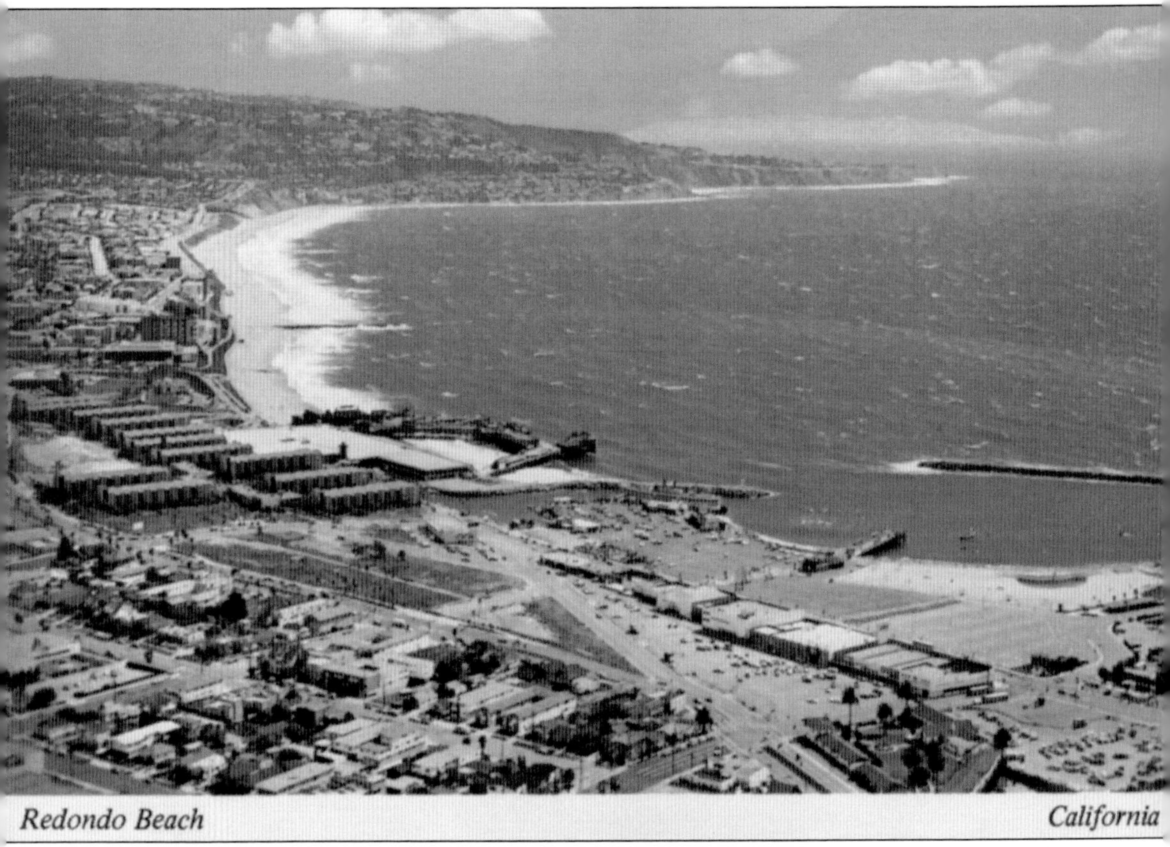

This aerial view of Redondo Beach and whitecap-filled South Santa Monica Bay points southwest, over Palos Verdes Peninsula and toward Santa Catalina Island. The reverse-side caption points out Fisherman's Wharf and the Princess Louise Ship Restaurant. (Courtesy Marilyn Ron; published by the Continental Card, Mike Roberts, Berkeley, California.)

On the Cover: The front cover depicts a northward view of Pacific waves rolling ashore from the vantage point of what is today Palos Verdes Estates. The resort area to the right in what is today south Redondo Beach was once known as Clifton by the Sea, home of the Sea Gull Inn, which the map on the back cover points out. Also marked on the back cover are the Palos Verdes Peninsula, Redondo Beach, Lawndale, Torrance, Gardena, Los Angeles Harbor, and, at the top left and 20 miles distant, downtown Los Angeles. (Both, courtesy Marilyn Ron.)

POSTCARD HISTORY SERIES

The South Bay

James Osborne, Marilyn Ron, and Jerry Roberts

ARCADIA
PUBLISHING

ISBN 978-0-7385-6905-5

Published by Arcadia Publishing
Charleston, South Carolina

Printed in the United States of America

Library of Congress Control Number: 2008941505

For all general information contact Arcadia Publishing at:
Telephone 843-853-2070
Fax 843-853-0044
E-mail sales@arcadiapublishing.com
For customer service and orders:
Toll-Free 1-888-313-2665

Visit us on the Internet at www.arcadiapublishing.com

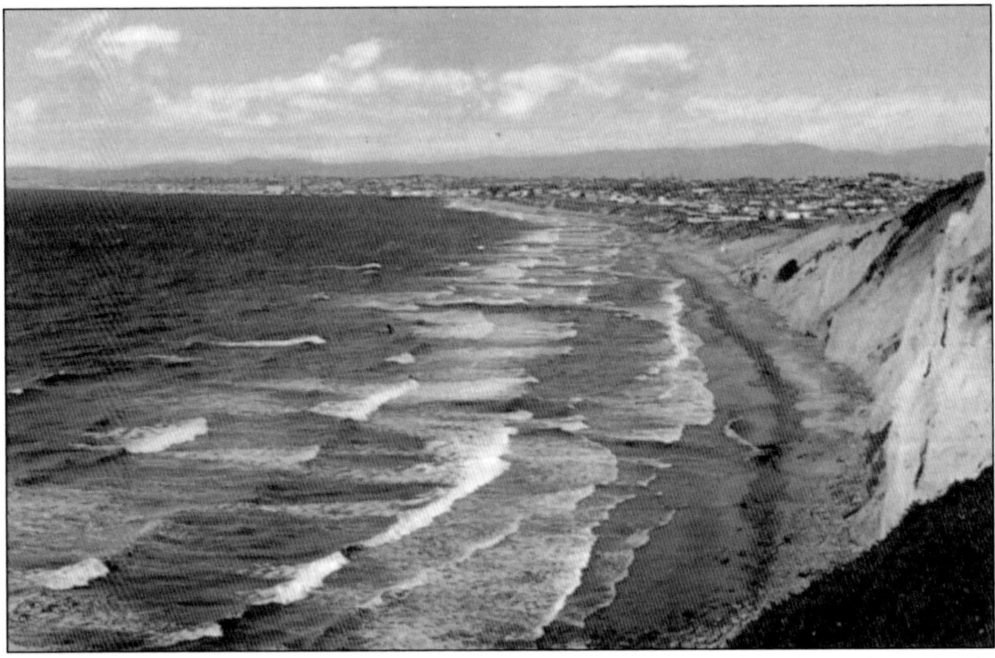

Similar to the view on the book's front cover, this image was taken from the Palos Verdes Peninsula, showing Redondo Beach and, as the shoreline diminishes north and to the left, Hermosa Beach and Manhattan Beach. Postmarked on October 14, 1955, the card's message carries a complaint from one "Nathan" to his mother in Alameda, California, that the area is either "dull and smoggy or very hot." Perhaps Nathan moved to Iowa. (Courtesy Marilyn Ron, published by Color Photo by George E. Watson.)

Contents

Acknowledgments

The authors would like to acknowledge the following persons for their help and goodwill toward the completion of this project: Bill Ron of Bill Ron Bicycles in Redondo Beach, the late Helen Buss Thomas, Laura Osborne, Keith Nelson, Devon Weston, and Joanne Mallillin.

The majority of the postcards are owned by Lawndale City councilman James Osborne and by Marilyn Ron of Antique Attic in Old Torrance. Individual ownership is noted at the end of each caption.

While our bibliography contains recent works, the authors would also like to extend their gratitude to the efforts of past writers of South Bay history, particularly Jack Jerrils (1972) and Charlotte Trejos (1987) on Carson; Eileen Curry Hunter (1991) on El Segundo; Olive Hensel Leonard and Emily D. Cost (1934) on Gardena; Robert S. Hartman (1972) and Douglas T. Robertson (1987) on Hawthorne; Fern Rhein (1933) and Patricia A. Gazin (1991) on Hermosa Beach; Gladys Waddingham (1994) on Inglewood; James Carr (1975), Thomas G. P. Hansen and Robert P. Kruse (1979), and James Osborne (2004) on Lawndale; Jim Cole (2007) on Lomita; Jan Dennis (1987) and Bonnie Beckerson (2000) on Manhattan Beach; Augusta Fink (1966) and Delane Morgan (1983) on Palos Verdes Peninsula; Curt R. Richardson (1982), Dennis Shanahan (1982), and Michael H. McCandless (2000) on Redondo Beach; Roland G. Swaffield (1958) and A. E. Hanson (1978) on Rolling Hills; Henry P. Silka (1993) and Michael D. White (2008) on San Pedro; Dennis Shanahan and Chuck Elliot (1984), Peggy Coleman Dalton (1990), and Thomas Rische (2002) on Torrance; and Robert Cameron Gillingham (1961), William M. Mason (1991), Lorietta Louise Scheerer (1938), Donn Benjamin Tatum Jr., (1968), and Ann Elizabeth Wiedel (1980) on the rancho era. Among the places where these writers' books can be found are in the Palos Verdes Library District's Local History Collection, the El Segundo Public Library's Local History Room, the Centinela Adobe in Inglewood, and in the reference stacks at the Katy Geissert Civic Center Library in Torrance.

If the postcards carried a publisher's name and location, those were noted in the courtesy line.

Introduction

The South Bay historically has been as varied and picturesque in its landscapes as anywhere in Los Angeles County, with beautiful beaches, rolling ranchlands, precipitous sea cliffs, and vast flatlands. Some vistas remain in the areas that today are generally defined with a map glance as south of the Century Freeway (I-105) and west of the Los Angeles River. The region has been vital and important to the fortunes of Greater L.A. Important gains were made here in agriculture, transportation, petroleum, aviation, tourism, entertainment, and real estate.

South Bay cities have contained some of the nation's prime real estate as well as great swaths of industrialization—surrounded after World War II by the incrementally perpetuating suburban sprawl. Today's two cities in the region with more than 100,000 residents, Inglewood and Torrance, grew as models of postwar suburbia. Angelenos who do not live here often associate the region mostly with the picturesque oceanfront cities of Manhattan Beach, Hermosa Beach, and Redondo Beach or the affluent environs of the Palos Verdes Peninsula. Others only enter the South Bay for its two great portals of entry/exit and import/export on either end: Los Angeles International Airport on the seacoast to the north of El Segundo and the Port of Los Angeles on San Pedro Bay to the south, just east of Palos Verdes.

After the rancho period and a scant decade after the 1848 Treaty of Guadalupe Hidalgo ceded California to the United States, entrepreneur Phineas Banning founded the town of Wilmington on San Pedro Bay as one of only three outposts—including Los Angeles and El Monte—in all of what is today L.A. County. The Los Angeles and San Pedro Railway began operating in 1869.

The South Bay in the front half of the 20th century was heavily impacted by the Industrial Revolution as the Southern Pacific became the main cargo line and the Pacific Electric "Red Cars" became the region's chief passenger trolley system. Truck farming developed in Gardena; poultry raising in Inglewood, Lawndale, and Torrance; and flower farming on Palos Verdes and in other areas.

World War II created a paradigm shift in Southern California culture. The influx of families from other parts of the country and the growth of the aforementioned industries filled in the rural lands in a few decades. A few fast facts will help the reader get a sense of the cities of the South Bay. The years in parentheses are incorporation dates; the four intertwining Palos Verdes Peninsula cities were incorporated thusly: Palos Verdes Estates (1939), Rolling Hills (1957), Rolling Hills Estates (1957), and Rancho Palos Verdes (1973). San Pedro and Wilmington are large neighborhoods of the city of Los Angeles proper.

Carson (1968). *Name:* In 1857, namesake George Henry Carson married Maria Victoria Dominguez of the Dominguez Rancho family; they had 15 children. *Fame:* Academy Award–winning actor Forest Whitaker grew up here. *Game:* Carson is the mooring grounds of the Goodyear Blimp.

El Segundo (1917). *Name:* A tent city sprouted after 1911 when Standard Oil established the second ("El Segundo" in Spanish) refinery on the West Coast. *Fame:* The El Segundo blue butterfly is a poster insect for conservation. *Game:* Baseball Hall of Famer George Brett grew up here.

Gardena (1930). *Name:* The Dominguez Slough provided moisture for this "garden spot," but the exact nomenclature has not been thoroughly accredited, even to founder Abram Ehle Pomeroy. *Fame:* Residents included jazz sax–man Art Pepper and actress Polly Bergen. *Game:* Legalized casinos have been a huge draw.

HAWTHORNE (1922). *Name:* Laurine Woolwine, daughter of founder B. L. Harding, shared her July 4 birthday with novelist Nathaniel Hawthorne. *Fame:* Marilyn Monroe and the Beach Boys were raised here. *Game:* Mattel was founded in the city, debuting the Barbie Doll in 1959.

HERMOSA BEACH (1907). *Name:* Who did the naming is a mystery, but the why is very understandable: "Hermosa" is Spanish for beautiful. *Fame:* The greatest jazz names for a generation played Howard Rumsey's Lighthouse: Gillespie, Parker, Davis. *Game:* The Surfers Walk of Fame is located on the pier.

INGLEWOOD (1908). *Name:* Founder Daniel Freeman's city was once believed to have been named for a town in his native Ontario, Canada. *Fame:* The Hollywood list includes Esther Williams, Jeanne Crain, and Tyra Banks. *Game:* Hollywood Park Race Track is adjacent to the Great Western Forum, former home of the L.A. Lakers.

LAWNDALE (1959). *Name:* Founder Charles B. Hopper established the town in 1905 and named it after a Chicago suburb. *Fame:* Leonard Slye lived in town for a time and later changed his name to Roy Rogers. *Game:* Baseball slugger George Foster and L.A. Rams defensive end Fred Dryer attended Lawndale schools.

LOMITA (1964). *Name:* A surveyor's map of the Rancho San Pedro labeled the area "Lomita del Toro" or Little Hill of the Bull. *Fame:* The Lomita Railroad Museum, built in 1966, was the first of its kind on the West Coast. *Game:* One of America's greatest all-around athletes, Jim Thorpe, lived and died (1953) in Lomita.

MANHATTAN BEACH (1912). *Name:* Landowners George Peck and John Merrill flipped a coin around 1902; Manhattan beat out "Shore Acres." *Fame: Pulp Fiction* (1994) filmmakers Quentin Tarantino and Roger Avary clerked at the city's former Video Archives. *Game:* MB rivals Hermosa as beach volleyball heaven.

PALOS VERDES PENINSULA. *Name:* Don Jose Sepulveda in 1827 named it Rancho de los Palos Verdes or "Range of Green Trees." *Fame:* Swashbuckling financier Donald Trump opened Trump National Golf Club in 2000. *Game:* Champions include NFL's Joe Montana, USC's Pete Carroll, and NBA's Bill Laimbeer.

REDONDO BEACH (1892). *Name:* The original Rancho Sausal Redondo is translated from the Spanish as a ranch of pastures with a round willow grove. *Fame:* The Smothers Brothers, Demi Moore, and Ron Kovic have abided here. *Game:* George Freeth, who popularized surfing on the West Coast, was a resident.

SAN PEDRO. *Name:* "Pee-dro" was named by Spanish explorers after St. Peter of Alexandria, a fourth-century bishop. *Fame:* Authors include Richard Henry Dana, Louis L'Amour, Charles Bukowski, and Robert Towne. *Game:* Former Boston Celtics Willie Naulls and Dennis "DJ" Johnson have Pedro roots.

TORRANCE (1921). *Name:* Jared S. Torrance founded the town in 1911 specifically as the "Modern Industrial City." *Fame:* The range is wide, from Academy Award winner Denzel Washington to Chuck Norris. *Game:* For role models, it is hard to beat Torrance's own renowned figure skater, Michelle Kwan.

WILMINGTON. *Name:* "Father of the Los Angeles Harbor" Phineas Banning was born in Wilmington, Delaware, in 1830. *Fame:* Chewing gum tycoon William Wrigley nurtured the Banning Wrigley Historic District. *Game:* Banning High turned out pro football stars Vince Ferragamo and Freeman McNeil.

Defining the South Bay has depended on who drew the boundaries. It has been defined by the South Bay Council of Governments and the *Daily Breeze* newspaper's coverage area. Configurations through the years have included selective utility coverage, often depicted on telephone book covers.

The south and west boundaries are not issues as the shoreline is definite. In the east, the Long Beach border is definite. For the purposes of this collection, the northern extents of the South Bay include El Segundo and Inglewood, but not Westchester, LAX, or Compton. The postcards are arranged alphabetically by city within their respective chapters.

One

Beach Cities

Recreational visitors to the South Bay often equate the name for the region with its famous beach cities: Manhattan Beach, Hermosa Beach, and Redondo Beach, from north to south. Not surprisingly, most historic South Bay postcards depict the coast, particularly Hermosa but overwhelmingly Redondo.

Manhattan has evolved unto itself as an increasingly affluent community. Hermosa inherited the mantel of party town from early Redondo. In the 1950s, the Lighthouse in Hermosa enjoyed a reputation as the incubation chamber for West Coast jazz, and across Pier Avenue, the Insomniac was one of Southern California's counterculture hangouts. Redondo, which became a huge weekend resort city for Hollywood in the first half of the 20th century, is the largest beach city as well, in terms of population (about 63,000) and size (6.4 square miles).

The fourth city on top of this stack is El Segundo, which has fostered and maintained a small-town feel with tree-lined streets and mom-and pop businesses, even as its lands border Los Angeles International Airport to the north, and it contains the headquarters or major facilities of such worldwide corporate giants as Chevron, Boeing, Lockheed Martin, Raytheon, Northrop Grumman, Mattel, Xerox, and Hughes, as well as the Los Angeles Lakers of the NBA.

The wealth of postcards representing Redondo owes to the early-20th-century trend in postcards at a time when the city was a prime resort for Angelenos and the Hollywood crowd. The Roaring Twenties included Prohibition ("enforced" in the United States from 1920 to 1933), when Redondo was the southern terminus of the Pacific Electric "Red Car" line, far away from big-city strictures. This was when the "Plunge," a huge indoor pool and diving facility, and tycoon Henry Huntington's Hotel Redondo, an enormous resort, were in vogue. And, to borrow a phrase, what happened in Redondo, stayed in Redondo.

The authors largely eschewed repeating beach-area postcards that were collected in Arcadia Publishing's Postcard History Series, namely the Redondo Beach Historical Commission's *Redondo Beach* and Chris Miller, Jerry Roberts, and the Hermosa Beach Historical Society's *Hermosa Beach*. Postcards representing Manhattan Beach and especially El Segundo have been few.

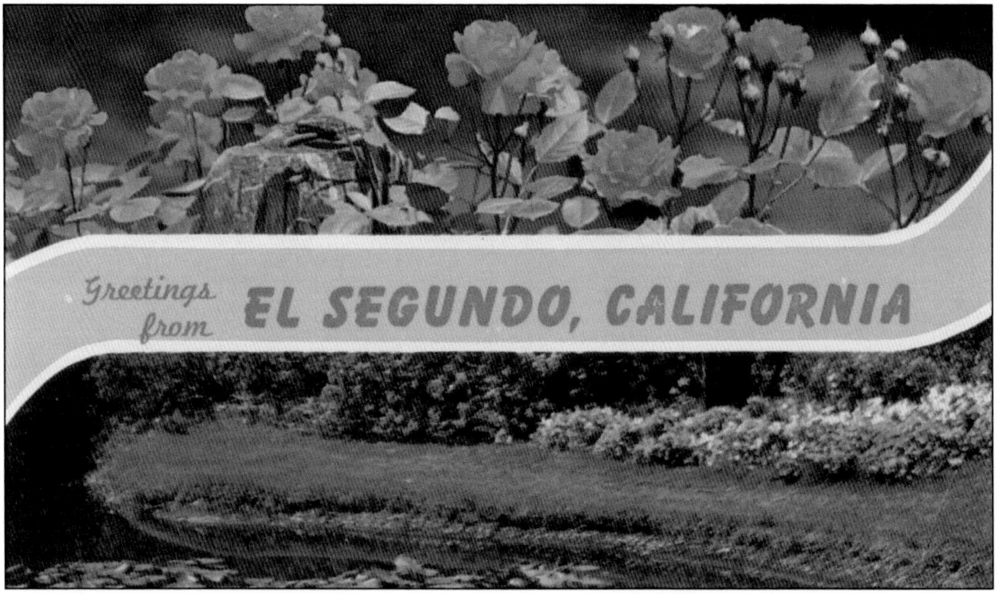

These flowers are rather picturesque on this "Greetings from El Segundo, California," postcard. (Courtesy James Osborne; published by Dexter Press, Inc., West Nyack, New York.)

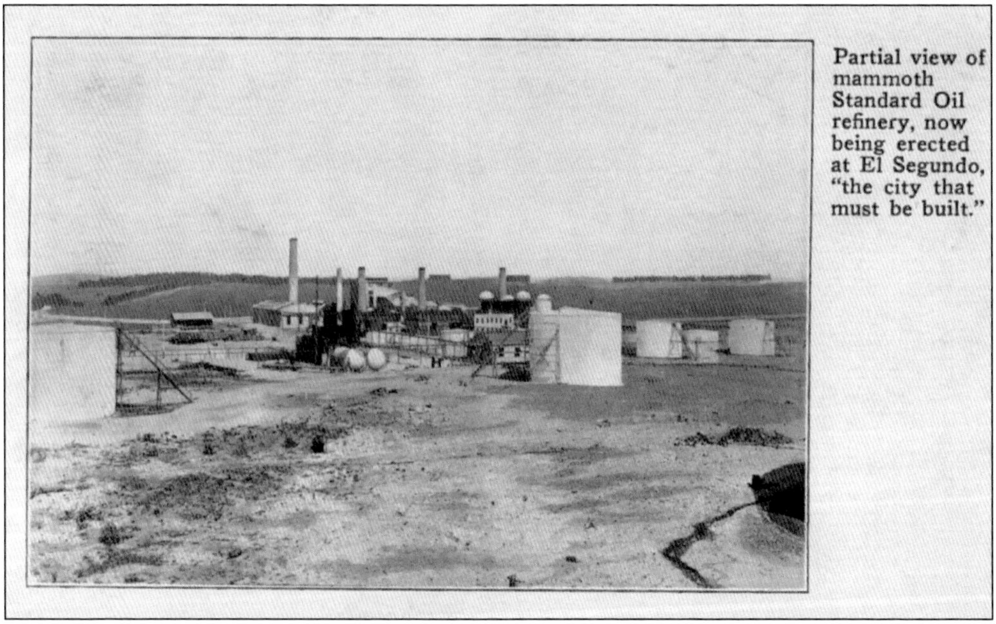

The caption on the reverse of this postcard reads, "El Segundo, Cal. Simply MUST go ahead. Every advantage and condition exists for its permanent progress. El Segundo has already attained tremendous momentum and nothing can stop it. The establishing of the Standard Oil Company's great refinery has created splendid values at El Segundo, but the pouring in of new industries, which is bound to result from the many permanent industries to be obtained by the manufacturer locating there, will increase realty values beyond the fondest hopes of any of the hundreds who have already purchased property here. Nothing in or near Los Angeles presents such attractive investment possibilities as lots or acreage at El Segundo." (Courtesy James Osborne; published by the Neuner Company, Los Angeles, California.)

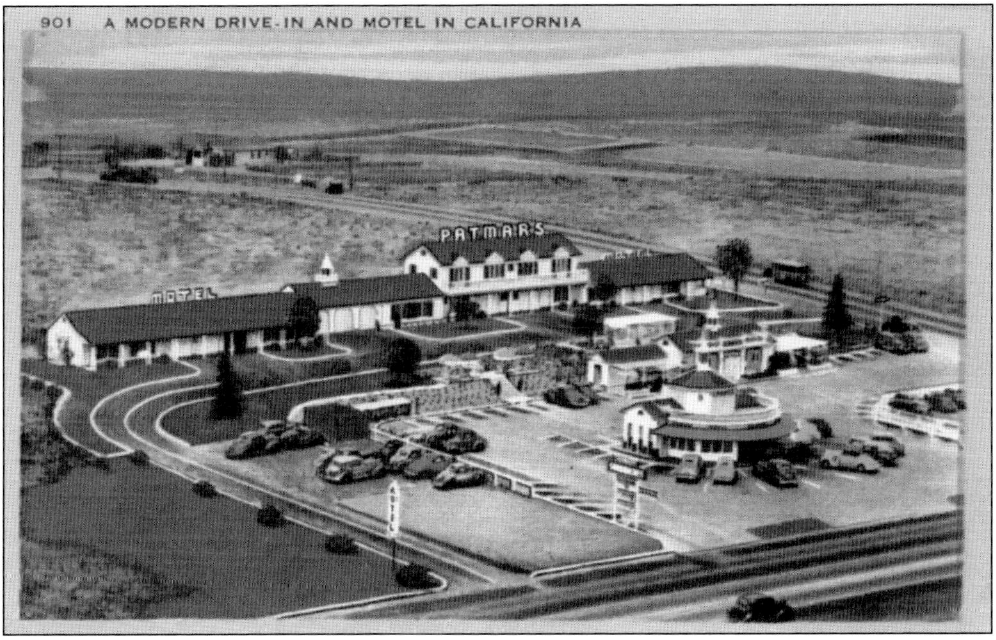

This linen-era postcard depicts Patmar's drive-in and motel, which was located at the corner of Imperial Highway and Sepulveda Boulevard. H. B. Patrick and Norman Marsh built the drive-in in 1939. Patmar's survived until 1959, when it was sold to developers. (Courtesy James Osborne; published by Longshaw Card Company, Los Angeles, California.)

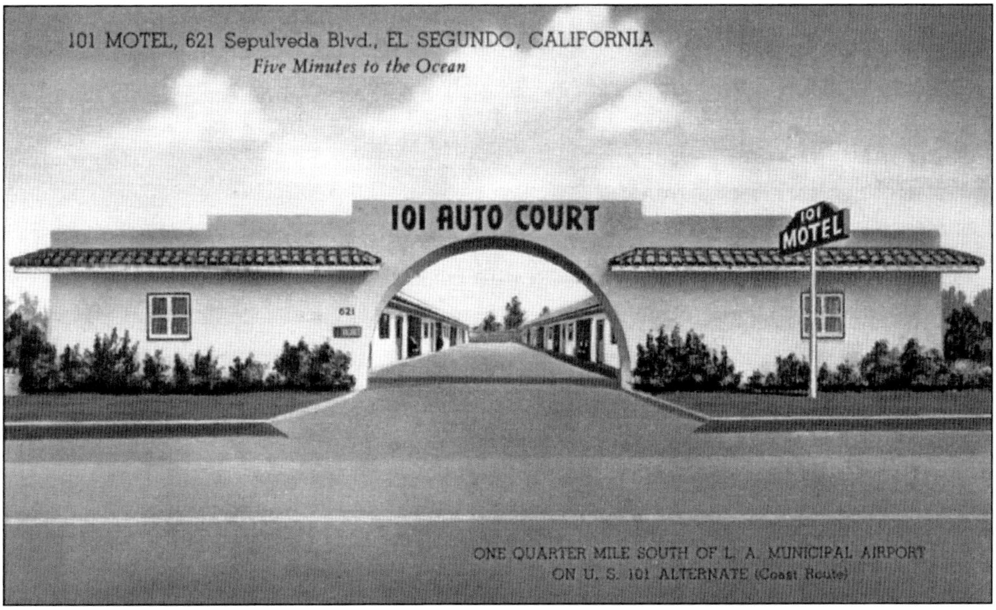

The caption on the reverse of this postcard reads, "101 Motel, 16 attractively furnished deluxe hotel apartments, individual and family type, with and without completely equipped kitchens. Attractive garages. Radio in each unit. Tiled baths. Near the beaches, airport, motion picture studios and Catalina Island terminal. Thirty minutes to Los Angeles and Hollywood. Café and service station next door. Mail address, 621 Sepulveda Blvd., El Segundo, California. Complete overnight car service." (Courtesy James Osborne; published by ASCO, Oakland, California.)

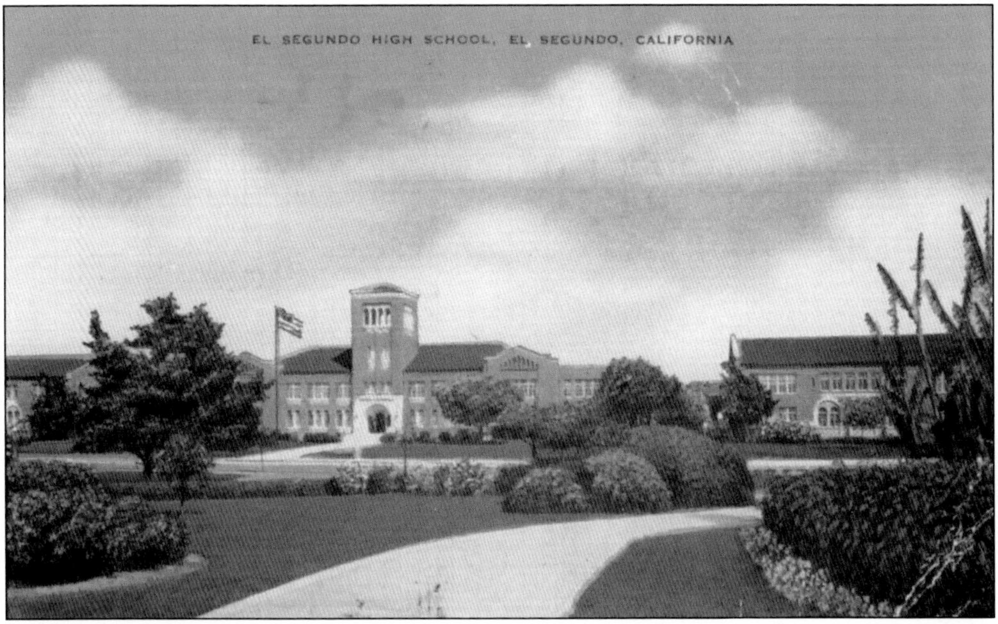

"El Segundo (pop. 7,000) is situated 17 miles southwest of Los Angeles, one mile from the ocean," reads the reverse of this postcard. "El Segundo Unified School District, with a total assessed value of $16,000,000, has expended more than $1,500,000 on buildings and ground. In 1947 the school enrollment was approximately 1,400. The high school campus includes home making and ship building, a gymnasium and an athletic field with football stadium." (Courtesy James Osborne; published by the El Segundo Parent-Teacher Association.)

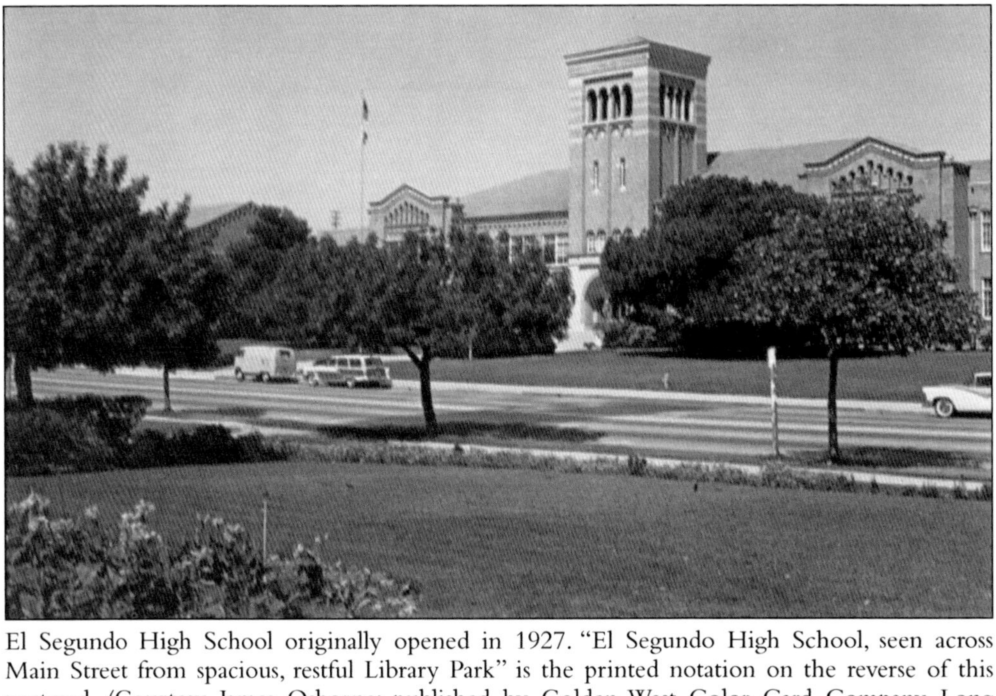

El Segundo High School originally opened in 1927. "El Segundo High School, seen across Main Street from spacious, restful Library Park" is the printed notation on the reverse of this postcard. (Courtesy James Osborne; published by Golden West Color Card Company, Long Beach, California.)

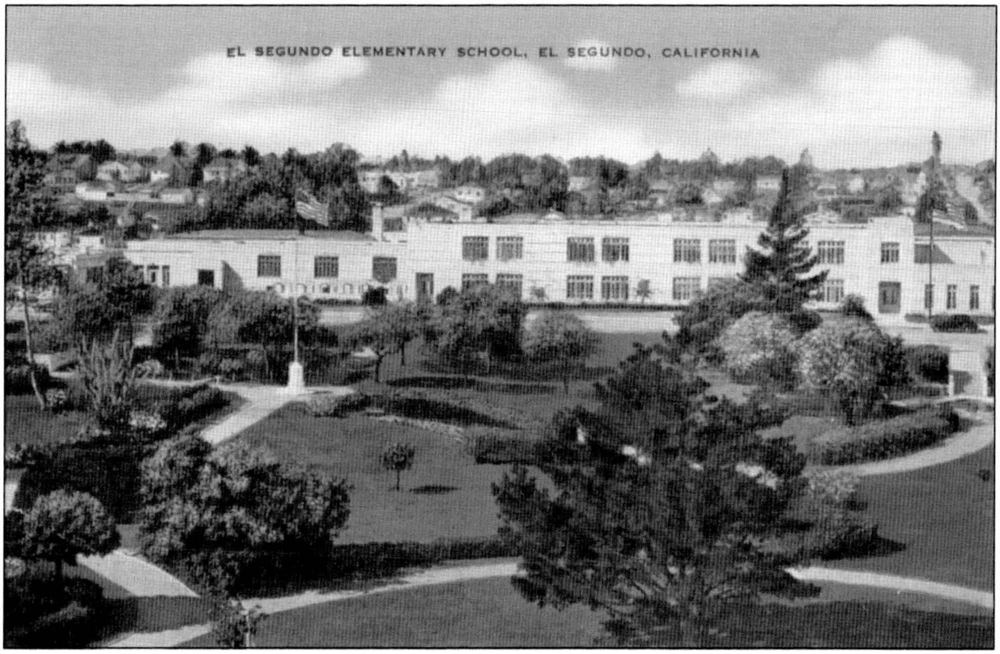

"The elementary campus includes a main building, a kindergarten unit, a plunge building, a recreation center, and a nursery school," reads a portion of the reverse side of this postcard. "All but the recreation center have been built since 1936." (Courtesy James Osborne; published by the El Segundo Parent-Teacher Association.)

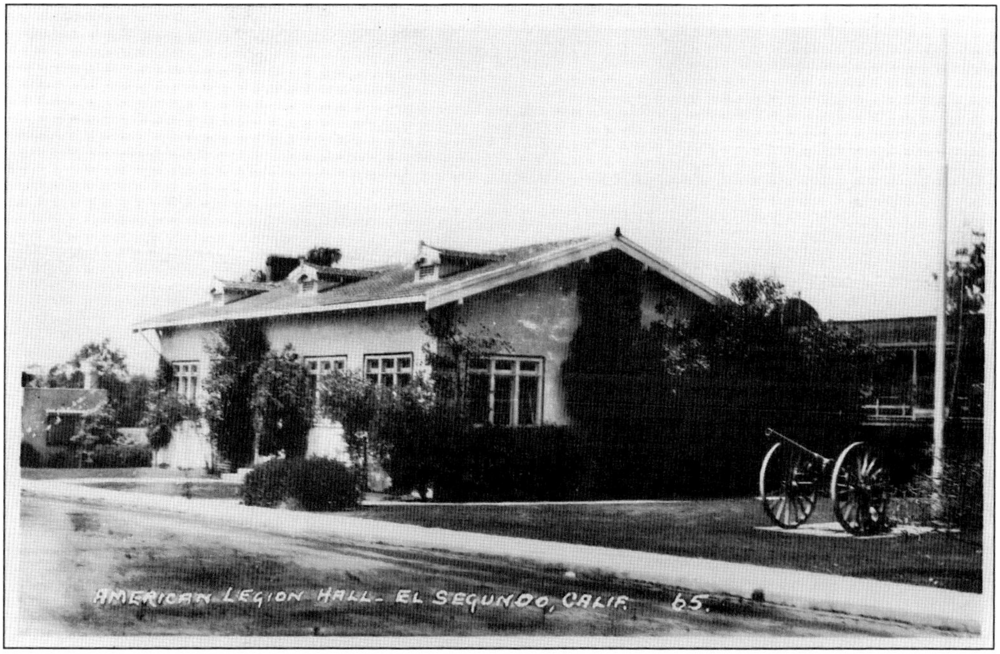

This real-photo postcard (RPPC) depicts the El Segundo American Legion Hall. The message on the reverse reads, "Dear Grandson, How are you? Do you go to the Boy Scout meetings anymore? Do you go to Sunday School? I would love to see all of you. I am getting homesick. I have had a good rest though. Love to all, Grandma." (Courtesy James Osborne.)

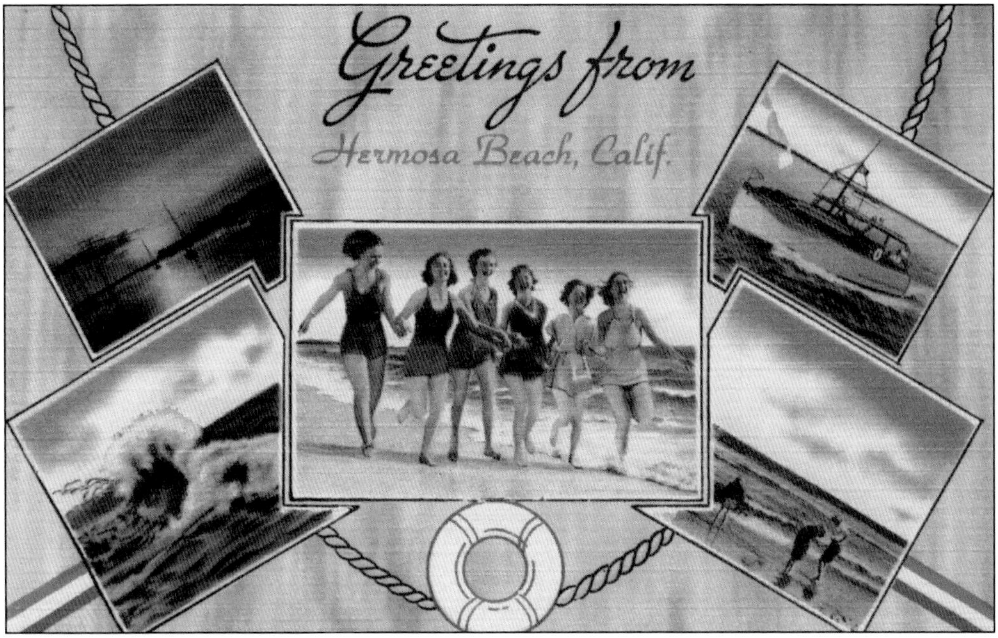

This 1920s-era postcard illustrates a fine summer day in Hermosa Beach. The 1¢ stamp was postmarked at Hermosa Beach on September 26, 1941, two months and two weeks before Pearl Harbor was attacked. (Courtesy Marilyn Ron; published by Independent Magazine Company, San Pedro, California.)

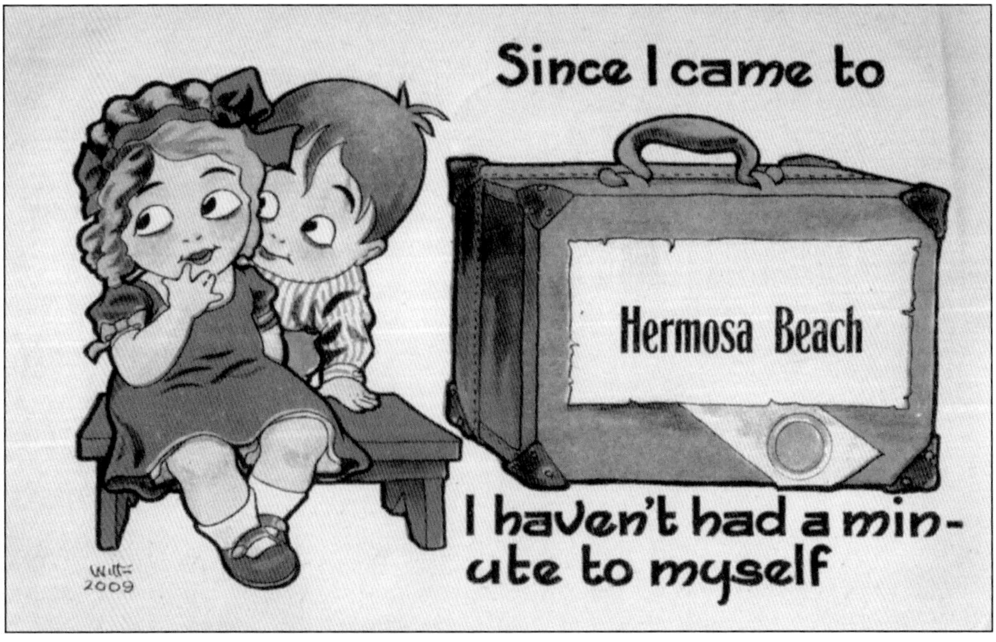

This postcard, postmarked at Los Angeles on July 9, 1914, depicts an aspect of the resort city that has never changed: It has always been a place for people to meet. (Courtesy Marilyn Ron.)

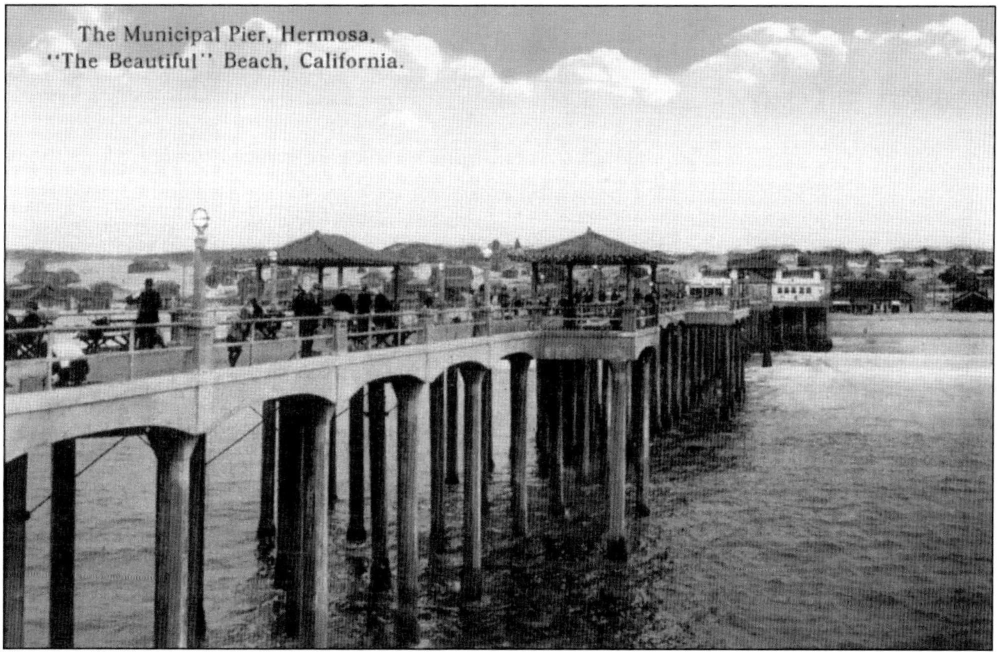

This undated postcard is from the early 1900s and shows the Municipal Pier at "The Beautiful" Beach, California. The pier was a popular tourist attraction of its day. (Courtesy Marilyn Ron; published by W. Robinson, Hermosa Beach, California.)

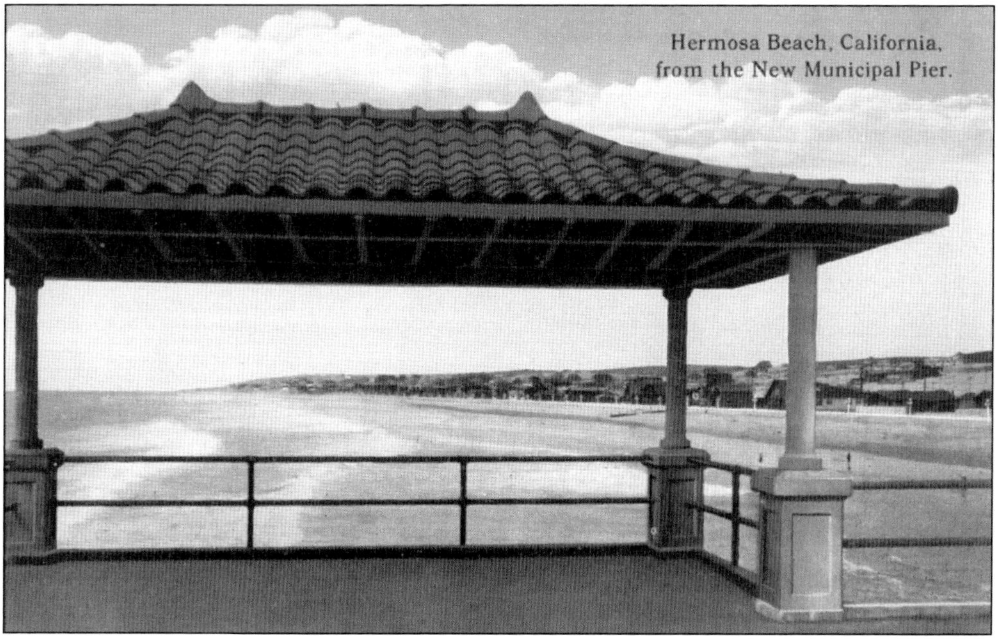

This postcard shows another view of the Municipal Pier, a close-up of one of the sheltering pagodas, and the homes in the background along the Strand. (Courtesy Marilyn Ron; published by A. J. James, Los Angeles, California.)

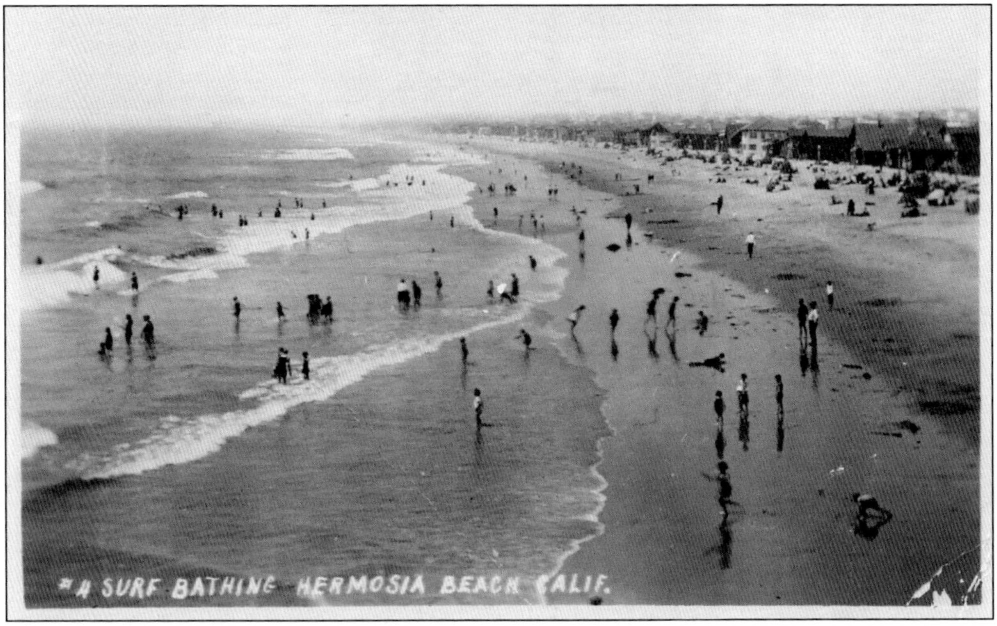

This postcard dated August 2, 1926, depicts "Surf Bathing" in Hermosa Beach. Note the houses in the background of this northward view, looking toward Manhattan Beach. (Courtesy Marilyn Ron; published by Wesley Andrews, Inc., Baker, Oregon.)

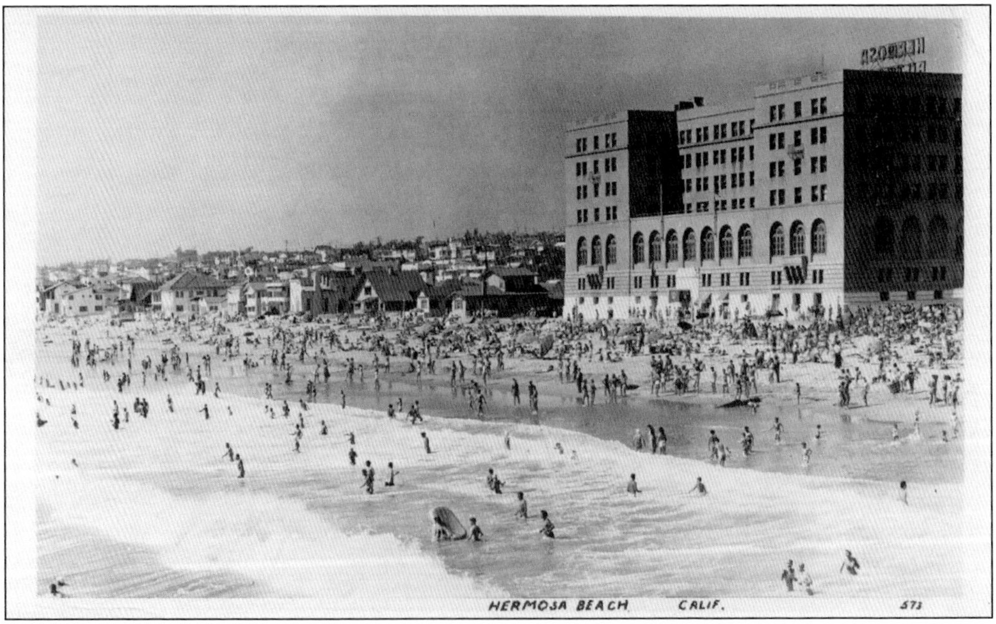

The Biltmore Hotel dominated the Hermosa Beach shoreline for generations. It was built in 1924 as the Sand and Surf Club at a cost of $840,000. It was one of the most luxurious hotels built on the West Coast, containing 150 rooms and famous for its private ballrooms, heated plunge, and a health studio with steam cabinets. In 1931, the Sand and Surf Club became the Hermosa Biltmore Hotel and was a popular spot with tourists. Unfortunately, nothing lasts forever, and in its later years, it became a home for vagrants. The hotel was demolished in 1969. This postcard is dated June 10, 1949. (Courtesy Marilyn Ron.)

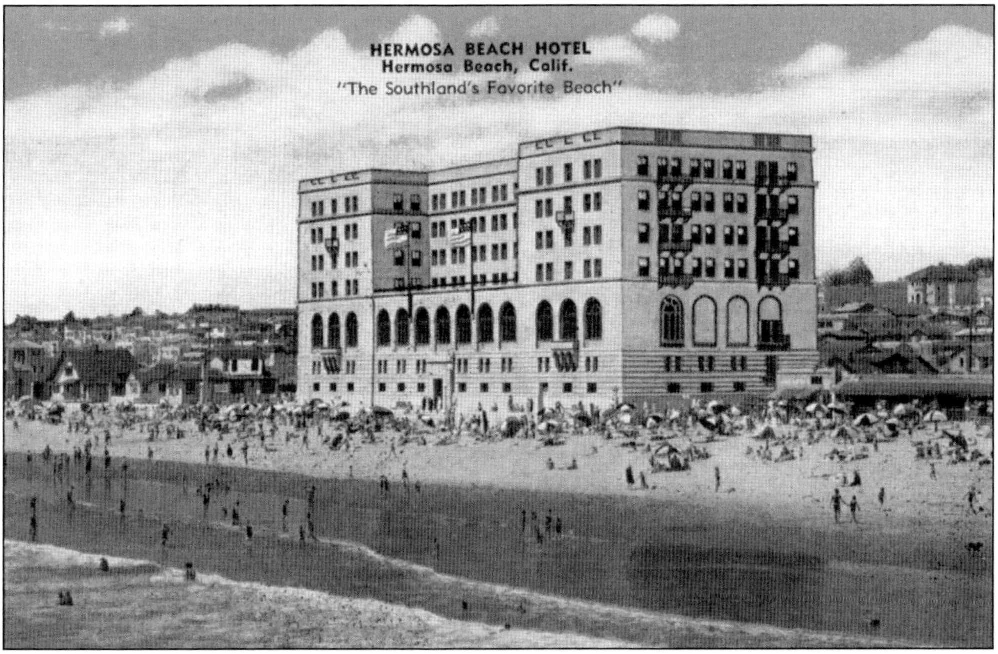

This artist's rendition of the Hermosa Biltmore is postmarked August 12, 1951, at Hermosa Beach. The flip-side caption boasts of the heated plunge, Red Giraffe Cocktail Lounge, private ballrooms, and coffee shops. (Courtesy Marilyn Ron; published by E. C. Kropp Company, Milwaukee, Wisconsin.)

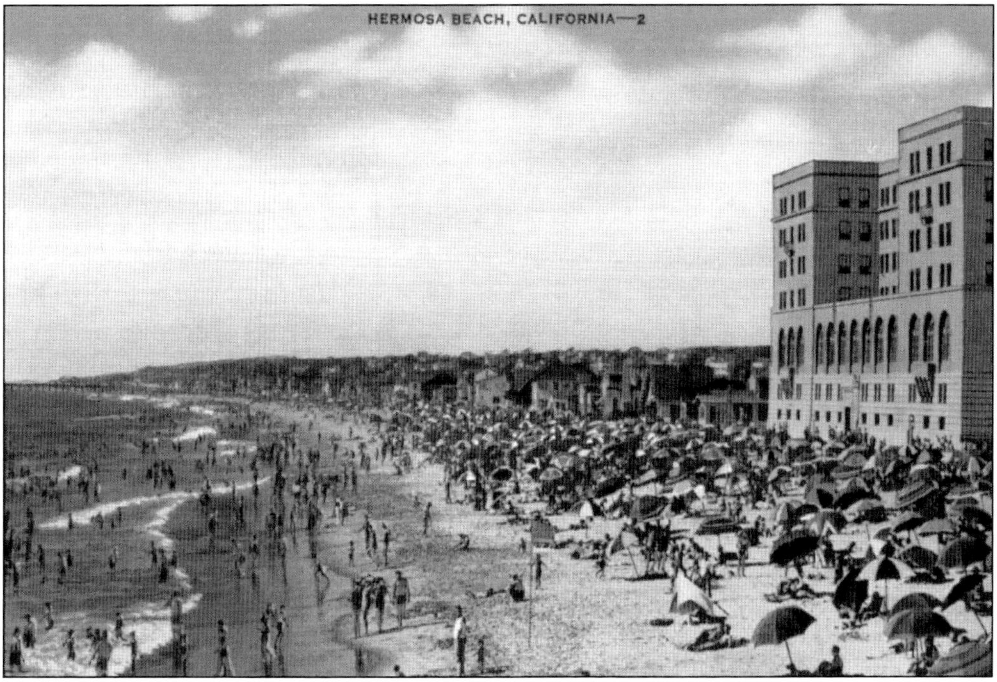

Another view northward from the Hermosa Beach Pier shows the Biltmore to the right and the houses along the Strand up into Manhattan Beach. (Courtesy James Osborne; published by Independent Magazine Company, San Pedro, California.)

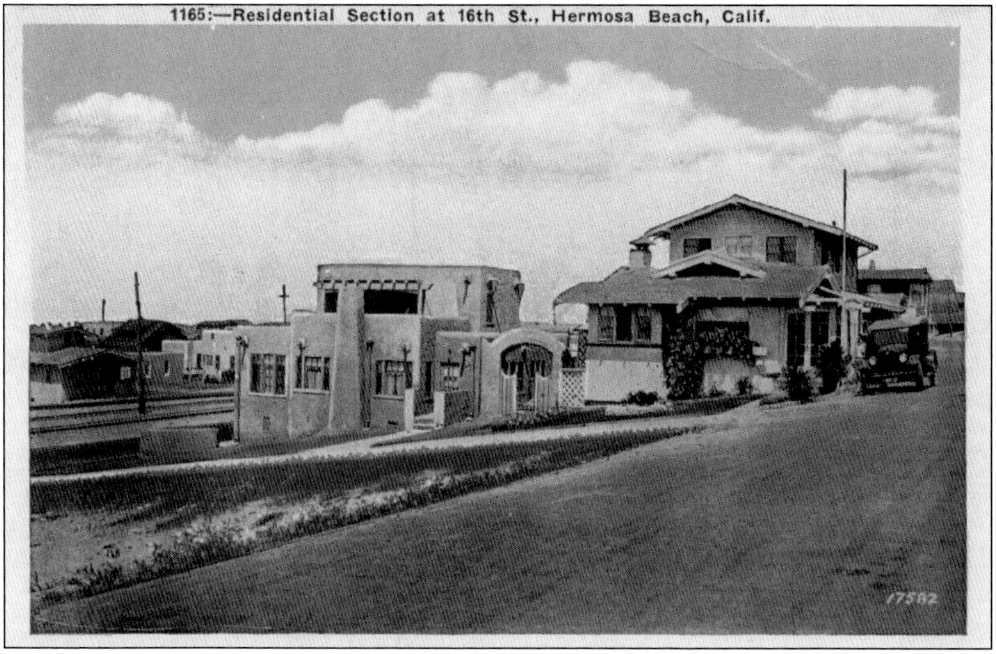

This card shows part of Hermosa's residential section at Sixteenth Street. Note the old car outside the residence. (Courtesy Marilyn Ron; published by M. Kashower Company, Los Angeles, California.)

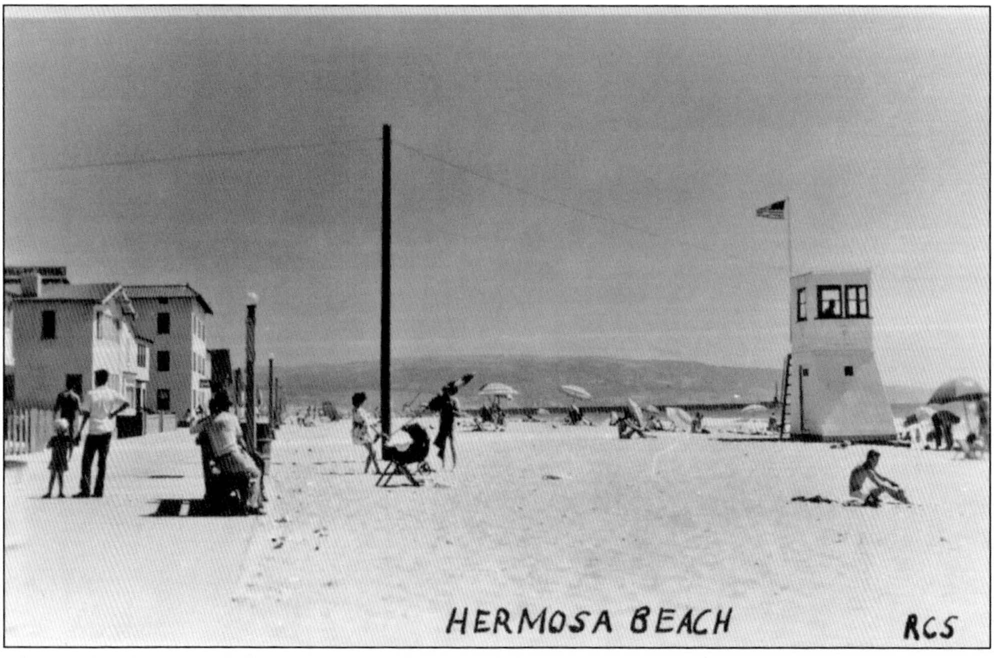

This undated postcard shows a view of some of the homes on the Strand and one of the early lifeguard towers. (Courtesy Marilyn Ron.)

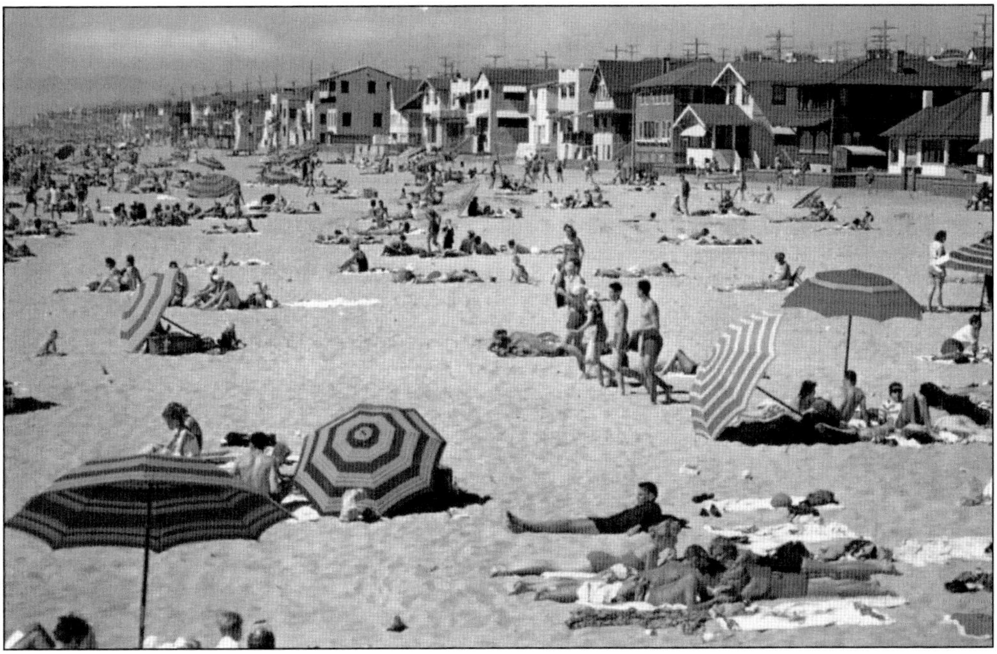

This postcard dated August 27, 1954, shows another later view of the public beach and homes along the Strand. Note the difference in the bathing attire in the two photographs. (Courtesy Marilyn Ron; published by Colourpictures, Boston, Massachusetts, and distributed by Golden West, Long Beach, California.)

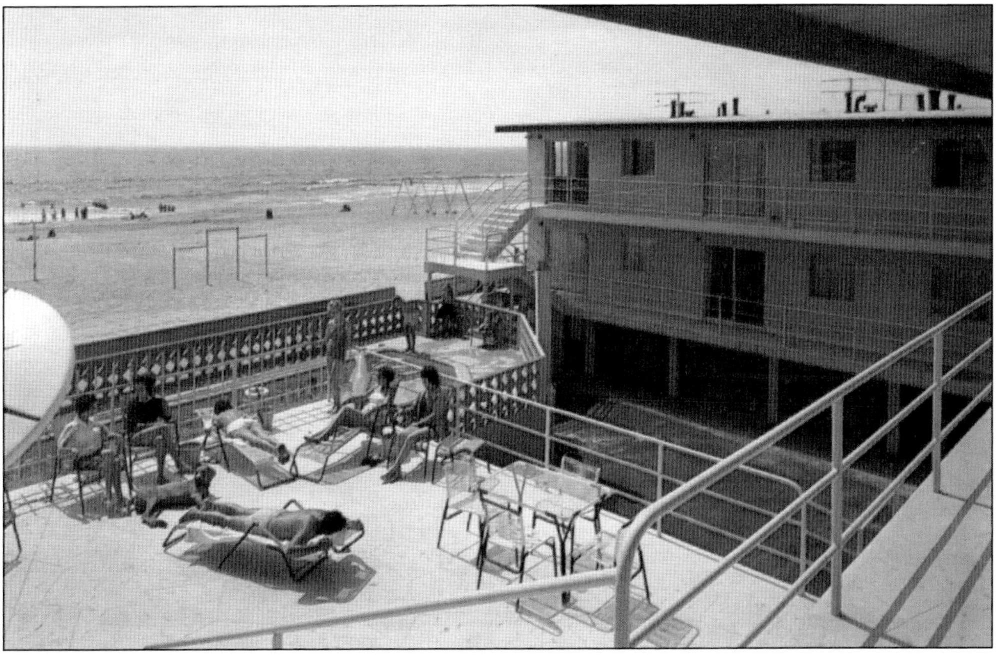

Another noted Hermosa hotel is the Sea Sprite, located at Tenth Street and the Strand. This card boasts, "Singles or Families, Kitchens or Light Housekeeping, Free TV and Heated Fresh Water Pool." (Courtesy Marilyn Ron; published by Forest Mathews "FOTO-COLOR" Cards, Pasadena, California.)

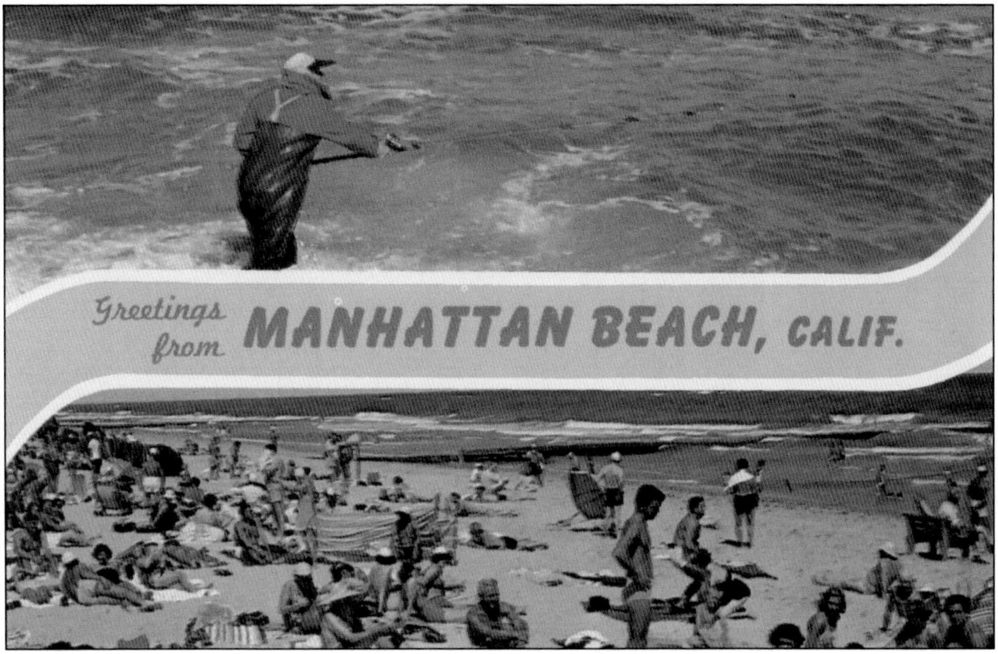

Surf fishing is a well-practiced sport and sunbathing a time-honored inactivity on the South Bay's beaches, so these depictions could very well be "Greetings from Manhattan Beach, Calif." (Courtesy James Osborne; published by Dexter Press, West Nyack, New York.)

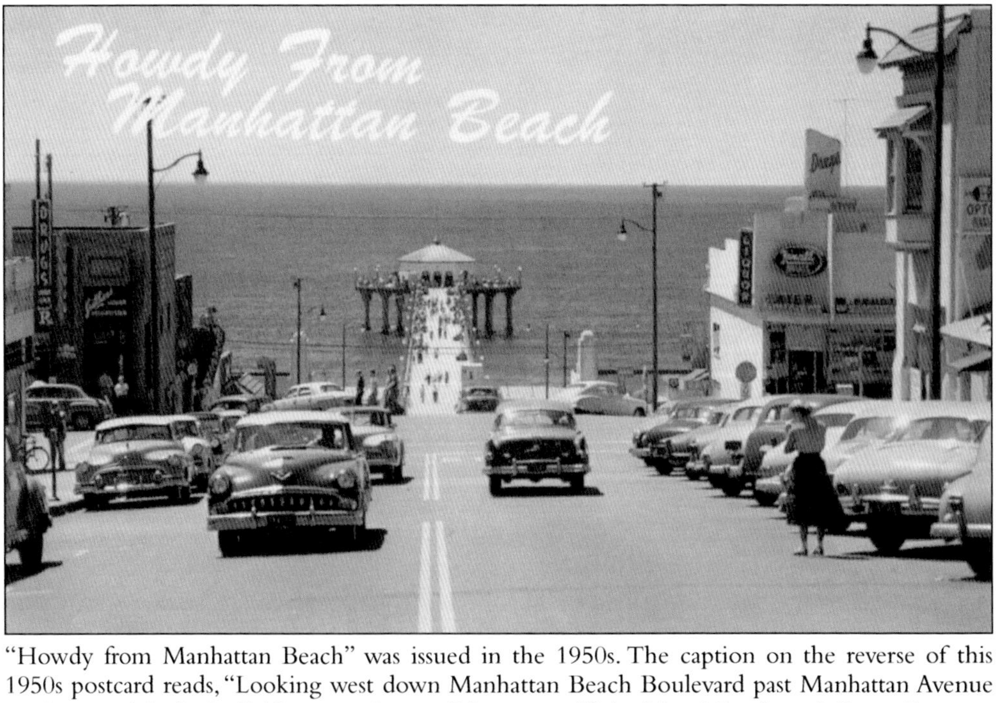

"Howdy from Manhattan Beach" was issued in the 1950s. The caption on the reverse of this 1950s postcard reads, "Looking west down Manhattan Beach Boulevard past Manhattan Avenue to the municipal pier." (Courtesy James Osborne; published by Mitock and Sons, Sherman Oaks, California.)

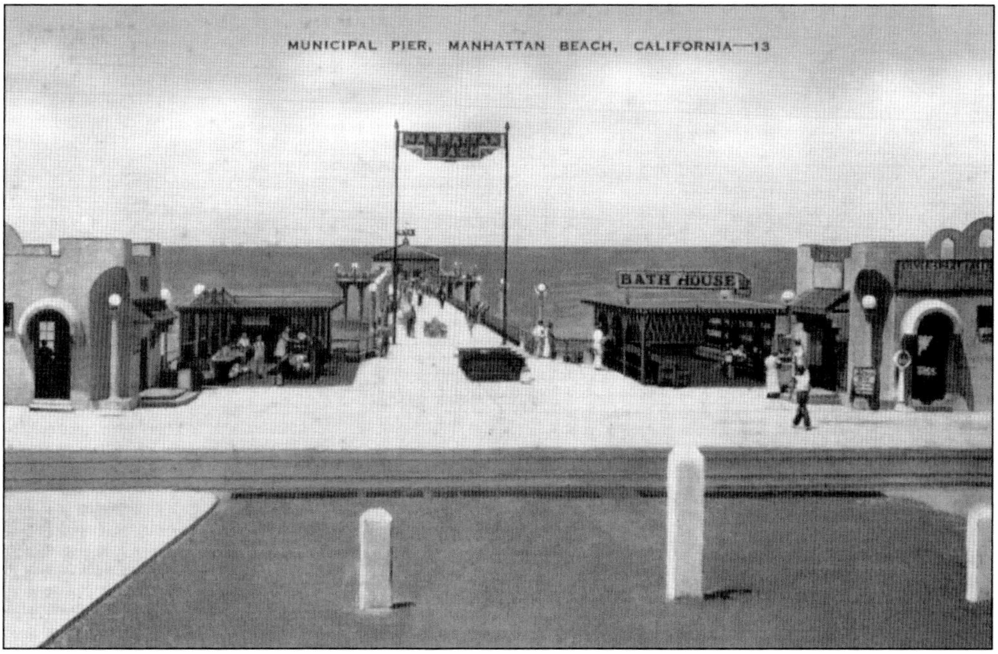

This postcard illustrates the Manhattan Beach Pier and adjoining Bath House. The Silver Spray Café is on the far right. (Courtesy James Osborne; published by Independent Magazine Company, San Pedro, California.)

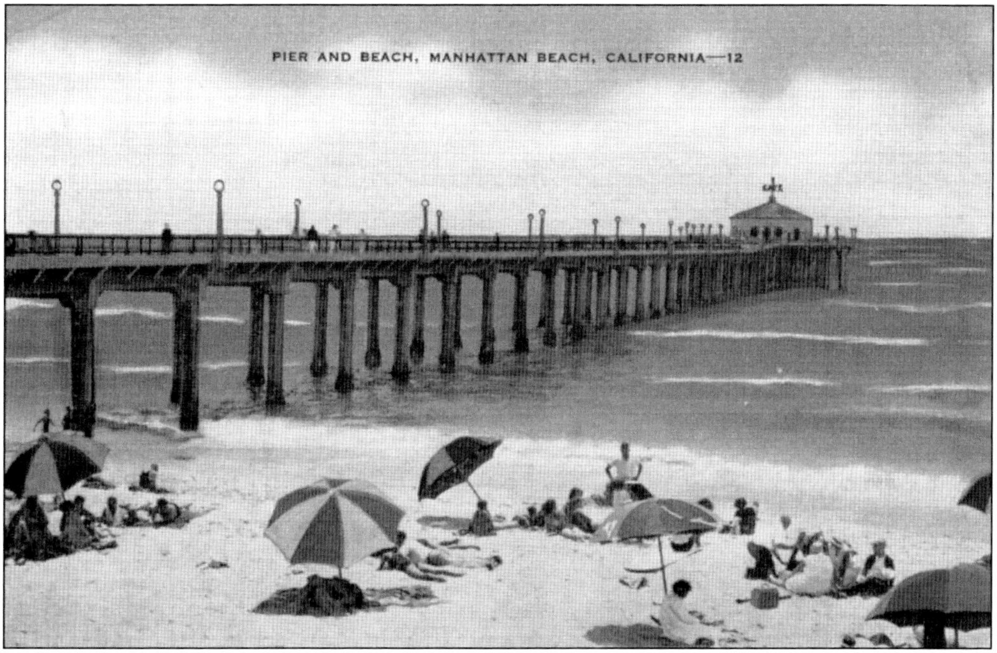

Beachgoers are pictured on the north side of Manhattan Beach Pier. The reverse side reads, "At the ocean edge of Los Angeles County, Manhattan Beach provides fun in the sun and sea all year long" (Courtesy James Osborne; published by Independent Magazine Company, San Pedro, California.)

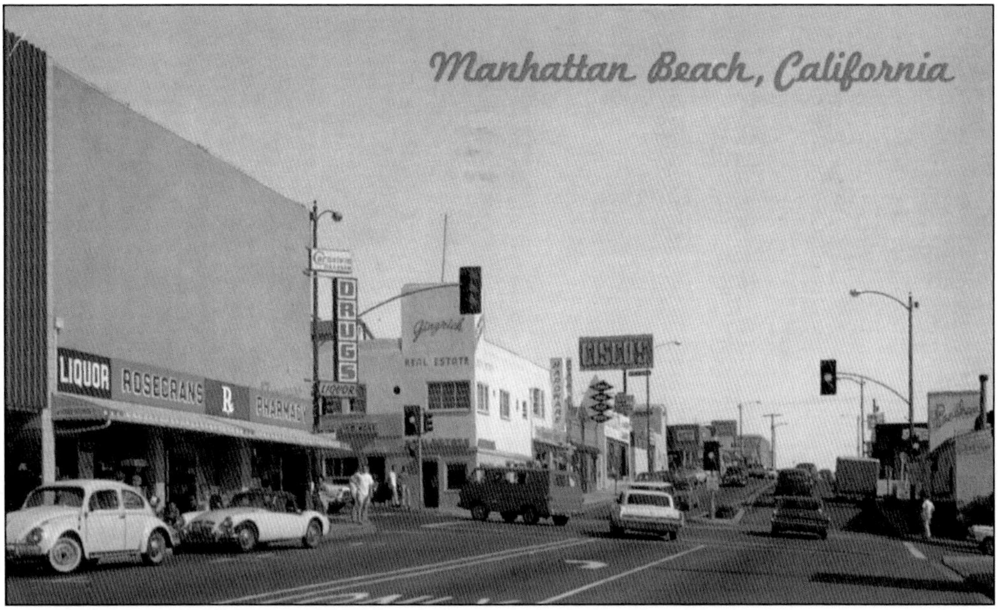

This image, postmarked on November 1, 1968, depicts the businesses on Highland Avenue looking south through the Rosecrans Avenue intersection in North Manhattan Beach, also known as El Porto. Note Pancho's Restaurant on the right on the southwest corner of Highland and Rosecrans. (Courtesy Marilyn Ron; published by Golden West, Long Beach, California.)

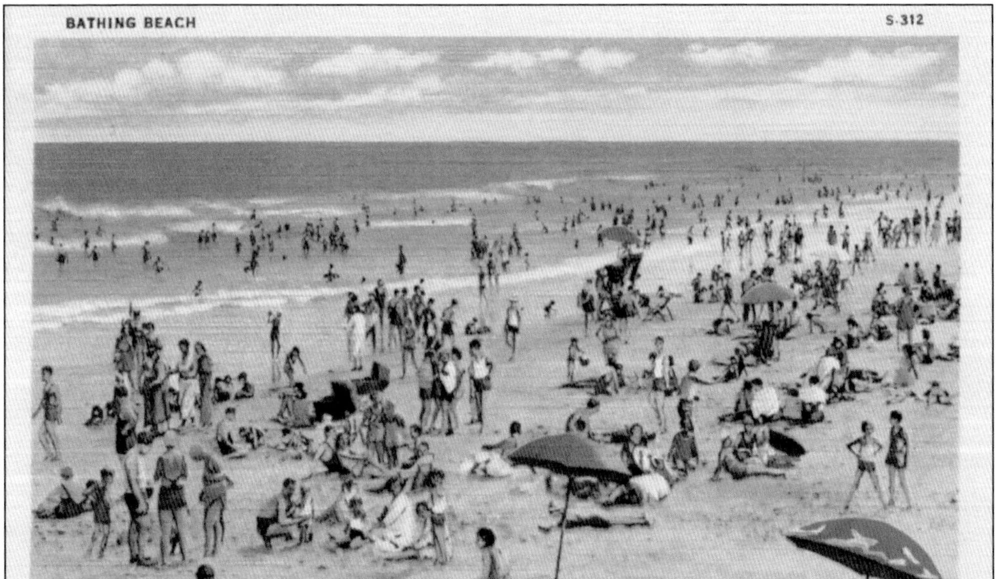

Postmarked on June 21, 1937, this northwest-view postcard labeled "Bathing Beach" depicts a crowded summer scene on Manhattan Beach. (Courtesy Marilyn Ron; published by Curt Teich and Company, Inc., Chicago.)

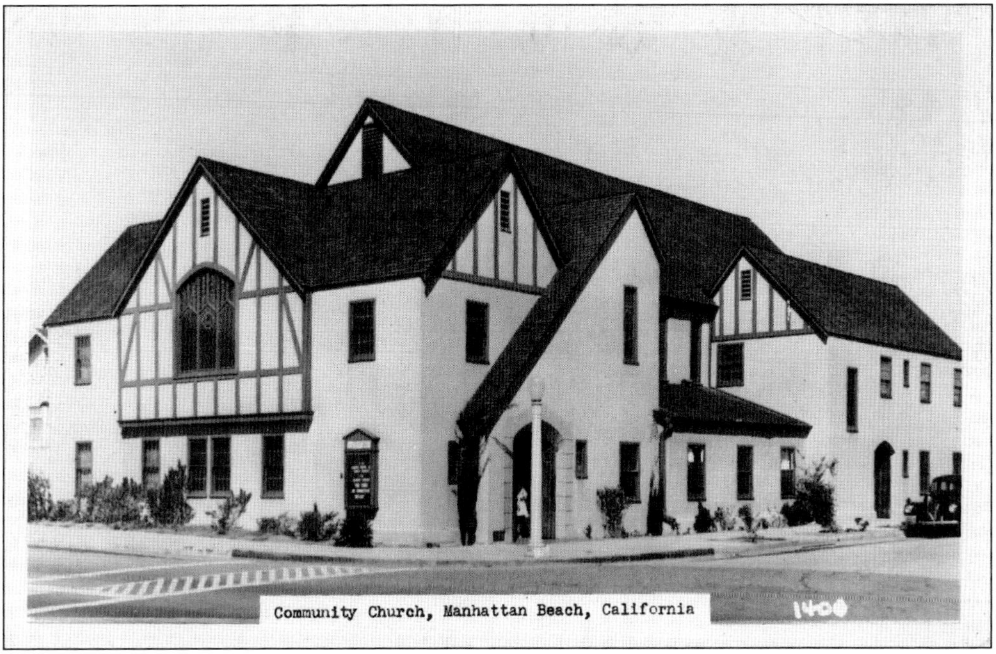

The Community Church building, seen in this real-photo postcard (RPPC) was built in 1937 at the corner of Ninth Street and Highland Avenue. It is still standing today. (Courtesy Marilyn Ron.)

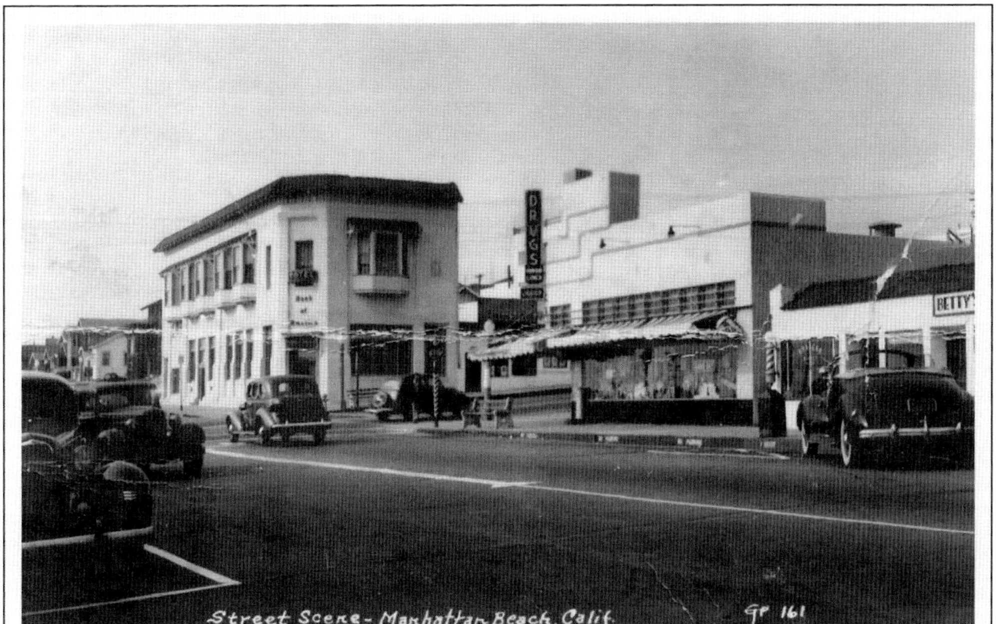

This RPPC depicts a street scene in Manhattan Beach during the 1930s. The intersection is Manhattan Avenue and Center Street, which today is named Manhattan Beach Boulevard. The old bank building seen at the left in this image was demolished in 1965. (Courtesy James Osborne.)

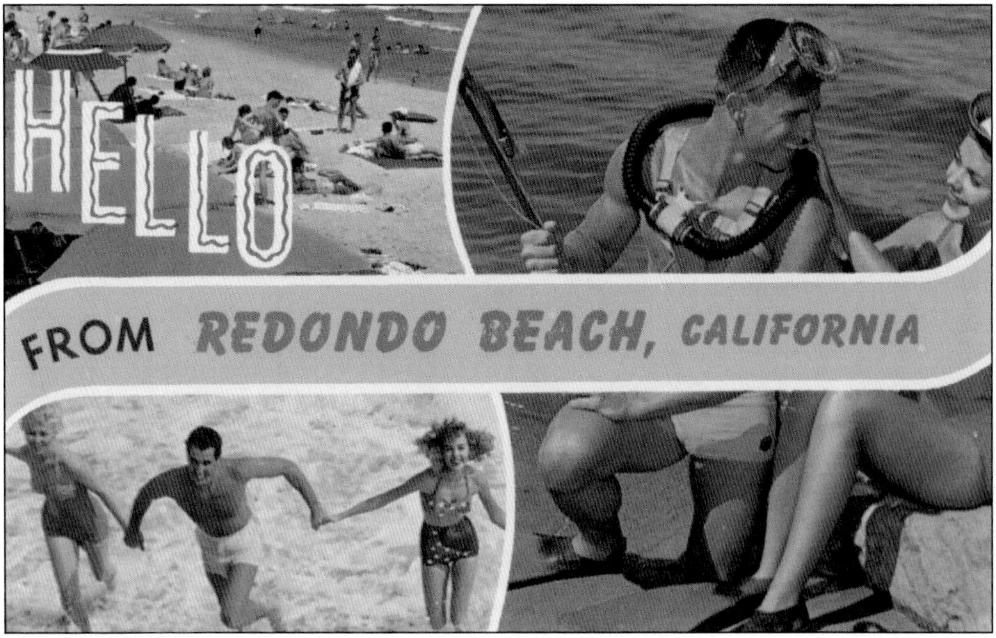

"Hello from Redondo Beach, California" depicts a few of the beach activities for which the city and its shoreline are justifiably known. (Courtesy Bill Ron; published by Dexter Press, Inc., West Nyack, New York.)

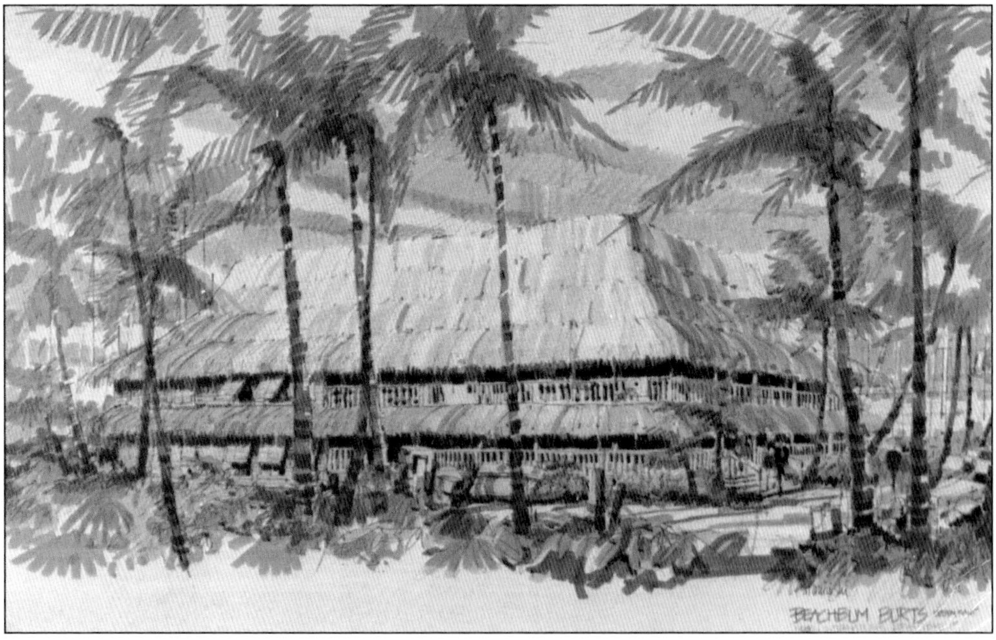

Beachbum Burt's was one of the more famous beach restaurants that no longer exist. It was located at 605 North Harbor Drive in Redondo Beach. This advertising postcard reads, "One of America's most unique restaurants overlooking Redondo Beach Harbor and the blue Pacific. This is the home of the international photographer Burt Hixson, whose menu features casual cuisine of the Pacific. Unusual entertainment nightly and magnificent décor creates dining pleasure you'll long remember. 12 minutes from Los Angeles airport." (Courtesy Marilyn Ron.)

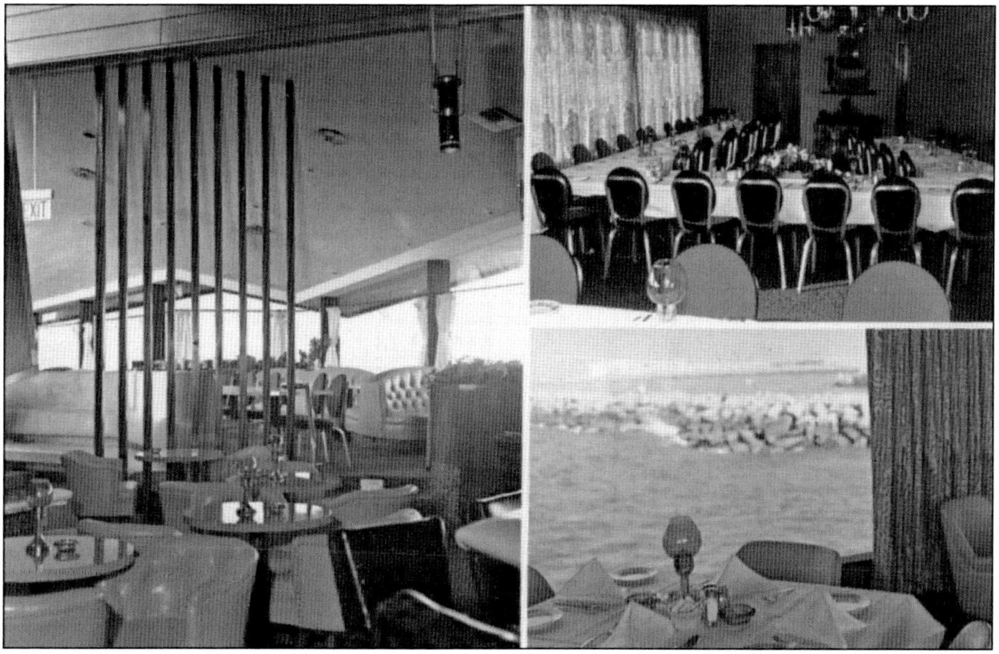

This advertising postcard for the Golden Hull reads, "Golden Hull—555 Fisherman's Wharf, Redondo Beach, California, Phone 376-8885. King Harbor's newest and finest gourmet restaurant. Picturesquely located out on the pier in Redondo Beach overlooking the blue Pacific. The Golden Hull has been acclaimed for its excellent cuisine and uniqueness of culinary specialties. . . . This combined with the Surf Room's relaxing atmosphere, makes 'Dining Out Over the Sea' a memorable occasion. The panoramic ocean view is worth a visit all by itself." (Courtesy Marilyn Ron; photograph by Keith Crowther.)

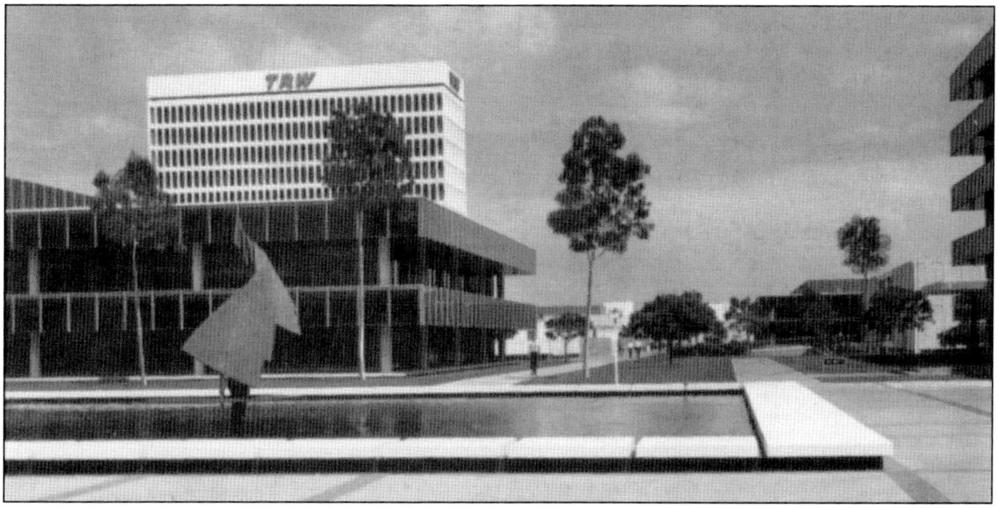

This postcard dated 1977 shows the TRW complex at One Space Park in Redondo Beach. It boasted of 200 acres of laboratories, offices, and engineering and manufacturing buildings in one of the world's foremost industrial centers for advanced technology. The 11,500 Systems Group people here represented nearly every scientific discipline needed to furnish products and services ranging from lasers and spacecraft to cancer detection equipment, from materials research to devices and processes to improve the environment. (Courtesy Marilyn Ron; published by TRW, Inc.)

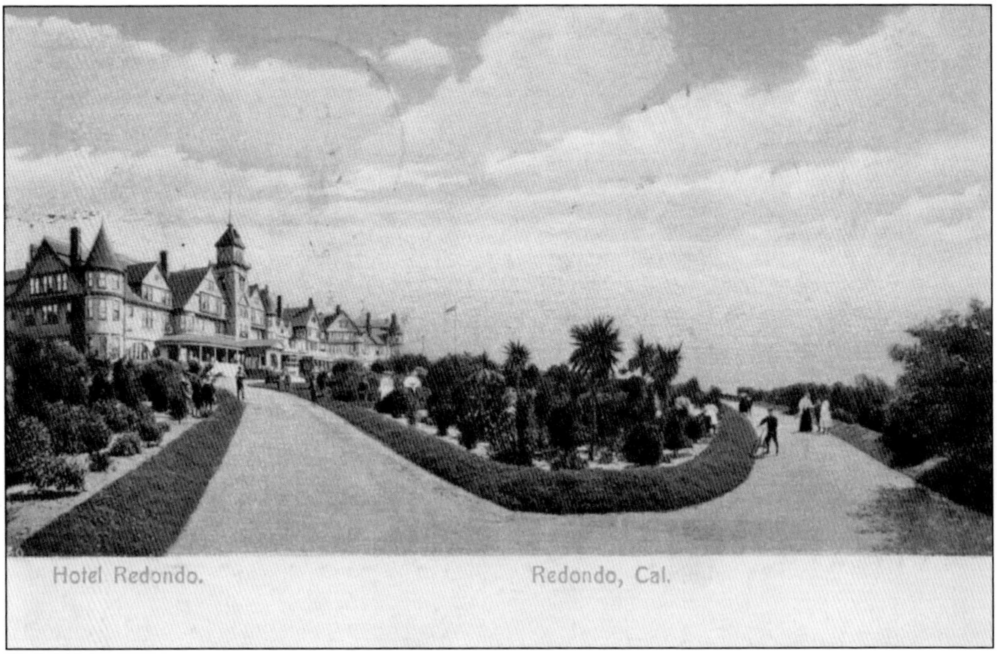

This 1908 view of the Hotel Redondo shows the grounds. The enormous hotel built by railroad tycoon Henry Huntington was located on the bluff where Veterans Park is today. (Courtesy Marilyn Ron; published by Newman Post Card Company, Los Angeles, California.)

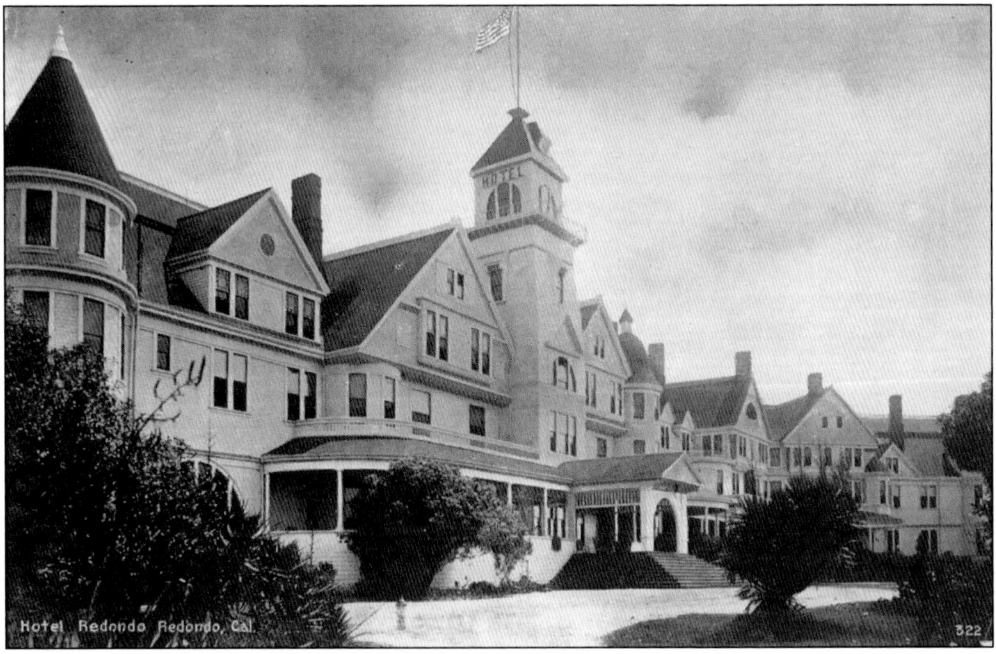

The Hotel Redondo opened on May 3, 1890. It featured 225 rooms, and the grounds included tennis courts and a golf course as well as sunken gardens. It was an ideal spot for vacationers. It was built at a cost of $500,000. This once magnificent hotel was torn down in 1924 and its remains sold for scrap. (Courtesy Marilyn Ron; published by Edward H. Mitchell, San Francisco, California.)

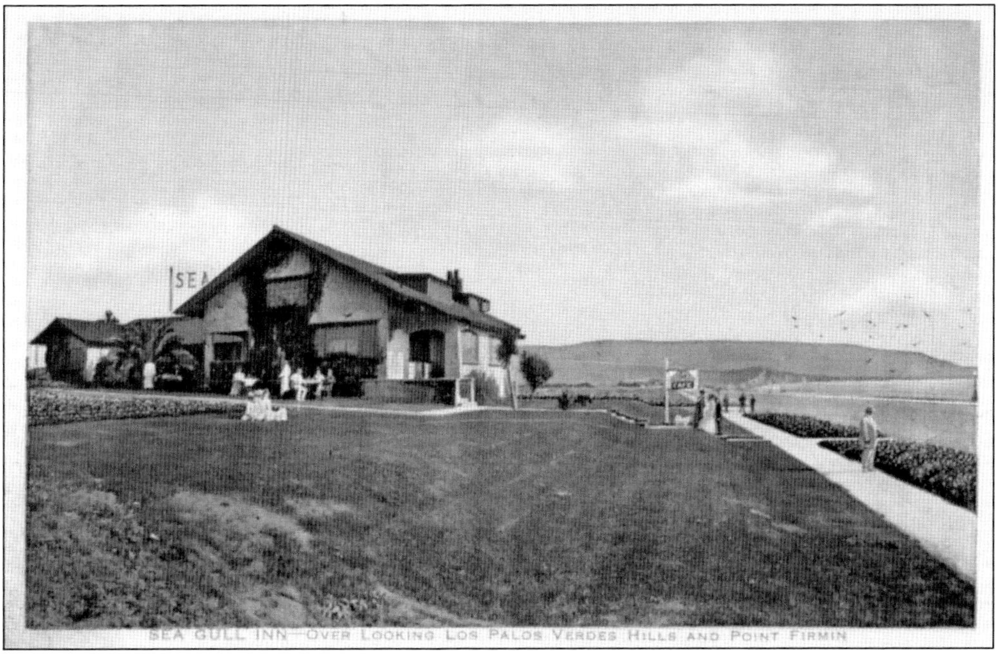

This 1915 postcard shows the exterior of the Sea Gull Inn at Clifton by the Sea, overlooking the Palos Verdes Peninsula. Note how very barren-looking Palos Verdes was in the background. (Courtesy Marilyn Ron; published by George Rice and Sons, Printers, Los Angeles, California.)

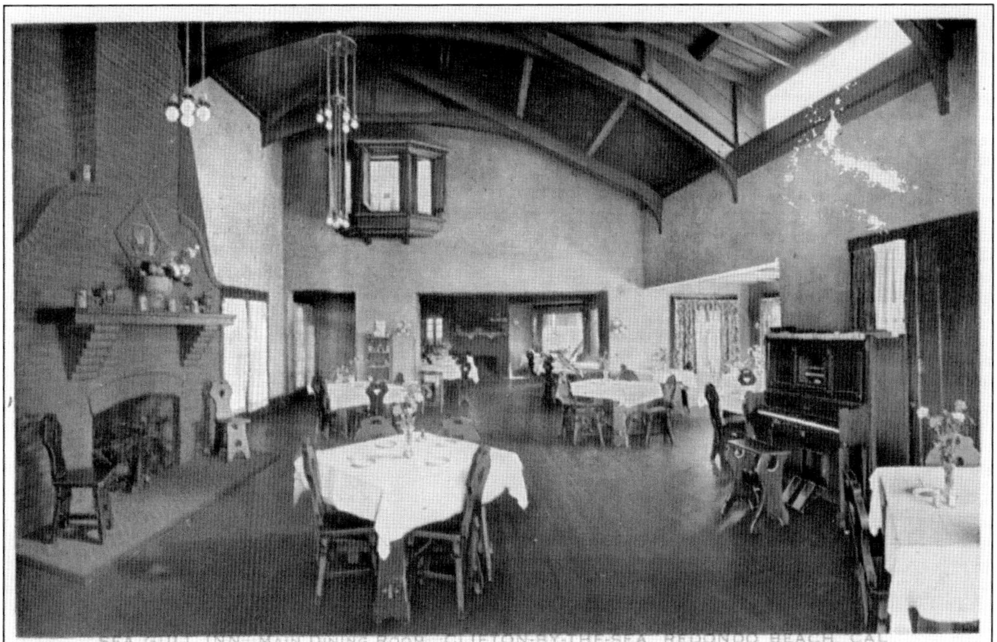

The main dining room of the Sea Gull Inn at Clifton by the Sea is seen in this RPPC. The postcard boasts the restaurant as being famous for salt-air-cured steaks, dancing, caterers, private dinner dances, and card parties. (Courtesy Marilyn Ron.)

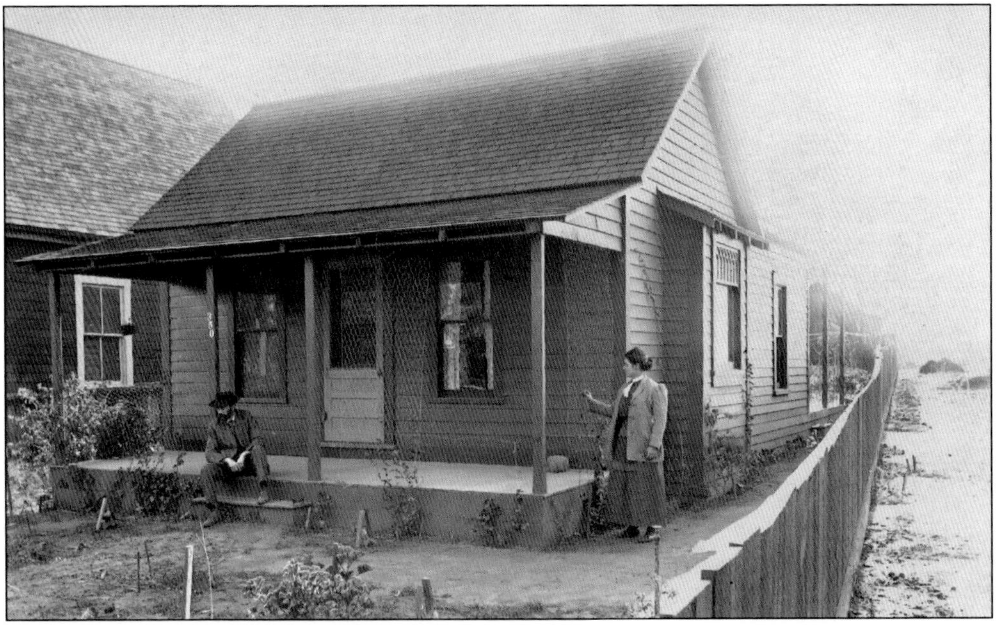

This real-photo postcard shows the home of Ruth Buxton at 350 El Redondo Street. Buxton worked for many years as a secretary at Redondo Union High School. She later moved to a two-story home at 813 El Redondo Street and lived there until her death. That home still stands today and was featured in several postcards. Shown is Ruth and her father, John Buxton. (Courtesy Bill Ron.)

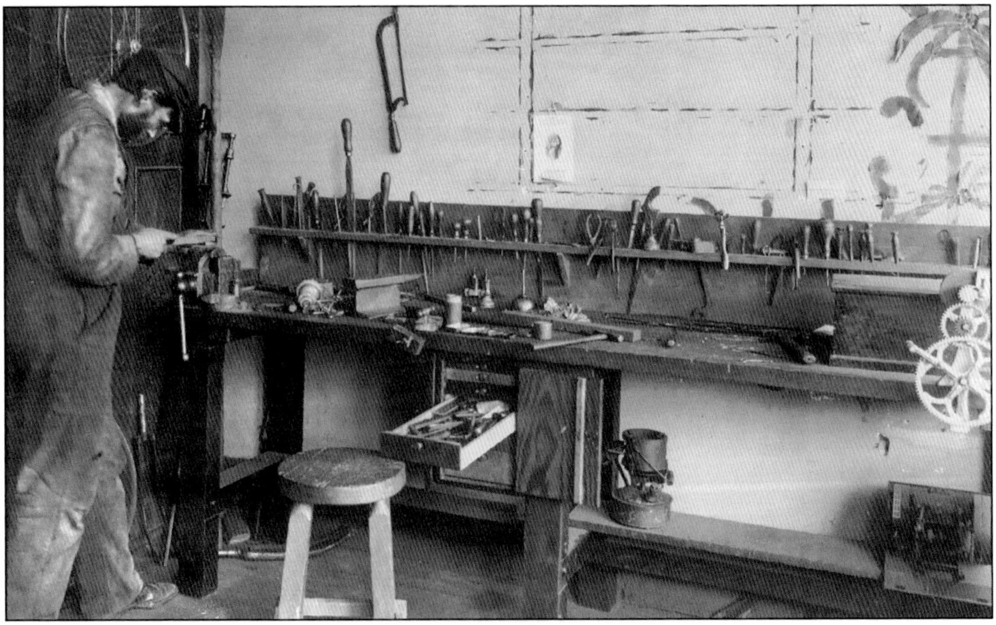

This RPPC dated February 19, 1910, shows a repair shop at 218 South Pacific Avenue in Redondo Beach. It is addressed to Ruth Buxton of Redondo Beach and reads, "My Dear Ruth, Hope to see you soon down to my place for repairs as I believe you are badly broken. With the best wishes of the proprietor who stands at his bench." This was sent to Ruth Buxton from her father, John Buxton. (Courtesy Bill Ron.)

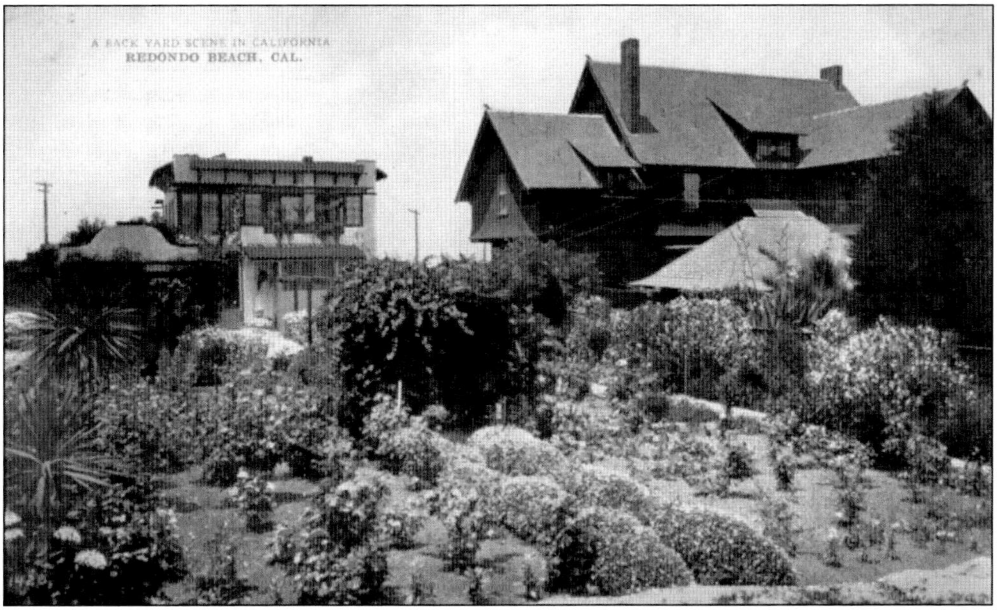

Although this photograph was previously published, the house on the left was the home of Ruth Buxton at 813 El Redondo Street. The home was purchased by Ruth's friend Barbara Barstow and was lovingly restored. The house still stands today and is a beautiful example of the homes that used to exist in Redondo Beach at the dawn of the 20th century. (Courtesy Marilyn Ron; published by the Benham Company, Los Angeles, California.)

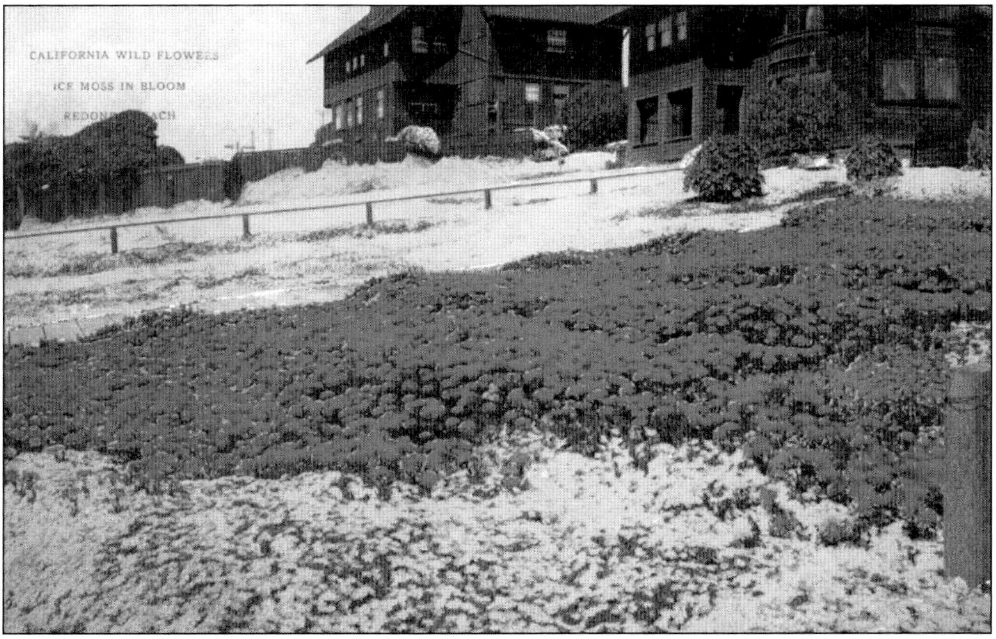

"California Wild Flowers—Ice Moss in Bloom," reads this card's caption. This postcard, dated July 28, 1909, to Dr. J. Allen Smith of Colorado from Ruth Buxton, states, "This is our backyard in the spring. The house does not show. The walk runs down to the edge of the bluff where we go down to go swimming. It is a beautiful sight." (Courtesy Bill Ron; published by the Benham Company, Los Angeles, California.)

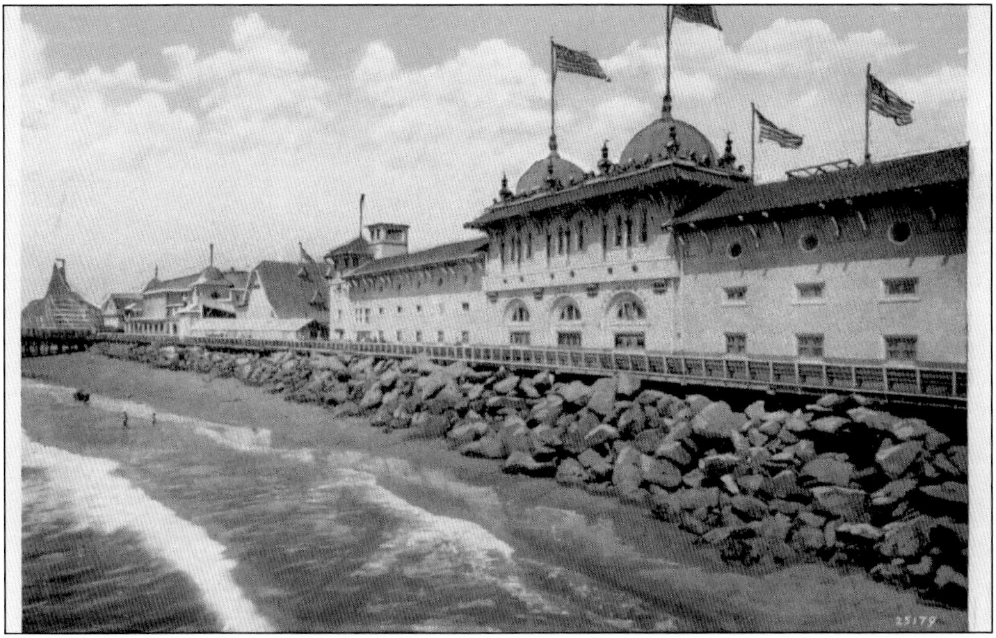

This oceanfront view of the Bath House in Redondo Beach illustrated what was billed as the largest such structure in the world. It was built in 1909 at a cost of $150,000 and contained 1,330 dressing rooms, warm and cold water, and 62 tub baths. The saltwater was heated by the nearby steam power plant. (Courtesy Marilyn Ron; published by M. Kashower Company, Los Angeles, California.)

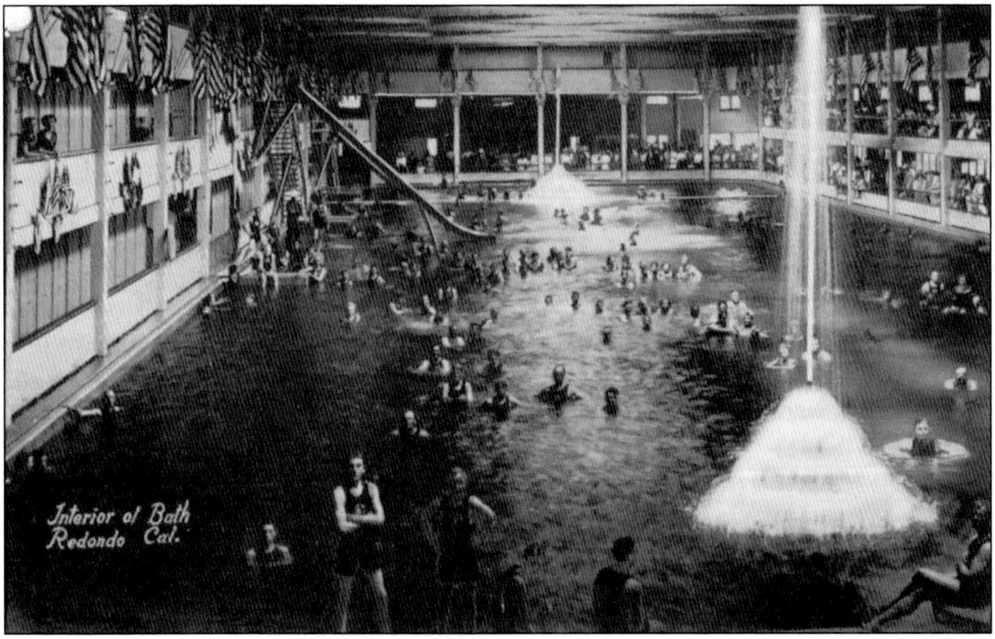

This postcard shows the interior of the first Bath House, which included the largest saltwater plunge in the world. The pool pumped more than a million gallons of seawater each day and was heated by the nearby Pacific Light and Power Steam Plant. The pool was replaced in 1909. (Courtesy Marilyn Ron; published by the Redondo Lapidary and Curio Store, William Kerrn.)

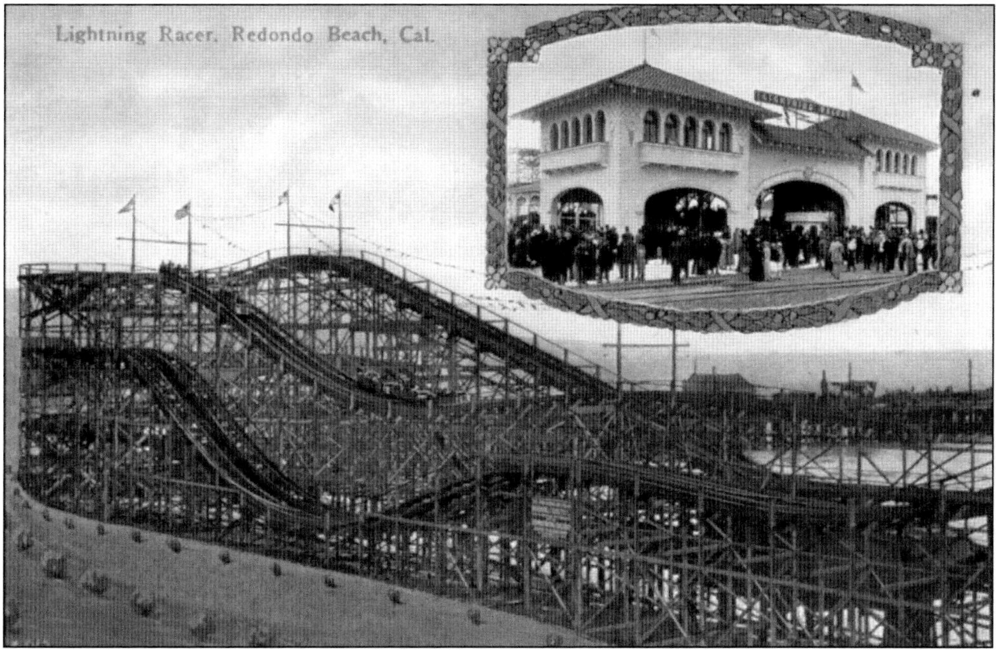

This advertising postcard reads, "You'll like Redondo Beach. Home of the Lightning Racer. The finest, fastest and safest ride ever built. It is on the ocean, over the surf, a most exhilarating and exciting ride. A magnificent panoramic view of miles of beach and surrounding hills with beautiful residences. Redondo Lightning Racer Company, J. A. Ellis, President and Manager." (Courtesy Bill Ron; published by George Rice and Sons, Printers, Los Angeles, California.)

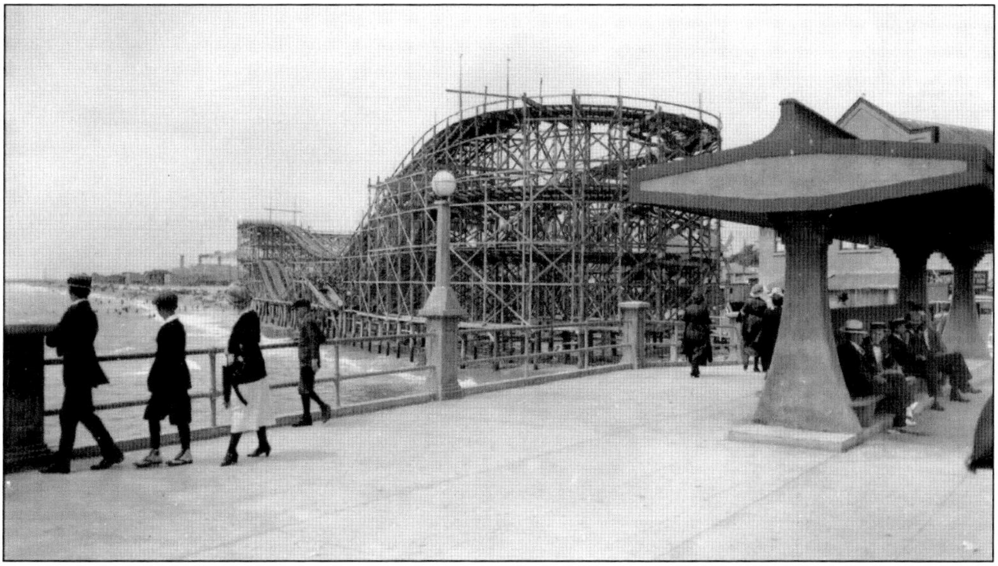

This photo postcard shows the Lightning Racer and the new Pleasure Pier in 1923. The Lightning Racer opened in 1913. It was located between Beryl Street and Coral Way on El Paseo. Many of the Redondo attractions were located along El Paseo, a street that no longer exists but which evolved toward southern Redondo Beach into the Esplanade. The Lightning Racer had 6,000 feet of track and was later destroyed by fire and storms. It was torn down in 1924. (Courtesy Bill Ron; published by Ilford Multigrade IV RC Portfolio.)

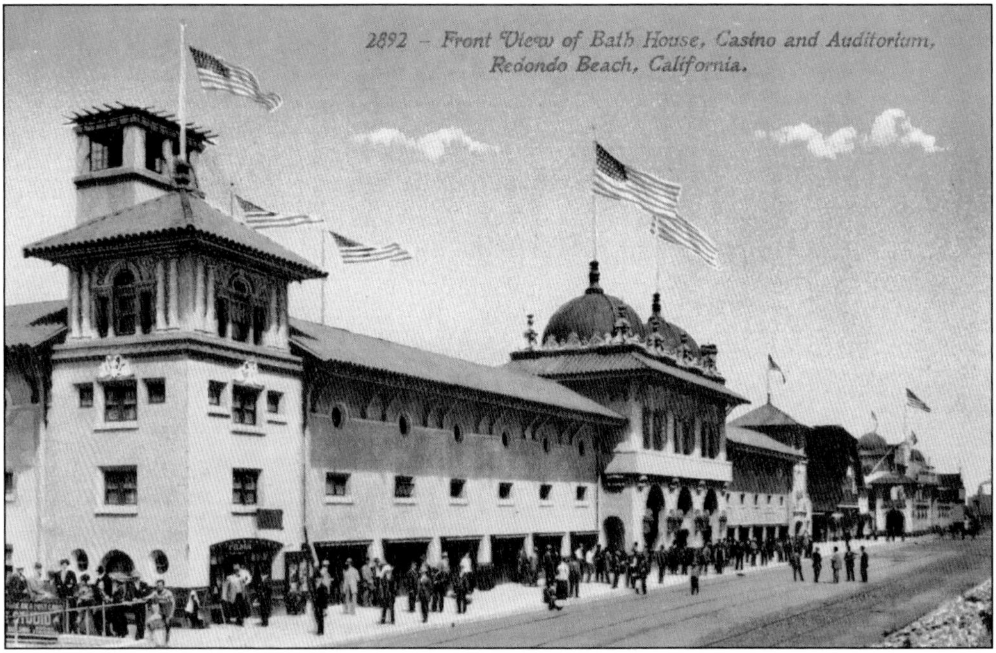

This postcard shows the front view of the Bath House, Casino, and Auditorium. Note the line on the left. The sign reads, "Put your picture on a postcard." This is one reason for the fact that Redondo Beach is depicted on more tourist cards than any other beach town in the South Bay. (Courtesy Marilyn Ron; published by Edward H. Mitchell, San Francisco, California.)

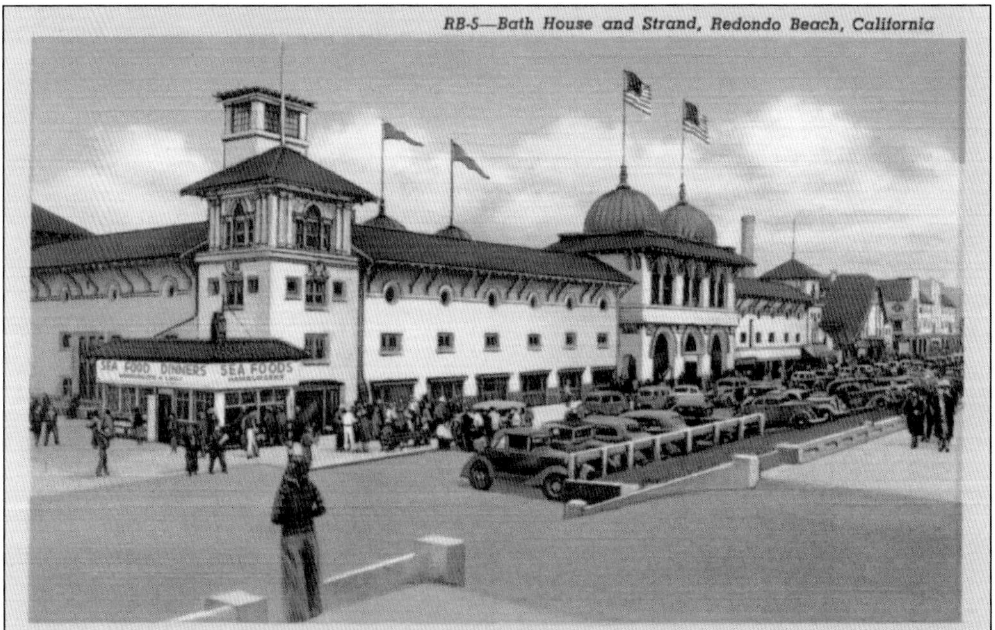

This view shows the Bath House and the Strand. Note that over time, seafood, hamburger, and chili restaurants were added to the area and cars began to be a popular form of transportation, eventually replacing the Pacific Electric "Red Cars." (Courtesy Marilyn Ron; published by Western Publishing and Novelty Company, Los Angeles, California.)

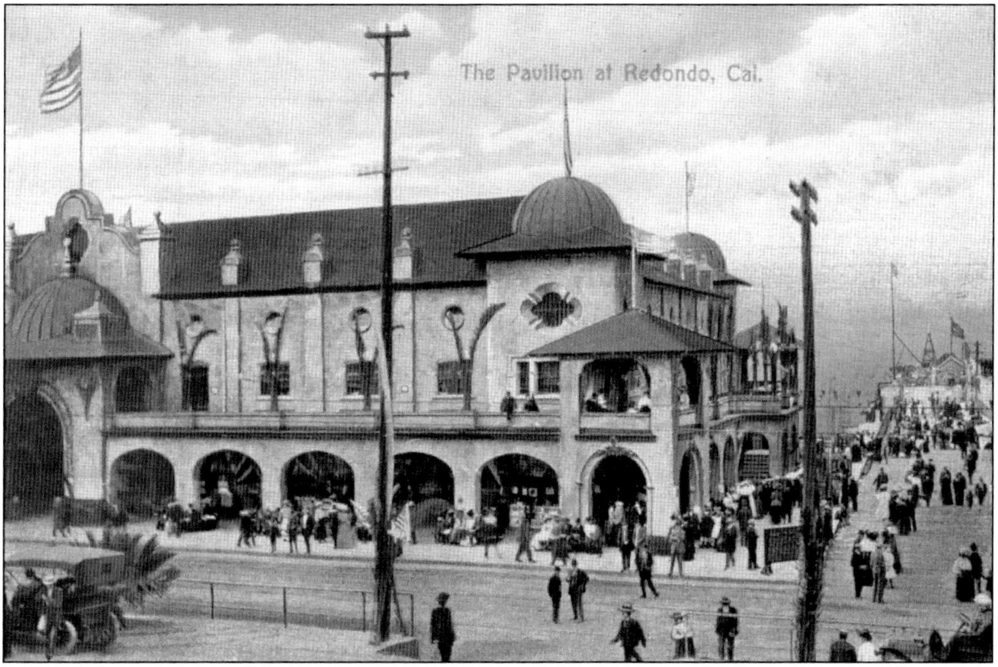

Postmarked April 24, 1910, this card depicts the exterior of the Pavilion and a portion of the Redondo Beach Pier. The Pavilion or Auditorium was famous for its upstairs Mandarin Ballroom. (Courtesy Bill Ron; published by Newman Post Card Company, Los Angeles, California.)

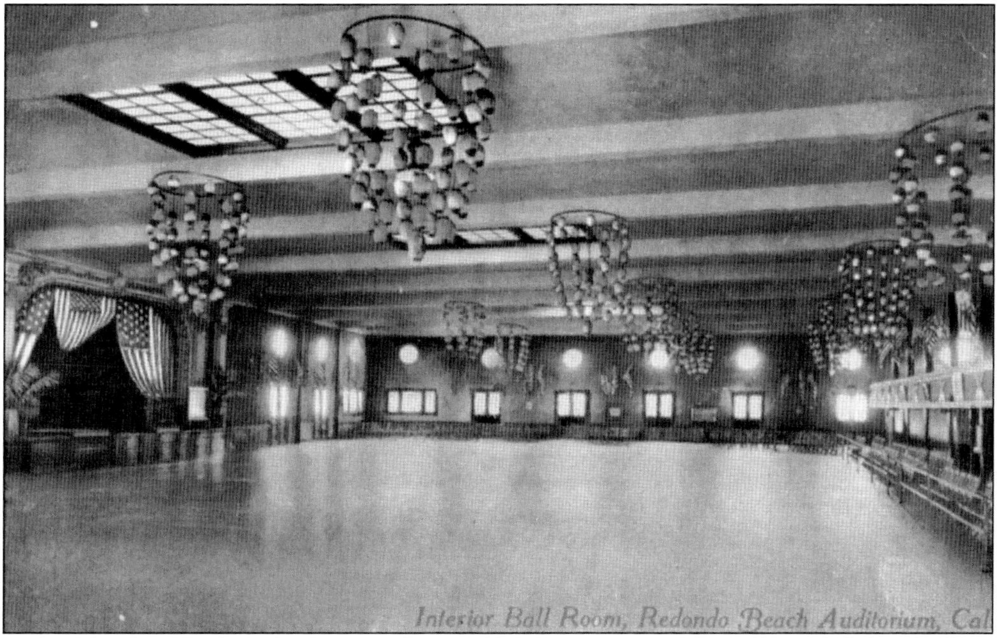

The Pavilion was built in 1892. The upstairs Mandarin Ballroom seated up to 4,000 people and had a beech wood dance floor that could accommodate up to 400 couples. Note the Chinese lantern chandeliers. (Courtesy Marilyn Ron; published by Newman Post Card Company, Los Angeles, California.)

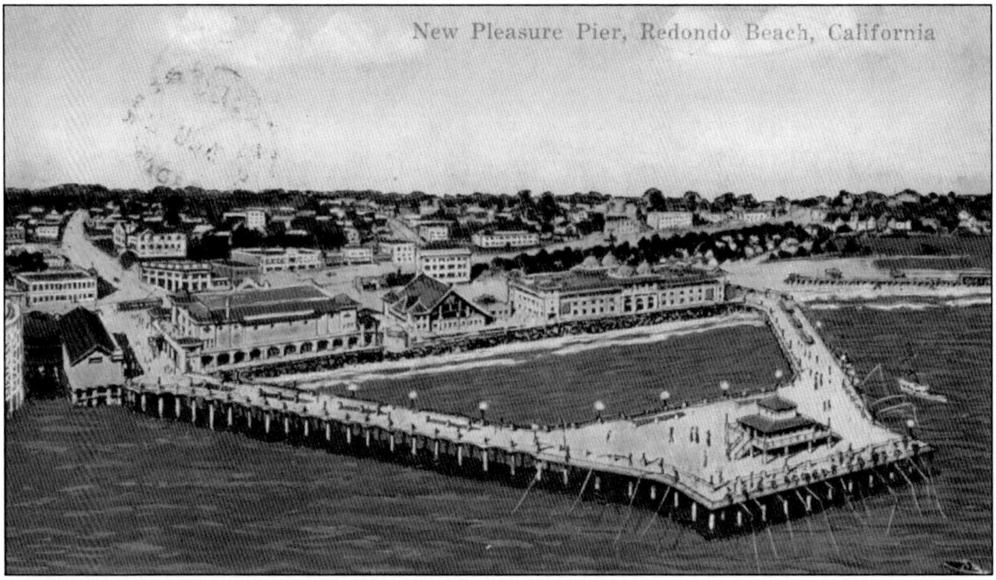

This postcard dated August 2, 1920, shows the full New Pleasure Pier with the amusement area in the background. The card was addressed to a Mrs. Niehaus in Anaheim, California, from General Del and reads, "We have arrived here today and having spent 5 hours looking for a room, at last located here. L.A. was hot enough to roast you and this is almost as bad. If you are still in Anaheim I will try to see you." (Courtesy Marilyn Ron; published by Van Ornum Colorprint Company, Los Angeles, California.)

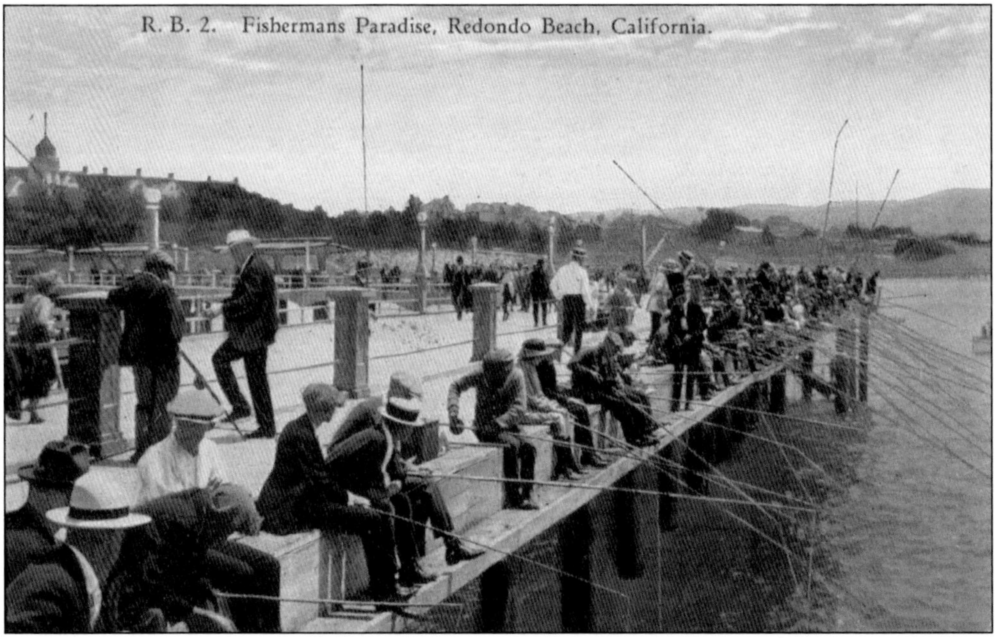

This postcard dated September 4, 1923, shows how popular fishing was on the Redondo Pier. The card, sent to Martin Hartings from a Mrs. L., reads, "Wonder if you like fishing? If so you would like this beach. It is famed for its good fishing. I do not think fish as firm and good as those caught in our own salt water as the water here is much warmer." (Courtesy Marilyn Ron; published by Western Publishing and Novelty Company, Los Angeles, California.)

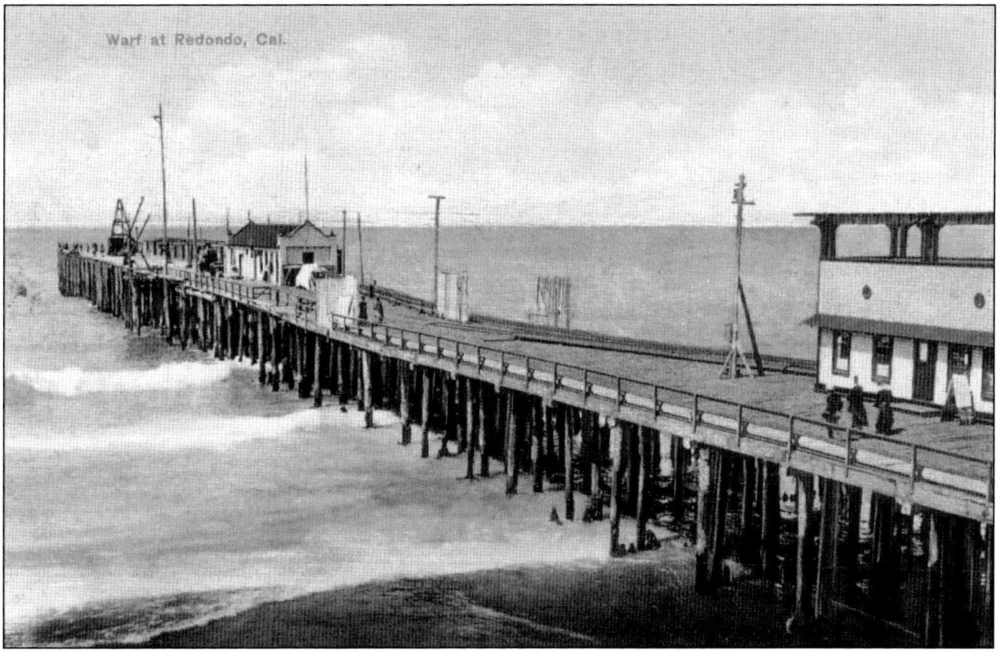

This card dated October 5, 1909, shows one of the many wharfs that used to exist in Redondo Beach. Wharf One washed out in the storm of 1915. Wharf Two was built in 1895 and Wharf Three in 1903. All had been destroyed by 1926. (Courtesy Marilyn Ron; published by Newman Post Card Company, Los Angeles, California.)

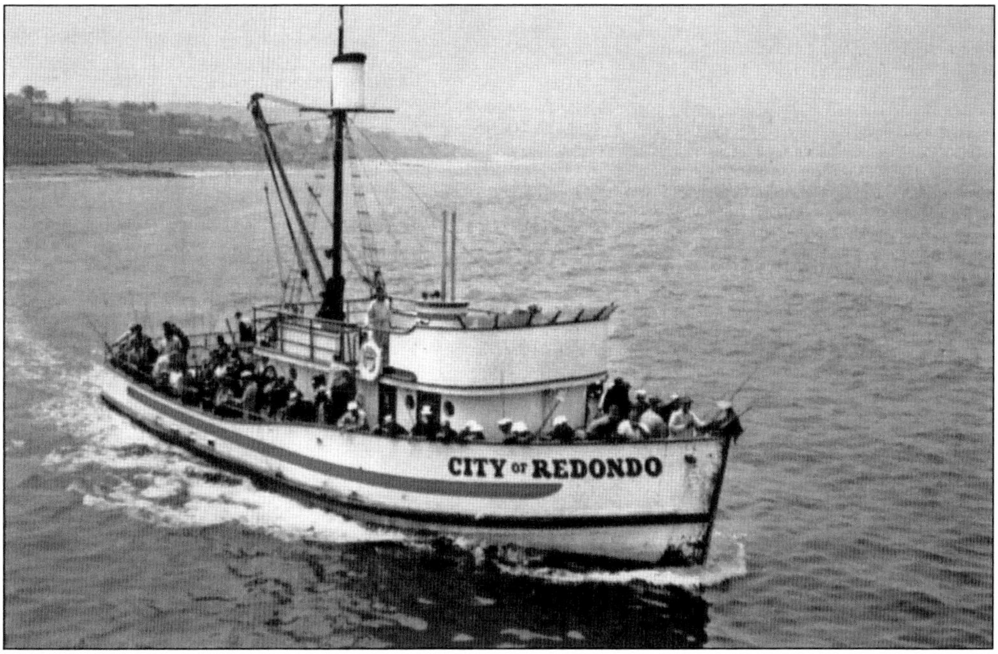

This 1950s postcard shows the fishing boat *City of Redondo*. The card states, "Leaves twice daily from the pier for deep sea fishing in one of the finest fishing areas off the California coast." (Courtesy Marilyn Ron; published by Western Publishing and Novelty Company, Los Angeles, California.)

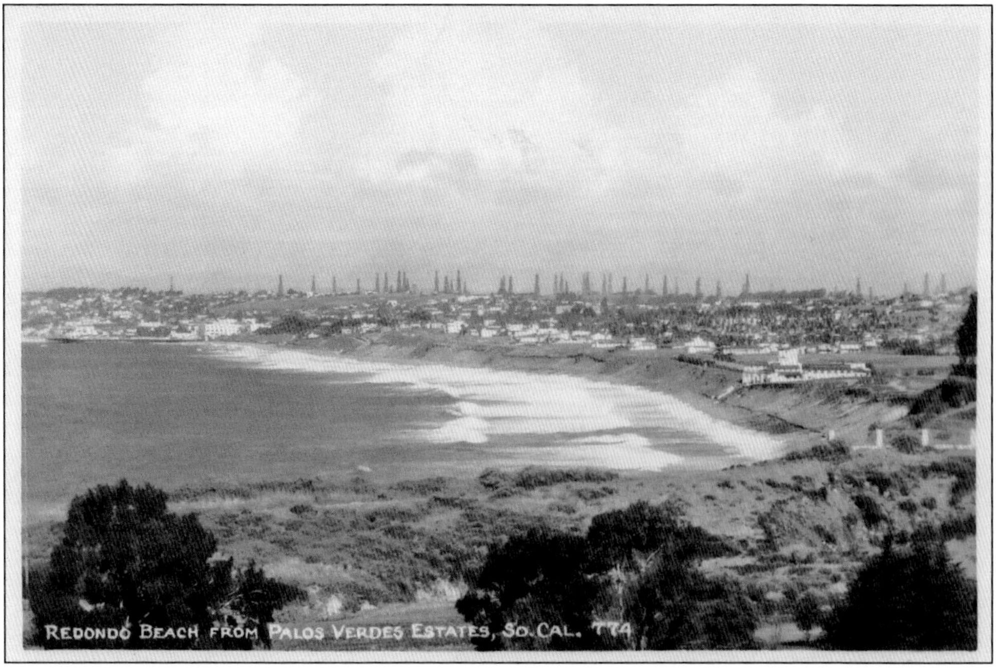

This scenic real-photo postcard shows Redondo Beach from the vantage point of Palos Verdes Estates. Note all of the oil wells in the background. (Courtesy Bill Ron.)

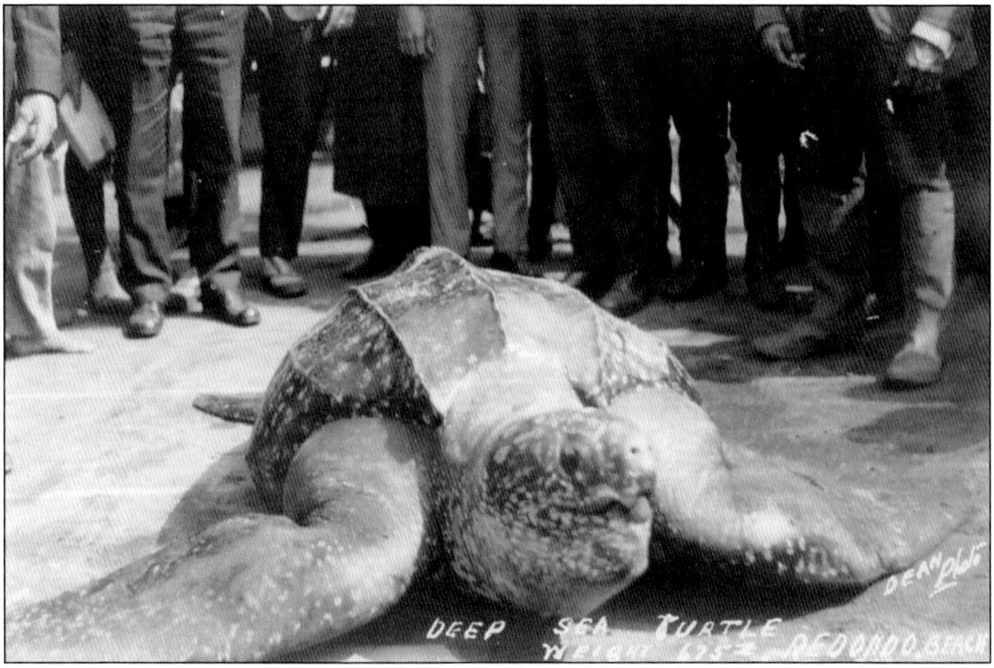

This Victorian postcard shows a giant deep sea turtle on the shore at Redondo Beach. The turtle weighed in at 675 pounds, according to the notation on the card. Hope this poor old guy did not end up in a soup pot. (Courtesy Marilyn Ron.)

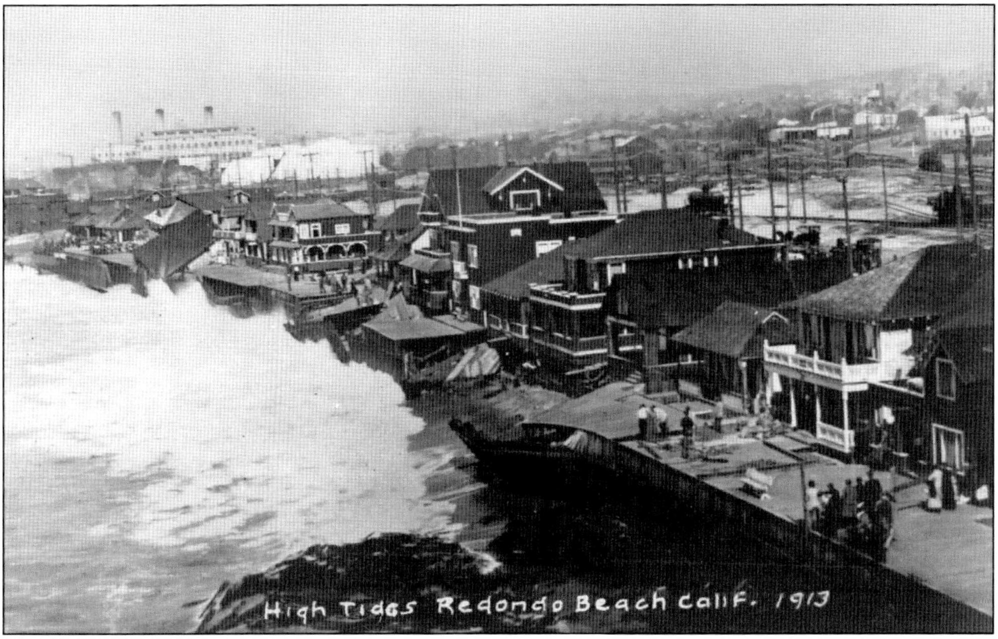

Redondo Beach has had a long history of destructive storms. This photo postcard dated 1913 shows the results of high tides on the residential area. Note the power plant in the background. The Pacific Light and Power Company Plant was built in 1907 at a cost of $500,000. The plant was acquired by Henry Huntington's Pacific Electric and later by the Edison Company. This plant was torn down in 1946 and replaced by the present plant in 1948. (Courtesy Bill Ron.)

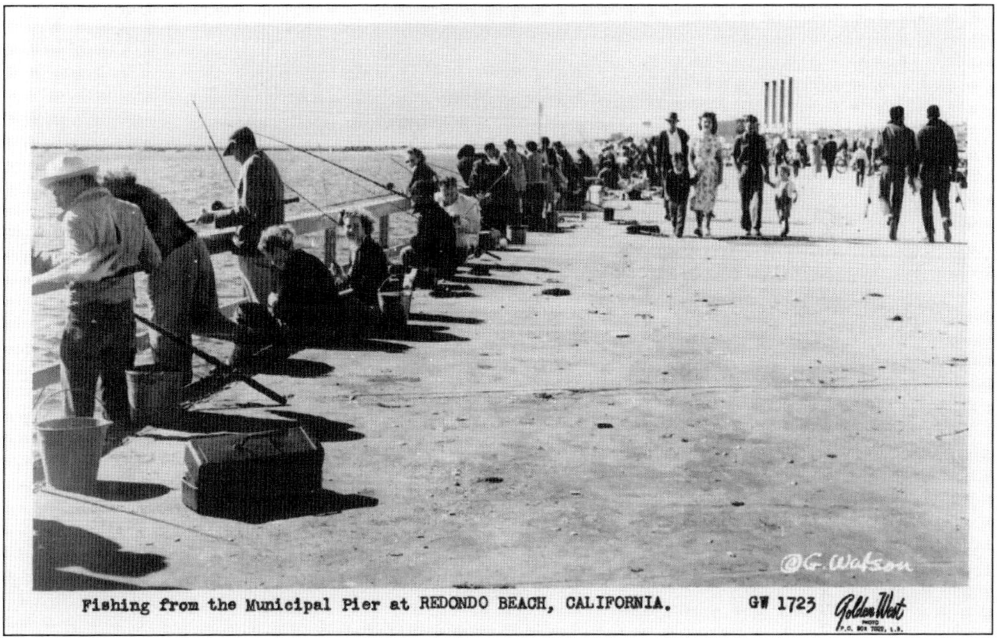

Fishing from the Municipal Pier at Redondo Beach is depicted. This early-1950s card shows the popularity of the area with tourists as well as fishermen. Note the stacks from the Edison Power Plant in the background. (Courtesy Bill Ron; published by G. Watson, Golden West, Long Beach, California.)

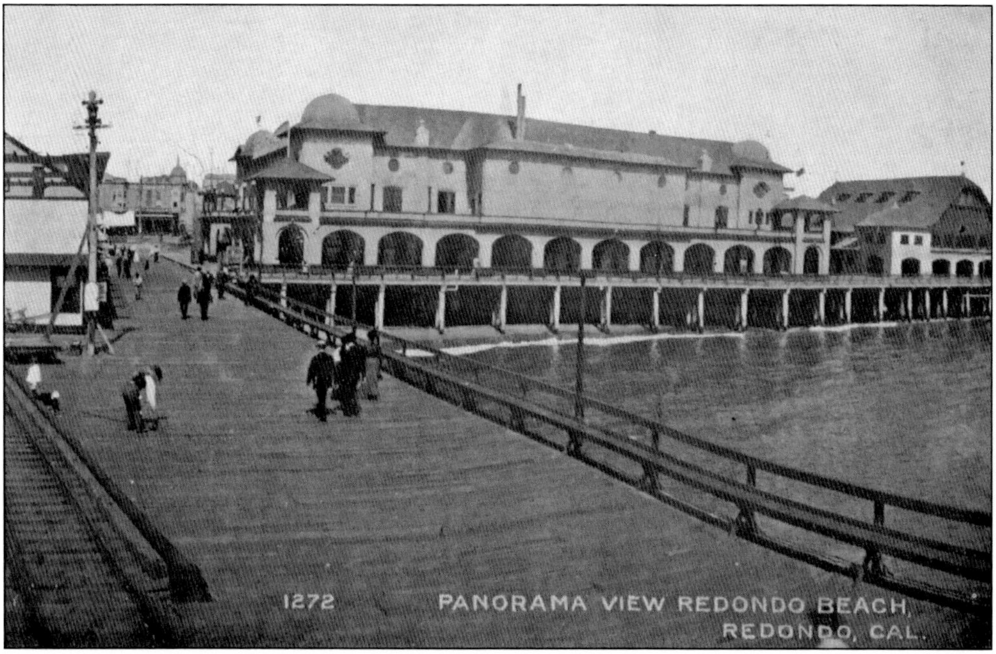

The back of this card reads, "Dear May, This is a dirty card, but they only had a few left and they were all dirty. This is Pier One where we go the most. Our rooms are straight up the street 3 blocks from this pier. On the left of the pier where you see the open bench is covered with roller coasters. It is quiet here except Sunday then the ocean front is crowded and every thing is wide open." (Courtesy Bill Ron.)

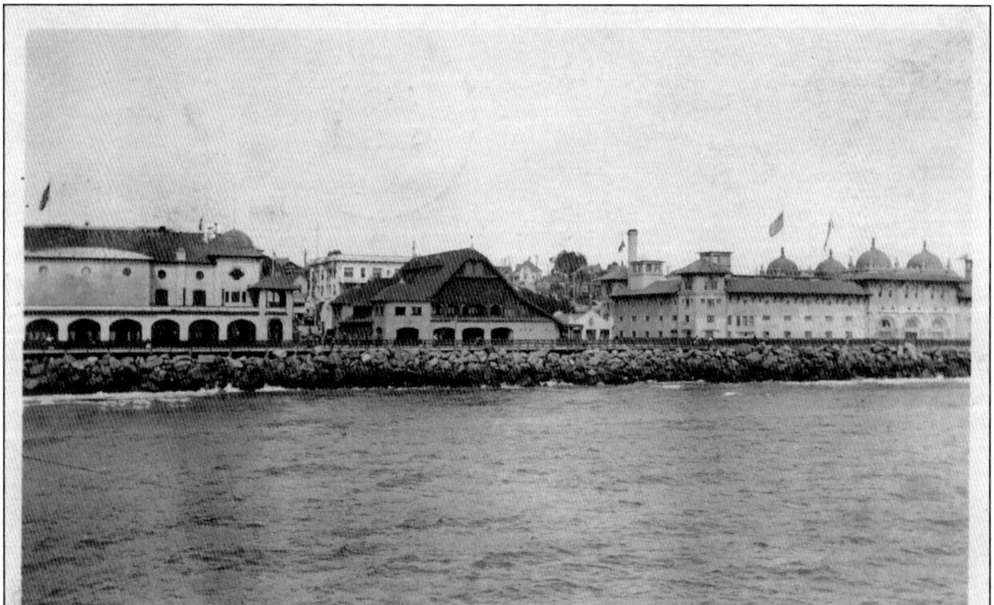

This RPPC shows the ocean view of the Auditorium, the Casino, and the Bath House. It was sent to Des Moines, Iowa, on August 8, 1910. (Courtesy Marilyn Ron.)

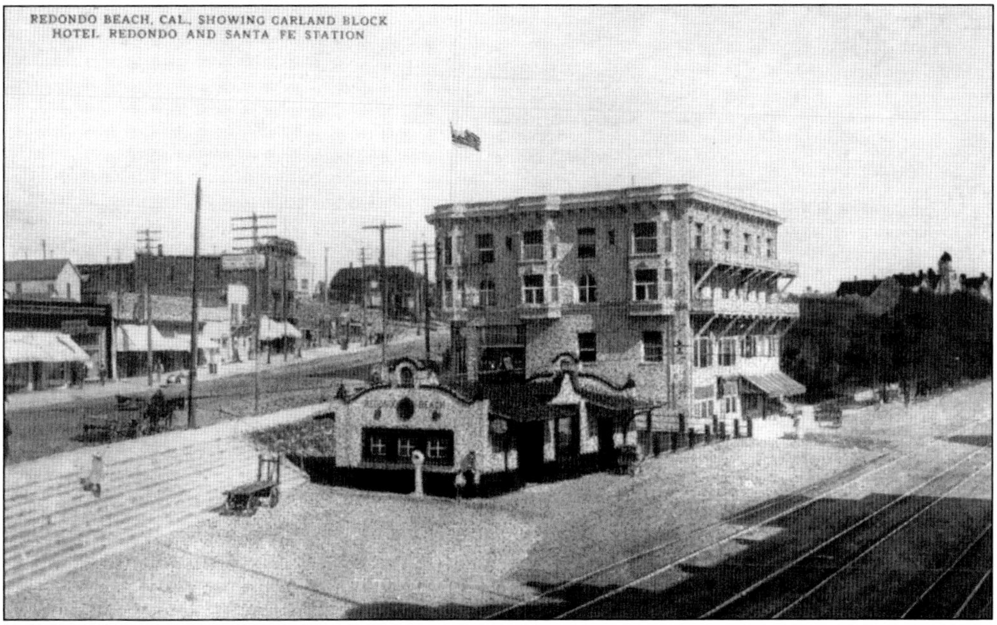

The Garland Block Hotel and the Redondo and Santa Fe Station were located side by side in old Redondo Beach. The notation at the bottom right dates this card to 1905. Note the horse and buggy to the left. The Hotel Redondo can be seen in the background on the far right. (Courtesy Bill Ron.)

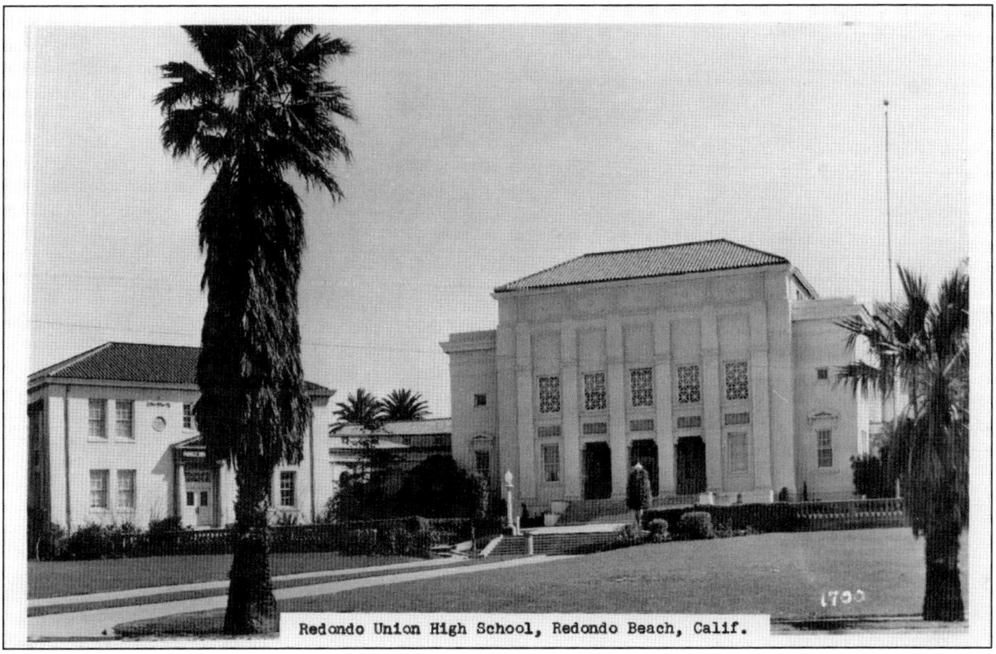

The Redondo Beach Union High School was opened in 1905 and moved to this location in 1907. The postcard reads, "Redondo Beach now has a population of over 37,000. When we came here about 5,000. This is one of our many buildings. Redondo Beach and Hermosa and Manhattan Beaches send their high school age students to our schools. We now have a group in Manhattan Beach and are planning for a third high school." (Courtesy Bill Ron.)

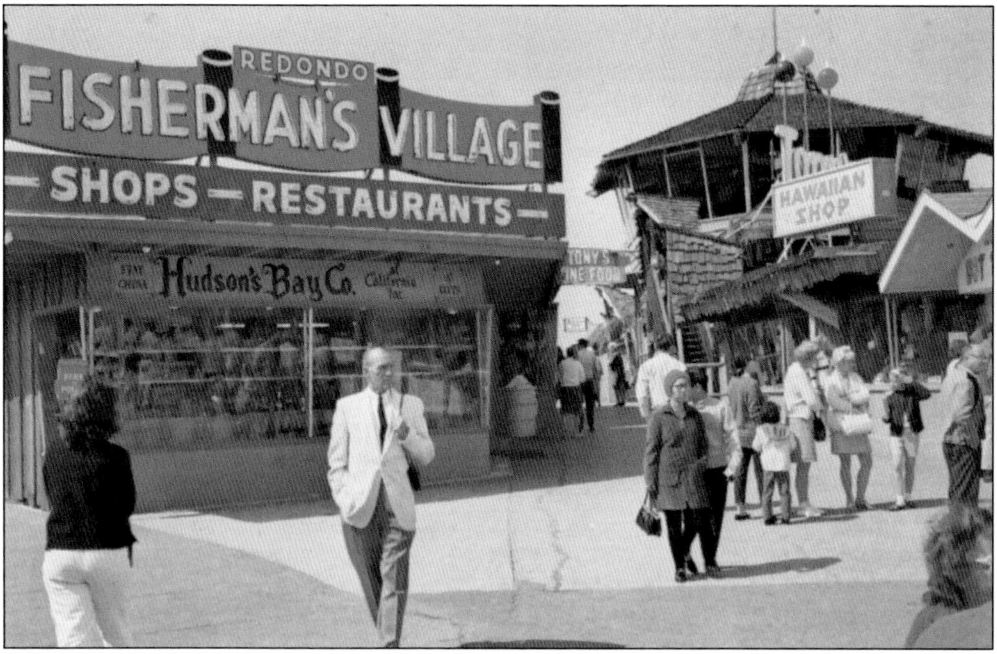

Fisherman's Wharf appears here mostly as it does to this day. The second story of Tony's can be seen in the upper right corner. (Courtesy Marilyn Ron; published by George E. Watson, Golden West, Long Beach, California.)

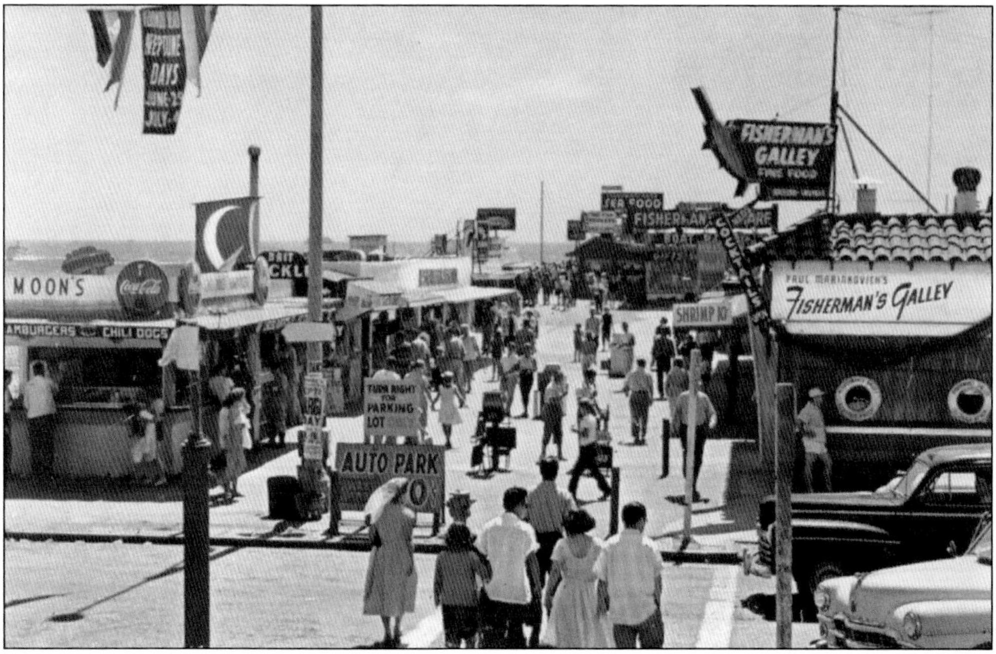

The old main entrance to Fisherman's Wharf is depicted here in 1964. Note Paul Marinovich's Fisherman's Galley. In those days, patrons could park all day for $1. (Courtesy Bill Ron; published by Western Publishing and Novelty Company, Los Angeles, California.)

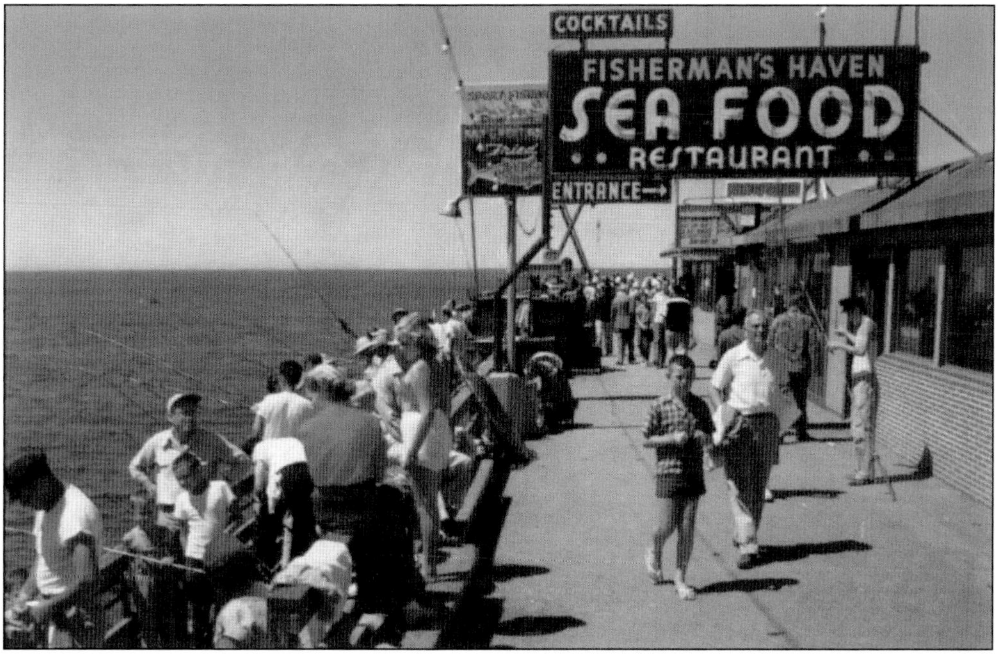

The Monstad Pleasure Fishing Pier was one of the popular draws on Fisherman's Wharf. (Courtesy Bill Ron; published by George E. Watson, Golden West, Long Beach, California.)

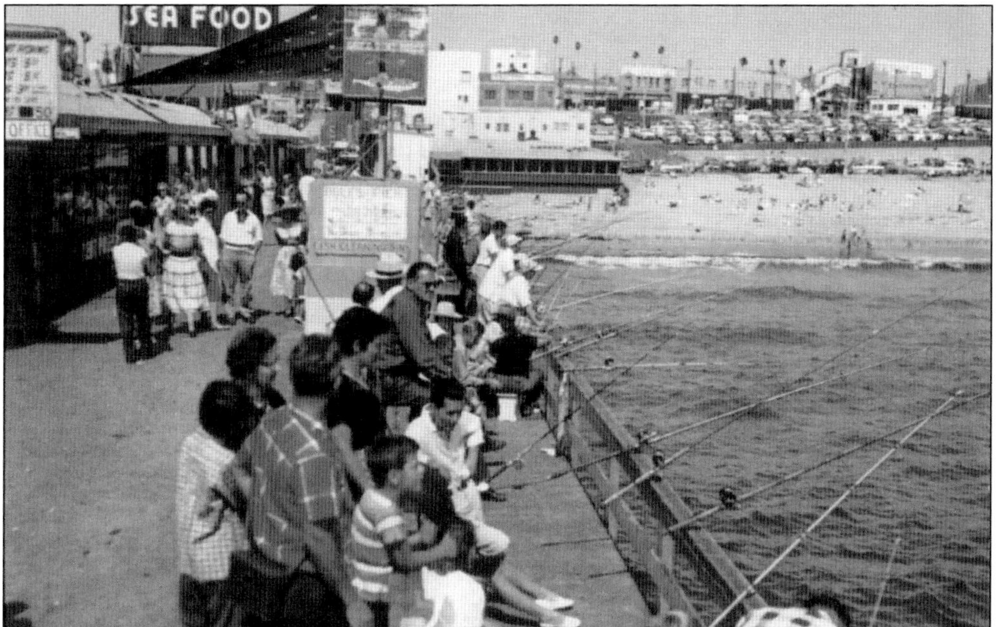

Fishing off the south end of Redondo Beach Pier was as popular in this image, perhaps from the 1950s, as it is from today's version of the pier. (Courtesy Bill Ron; published by Western Publishing and Novelty Company, Los Angeles, California.)

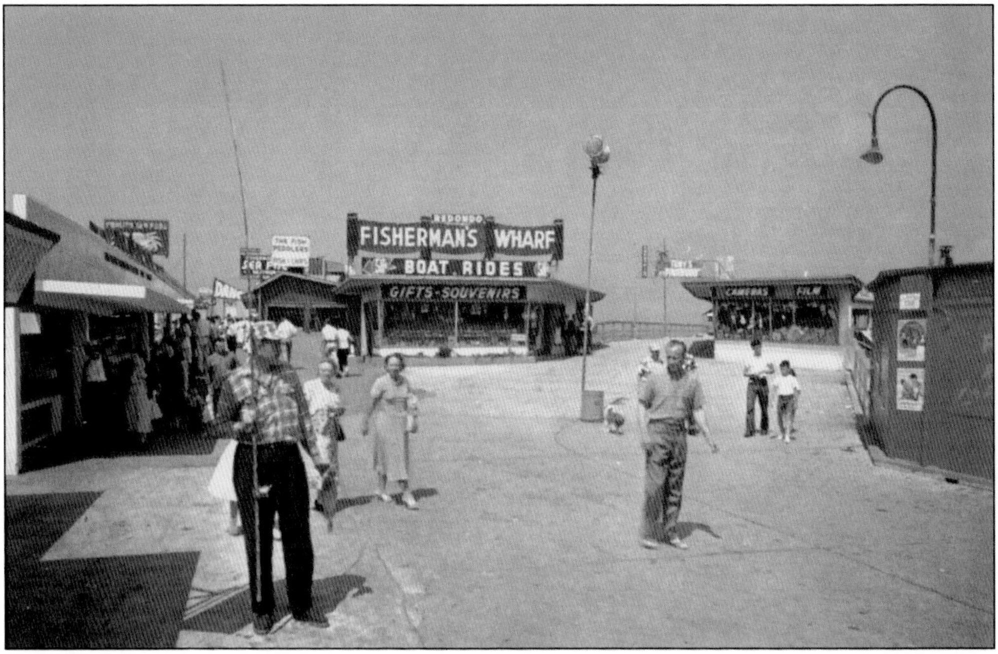

This card shows more buildings have been added, such as the camera shop in front of Tony's. The sign on the gift shop in the center now reads "Boat Rides." (Courtesy Marilyn Ron; published by Western Publishing and Novelty Company, Los Angeles, California.)

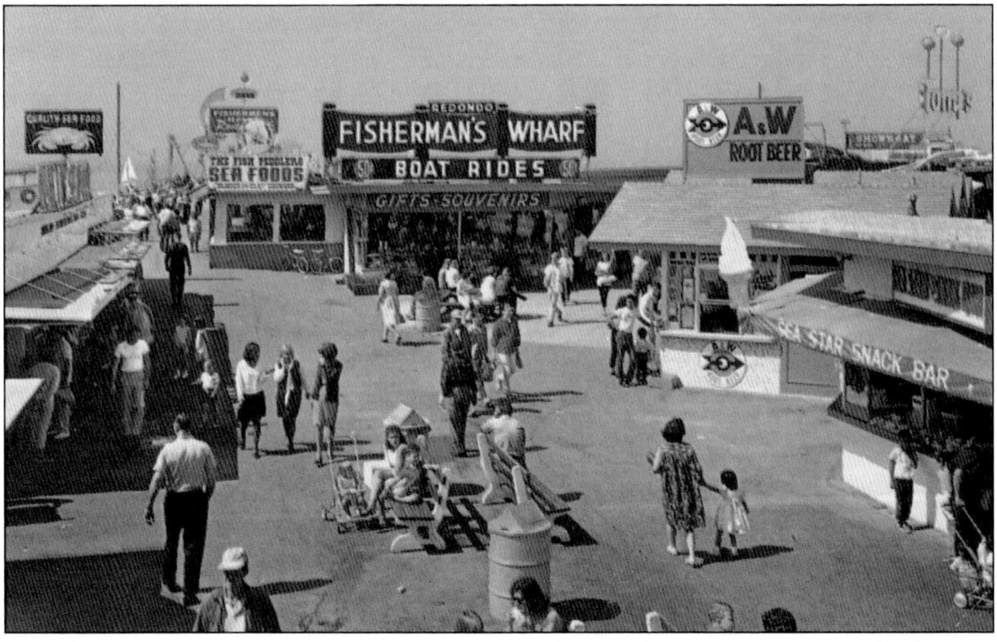

This 1960s postcard shows that A&W Root Beer and Sea Star Snack Bar have been added. Tony's has a new "space age" sign, and the Sea Food restaurant has been updated. Even with the passing of time, many of these building still exist today on the south end of the pier, which was spared from the 1988 fire that destroyed most of the center and north ends of the wharf. (Courtesy Marilyn Ron; published by Western Publishing and Novelty Company, Los Angeles, California.)

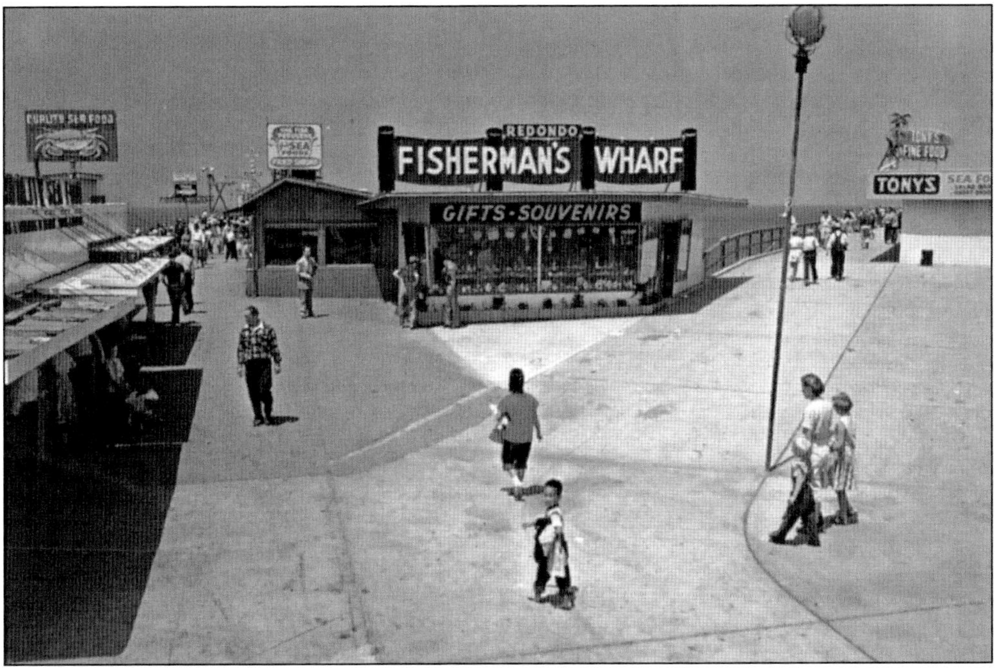

The reader can see some of the changes in the 1950s and 1960s in the look of the pier in the cards before and after this one. In this postcard, note how bare the right-hand side appears and the Tony's sign. (Courtesy Marilyn Ron; published by Colourpictures, Boston, Massachusetts.)

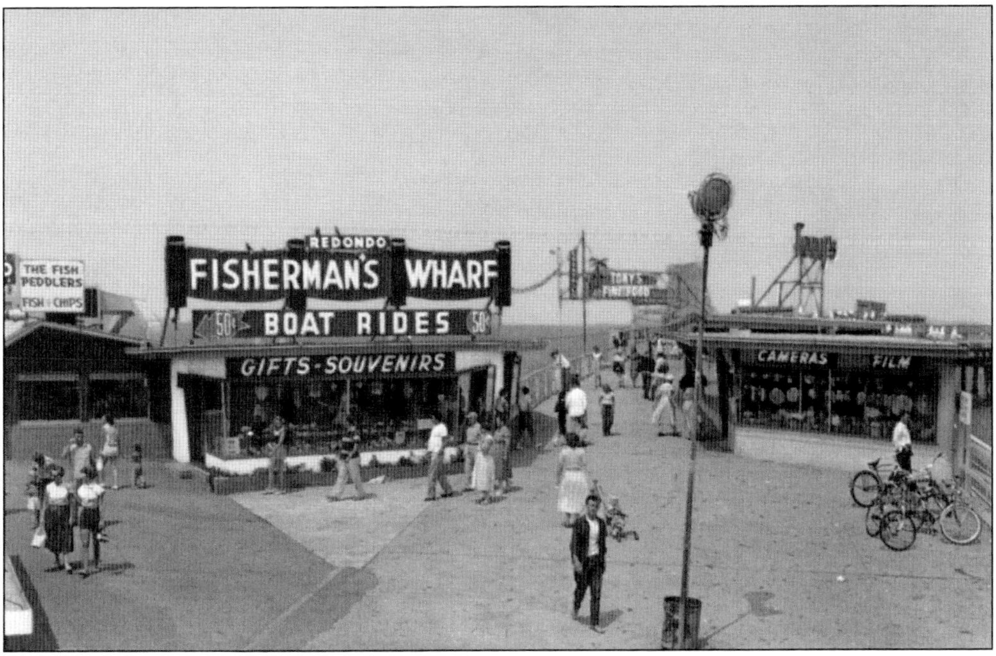

Another postcard of the Fisherman's Wharf Pier shows a closer look at the gift shop and camera store. Note that the Tony's sign is prominent on the roof. (Courtesy Marilyn Ron; published by Western Publishing and Novelty Company, Los Angeles, California.)

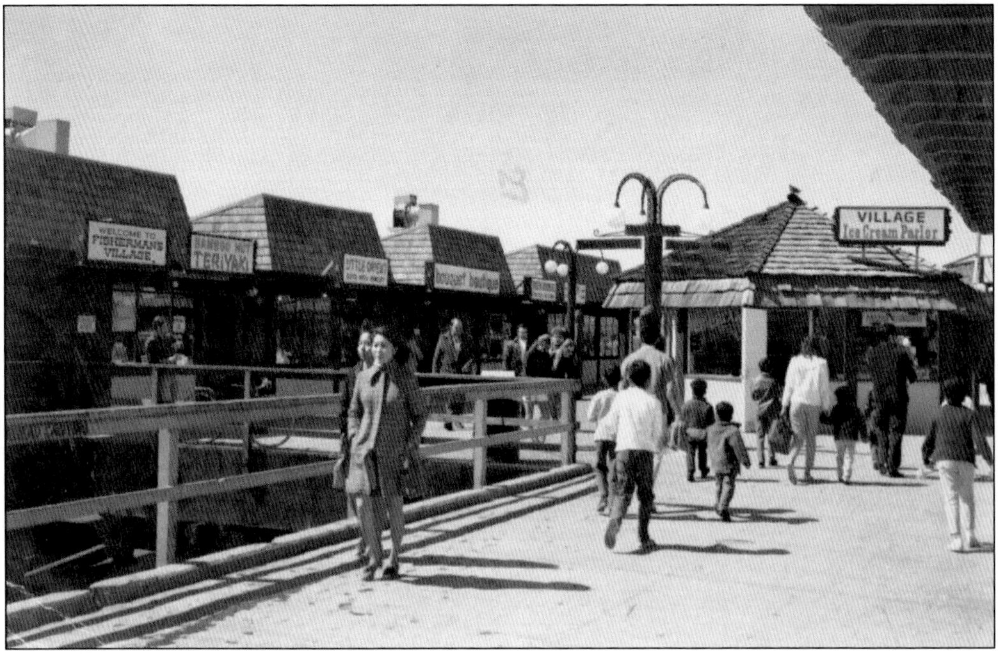

This 1972 vintage postcard depicts Redondo Beach Fisherman's Village, which was as popular then for strolling as it is today for joggers. (Courtesy Bill Ron; published by Golden West, Long Beach, California.)

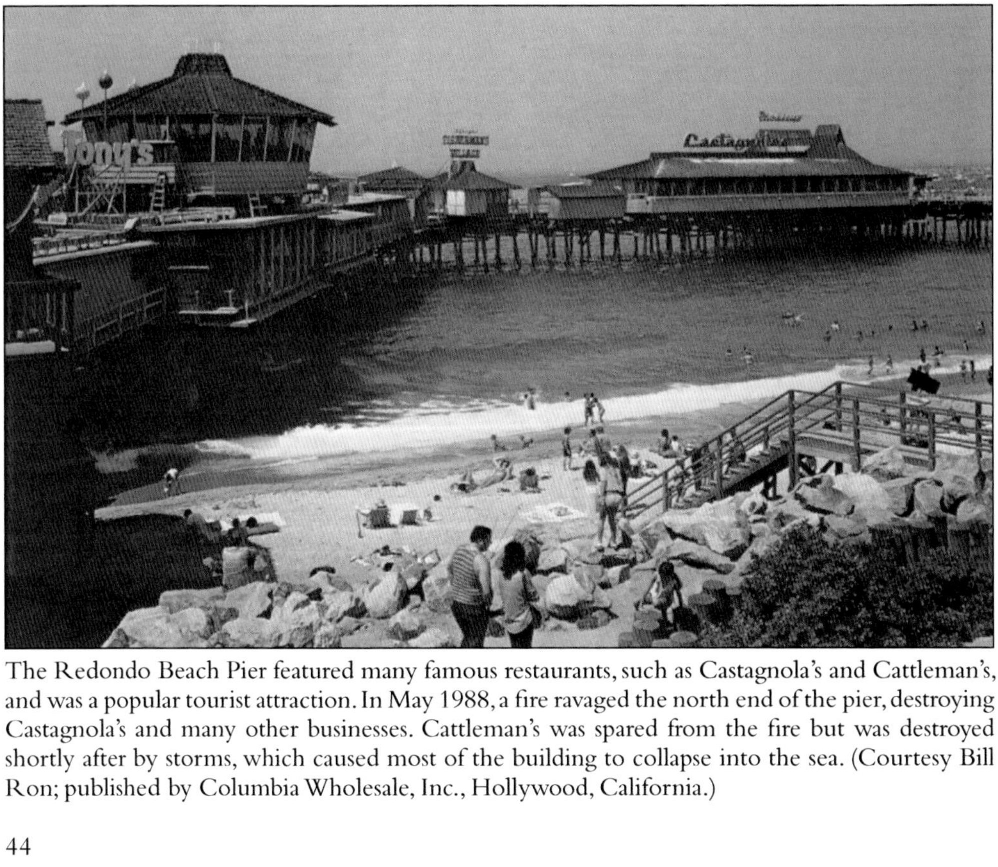

The Redondo Beach Pier featured many famous restaurants, such as Castagnola's and Cattleman's, and was a popular tourist attraction. In May 1988, a fire ravaged the north end of the pier, destroying Castagnola's and many other businesses. Cattleman's was spared from the fire but was destroyed shortly after by storms, which caused most of the building to collapse into the sea. (Courtesy Bill Ron; published by Columbia Wholesale, Inc., Hollywood, California.)

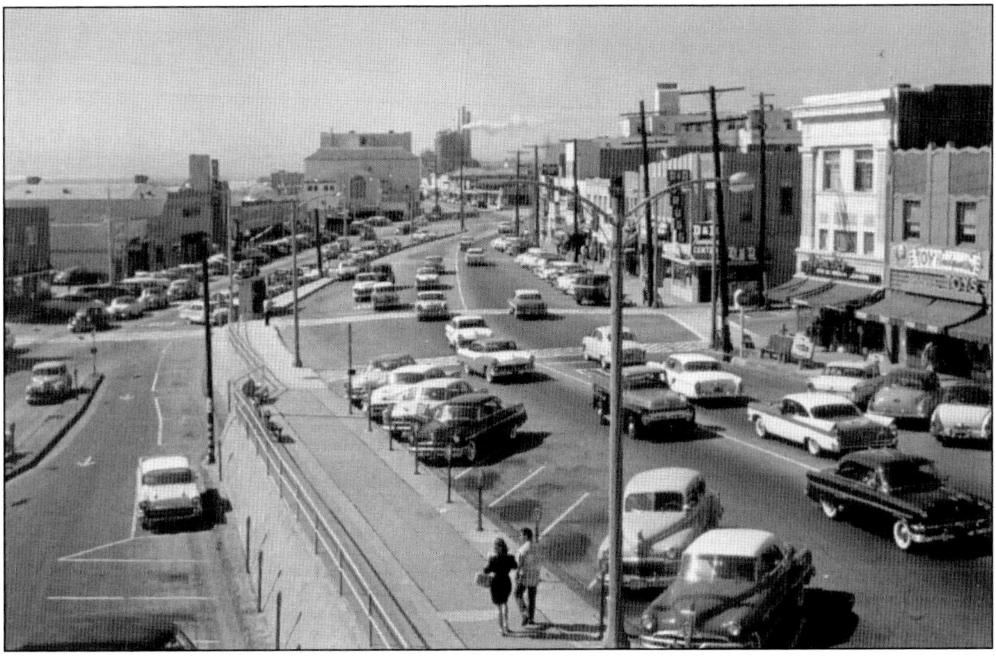

This view looks northward along Pacific Avenue at the "Triangle" in Redondo Beach. A main thoroughfare in Redondo, Pacific Avenue no longer exists. It was a casualty of the redevelopment of the 1970s that created the "new" Redondo Beach Pier area. Note the Fox Theatre and the power plant in the background. The Fox was torn down in 1973. D&D Drugs can be seen on the corner. (Courtesy Bill Ron.)

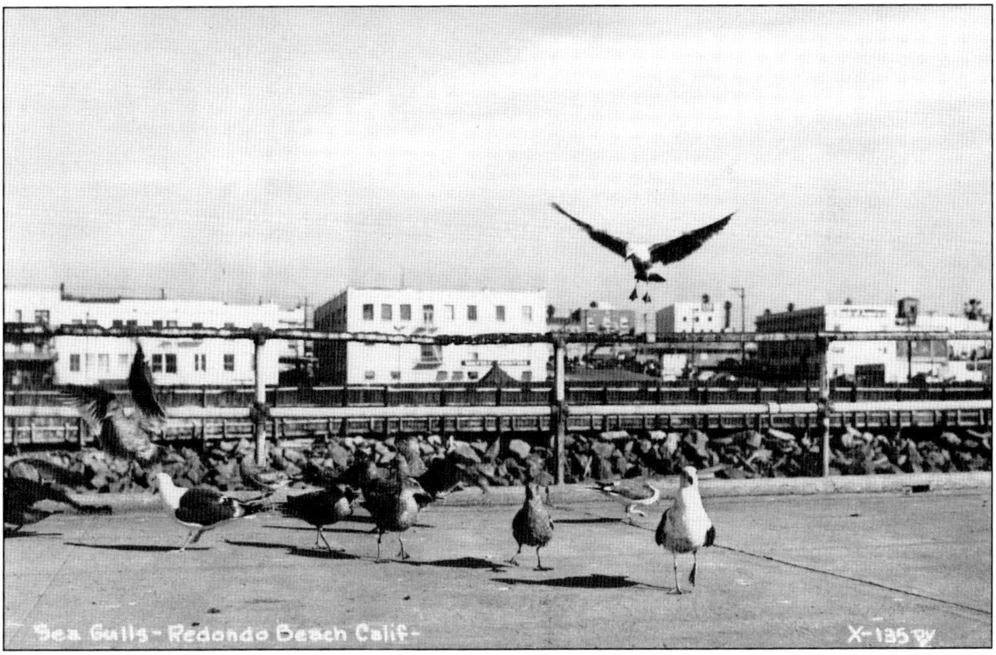

Among the most ubiquitous critters in Redondo Beach are the seagulls. This real-photo postcard looks toward Pacific Avenue sometime prior to the redevelopment that claimed that street in the 1970s. (Courtesy Bill Ron.)

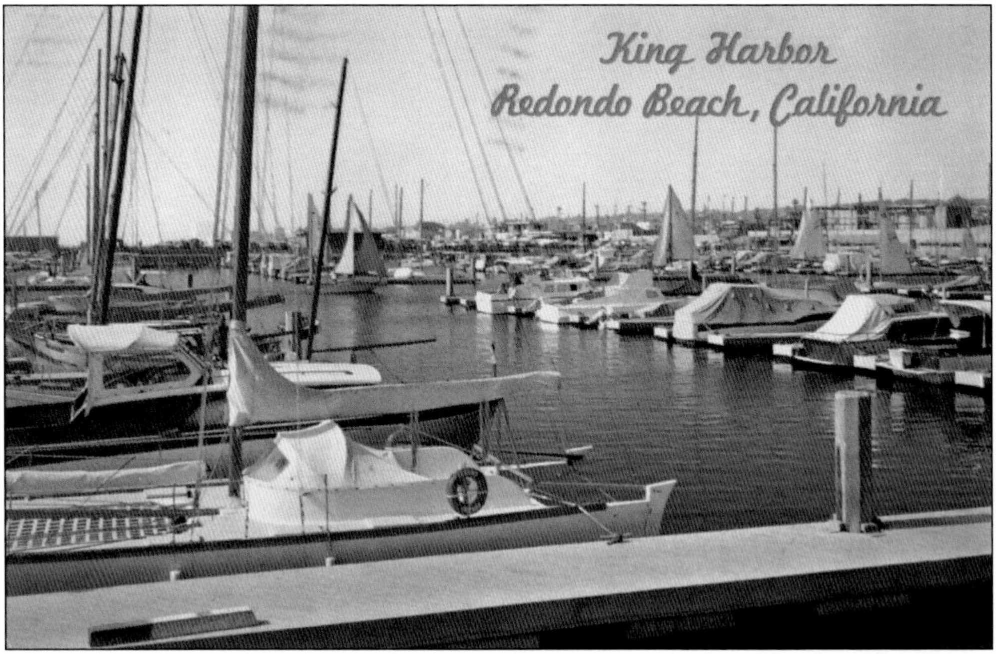

This 1968 postcard shows the King Harbor Marina area. It was sent to Al and Ann Spowart of Illinois from Gladys and Joe and reads, "Had a nice trip. Had dinner looking out at the Pacific Ocean. Went to Disneyland yesterday, Palm Springs tomorrow." (Courtesy Marilyn Ron; published by Golden West, Long Beach, California.)

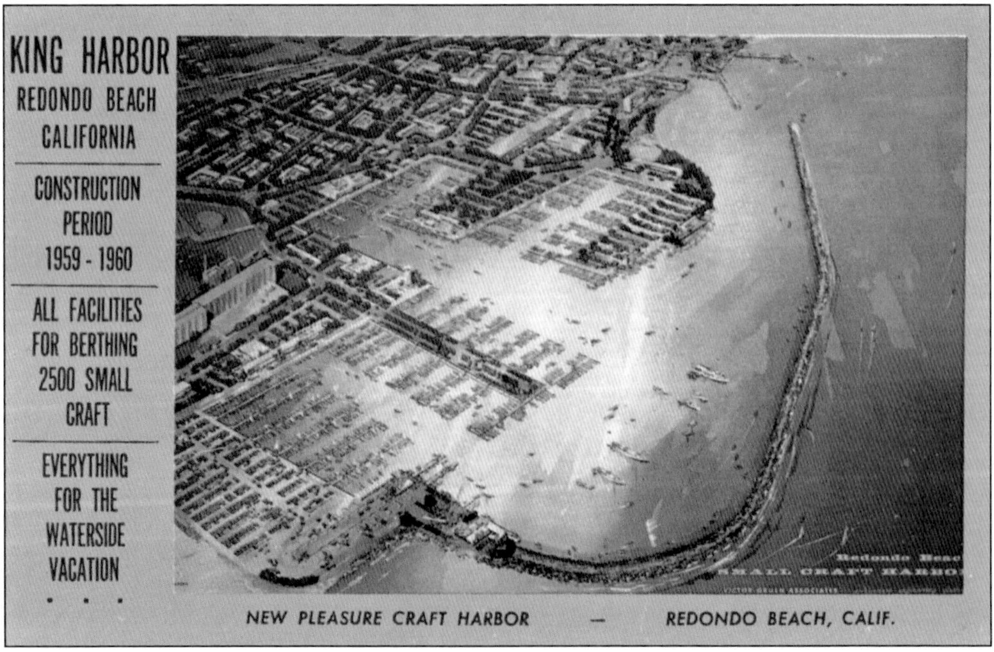

This advertising postcard depicts an artist's rendering of the new pleasure-craft harbor during the construction phase in 1959 and 1960. The marina was to contain berthing for 2,500 small craft and everything for waterside vacation needs. (Courtesy Bill Ron; published by Western Publishing and Novelty Company, Los Angeles, California.)

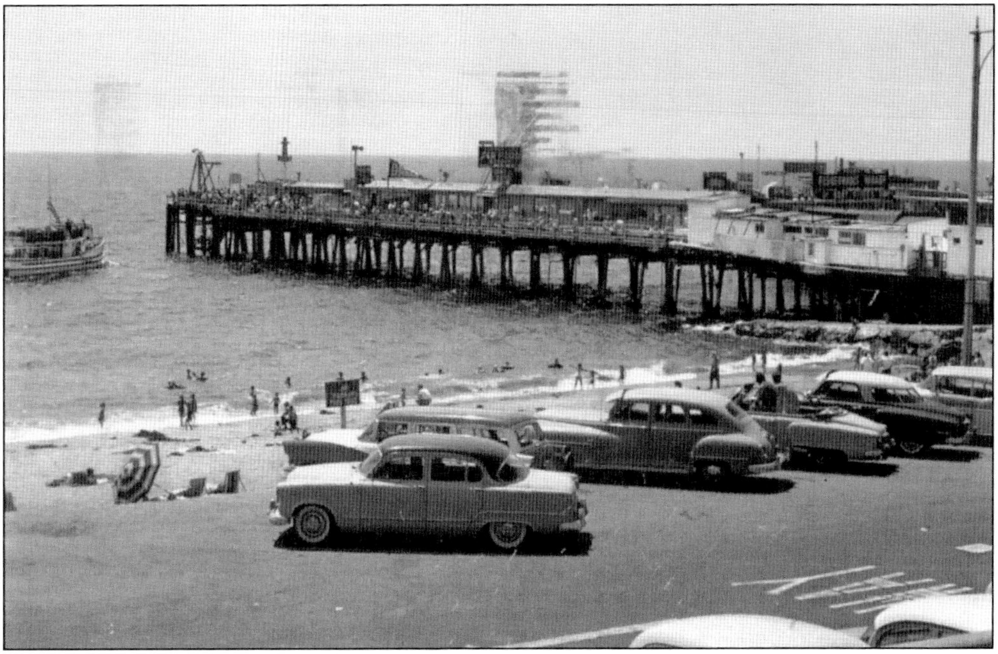

This 1963 postcard's caption reads, "El Paseo and Pier: Redondo Beach, California. A fine sandy beach and excellent fishing attract many to this popular seaside resort." (Courtesy Bill Ron; published by Western Publishing and Novelty Company, Los Angeles, California.)

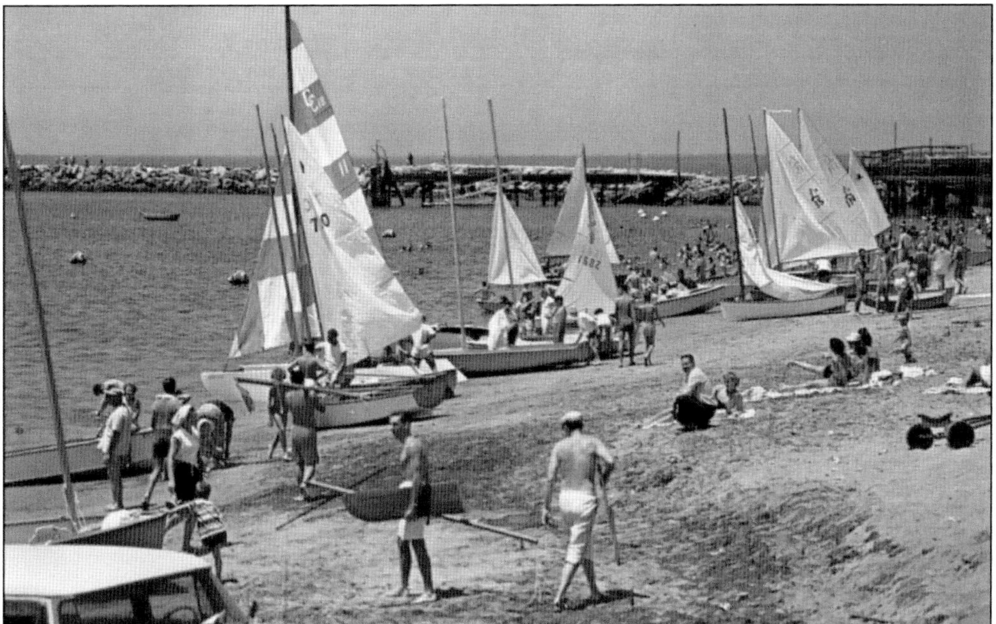

King Harbor's small boat launching area, located at the foot of Tenth Street in Redondo Beach, is depicted on this 1960 vintage postcard. (Courtesy Bill Ron; published by George E. Watson, Golden West, Long Beach, California.)

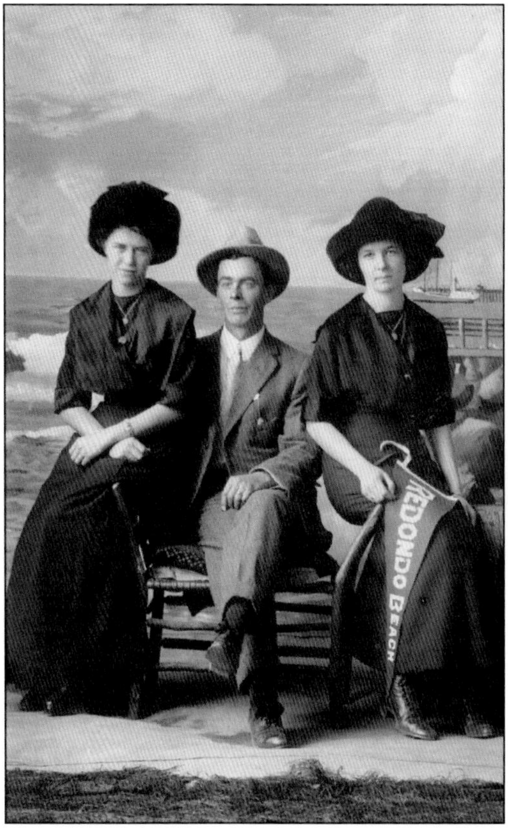

This real-photo postcard was taken on January 7, 1912, at Lemon's Studio in Redondo Beach. On the left is Helen Buss, who later became the founding librarian of the Lawndale Library on December 26, 1913. Her friend Nellie Dickey is seen at the right holding a Redondo Beach pennant. The gentleman in the middle is unidentified. (Courtesy James Osborne.)

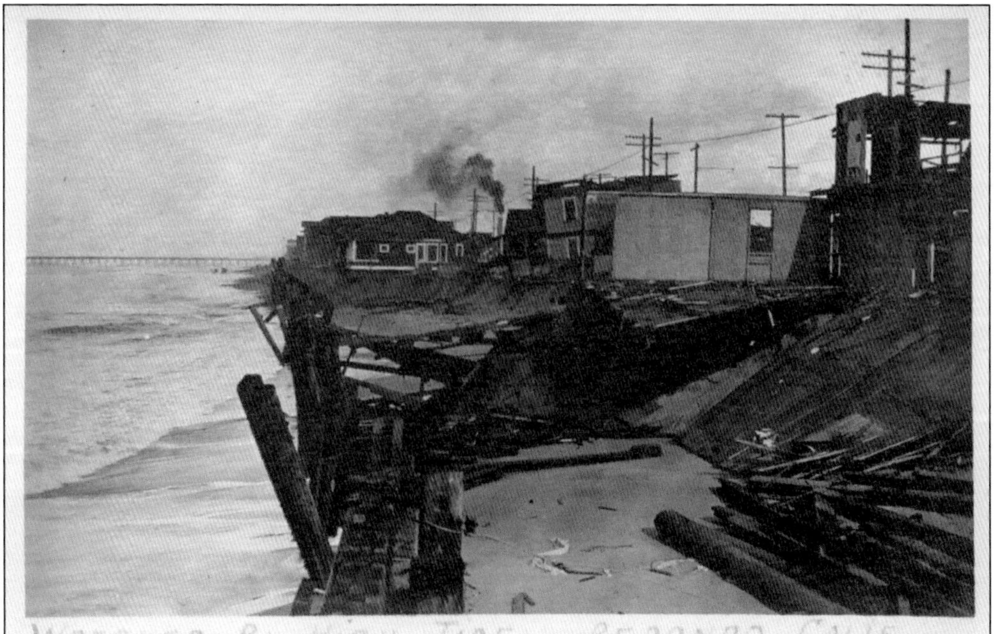

This RPPC scene shows storm damage in Redondo Beach and carries the notation, "Wrecked by high tide, Redondo, Calif." (Courtesy James Osborne.)

Two

INLAND CITIES

Getting from point A to point B in the South Bay has usually meant traveling through Torrance. That was via the old El Camino Real in the rancho days, the Southern Pacific Railroad thereafter, and on famous Pacific Coast Highway or California Highway 1 when it was the great thoroughfare of the 20th century. Now, for two generations, traversing the South Bay has often meant on the world's busiest road—or largest "parking lot"—the San Diego Freeway or I-405.

As a city on the go, as they say, Torrance has been integral to transportation in many ways, as it once was the location of a main shop for the Pacific Electric "Red Cars" and today contains the U.S. headquarters of American Honda Motor Company and Toyota Motor Sales USA as well as Robinson Helicopters, located at Torrance Airport, and the enormous ExxonMobil Refinery. As a business and retail focal point, Torrance has also been home to the mall that was once the world's largest, Del Amo Fashion Center, along venerable Hawthorne Boulevard.

The anchor city of the South Bay, Torrance is the region's largest municipality since 2000 in terms of population (roughly 150,000) and area (20.5 square miles). Stretching from the beachfront known as Hollywood Riviera east to Harbor Gateway, Torrance is encircled, clockwise, by Redondo Beach to the west; Lawndale, Hawthorne (a few blocks north of the L.A. County community of Alondra Park or El Camino Village), and Gardena to the north; Carson (just east of Harbor Gateway) and Lomita to the east; and the Palos Verdes cities to the south.

Torrance incorporated as a city in 1914, followed by Hawthorne in 1922 and Gardena in 1930. Today's Old Torrance was a South Bay center of commerce at mid century as Hawthorne and Gardena were small towns surrounded by farmlands, which became suburbia after World War II. Growth caused other cities to incorporate: Lawndale (1959), Lomita (1964), and Carson (1968).

These cities all evolved as suburbia with relationships to oil production, aviation history, and the ancillary businesses of the Port of Los Angeles—railroads, trucking, storage, and maritime services—that have kept them vital into the 21st century. Some of the few postcards depicting these suburban corners appear on the following pages. The authors could not obtain any from Carson.

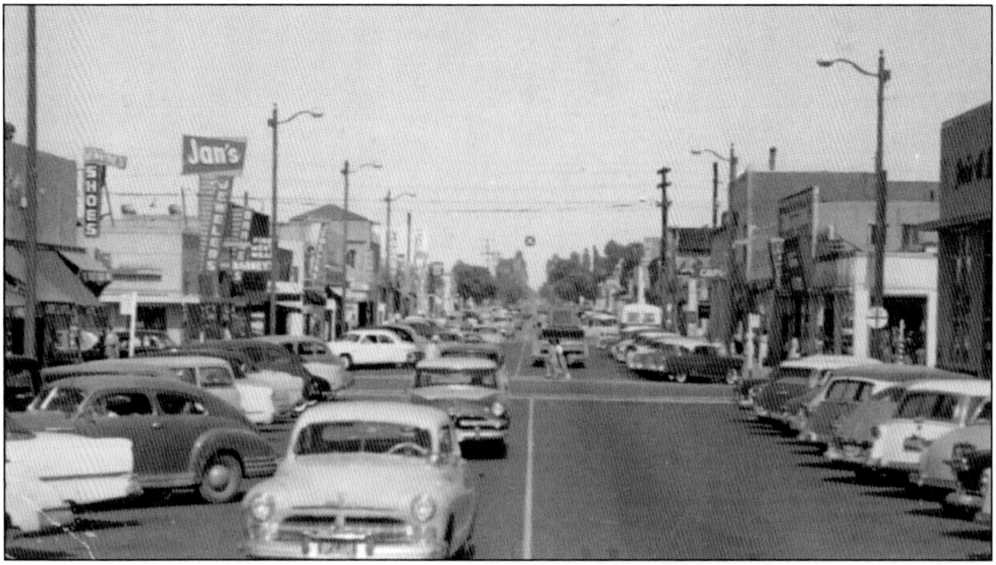

This 1950s view is of Gardena Boulevard looking east near New Hampshire Avenue. The message on the reverse is dated June 20, 1964, and reads, "We're down here for a few days with Elizabeth and her family, so you won't be hearing from me this week. Hope you are still making progress and that all is well in your household. Best wishes, Olive and Ward." (Courtesy James Osborne; published by Golden West, Long Beach, California.)

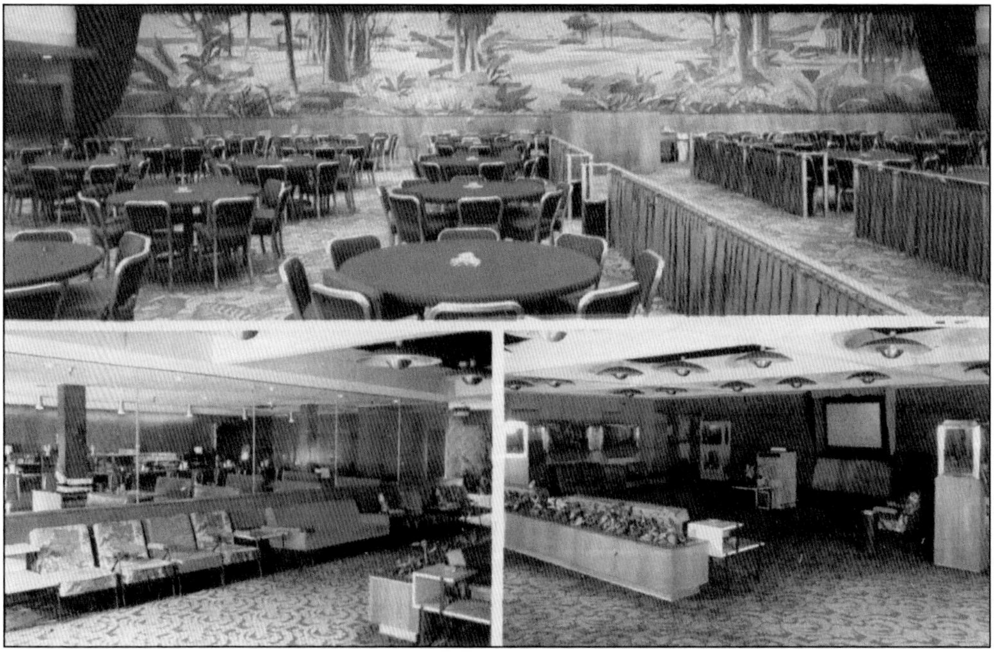

This view shows the interior of the Gardena Club, located at 15446 South Western Avenue in Gardena. The message on the reverse reads, "Hi Folks: This is the spot! It is ideal for recreation during your vacation. I do mean the Gardena Club in Gardena, California. Just enjoyed the fight on the huge 6 ft. by 4 ft. projected TV set. It came over like being at ringside. The food here is delicious—best in the country. See you soon." The postmark is November 1, 1957. (Courtesy James Osborne; published by Dexter Press, Inc.)

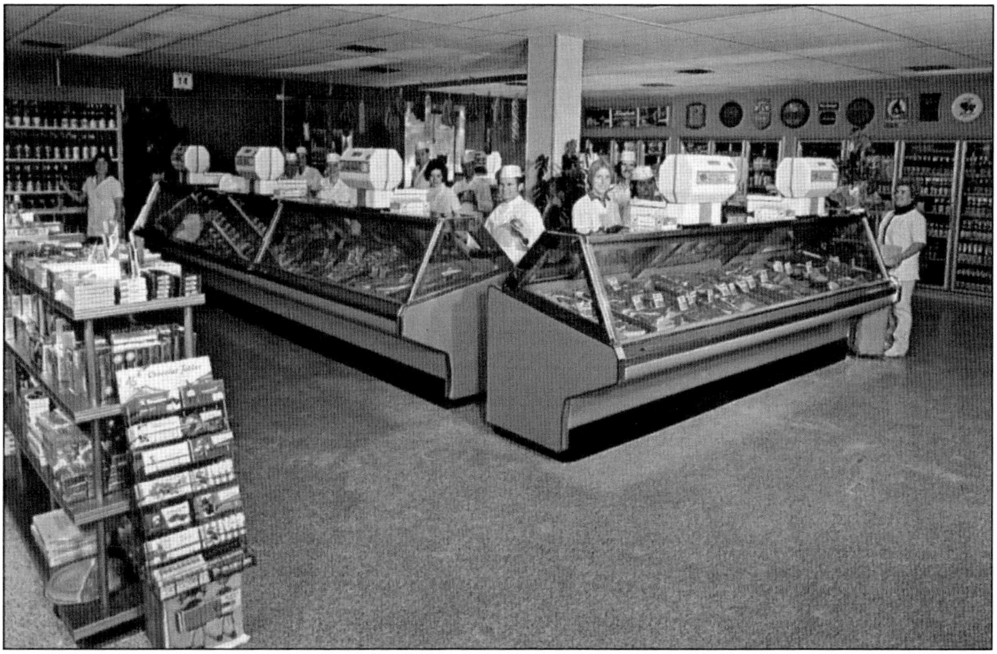

Eschbach Meat Products is depicted here, located at 18045 South Western Avenue in Gardena. The reverse reads, "We specialize in German and European sausages, gourmet meats, and delicatessen, large selection of international liquors, wines, and beer." (Courtesy James Osborne; published by John Rosenberger.)

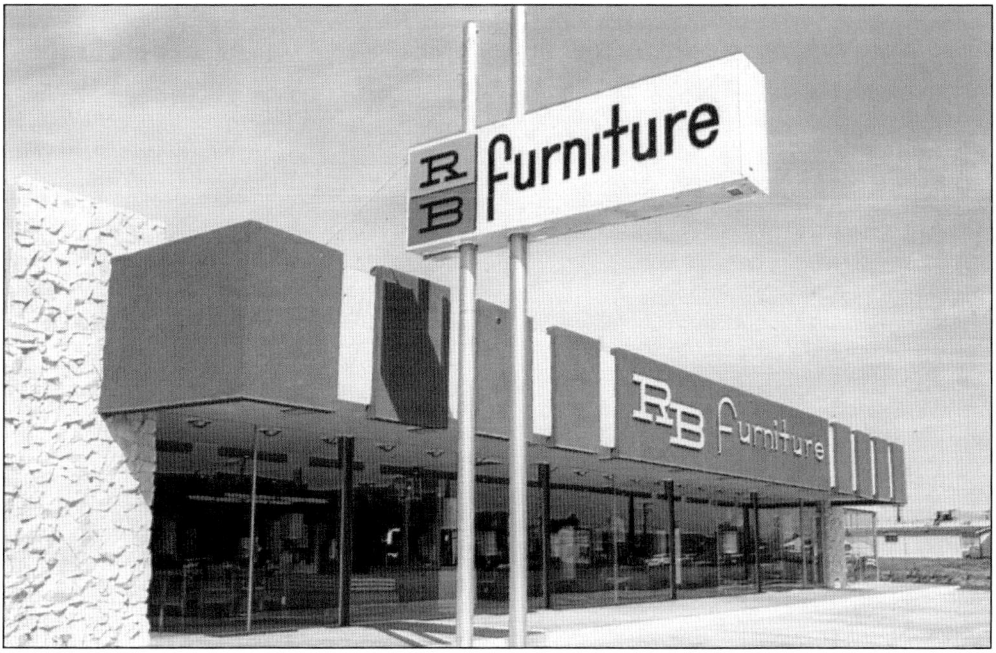

RB Furniture established its "Modern" store at 15533 Crenshaw Boulevard, Gardena. Not far away, at 15711 Crenshaw Boulevard, was RB's "Maple" store. (Courtesy James Osborne.)

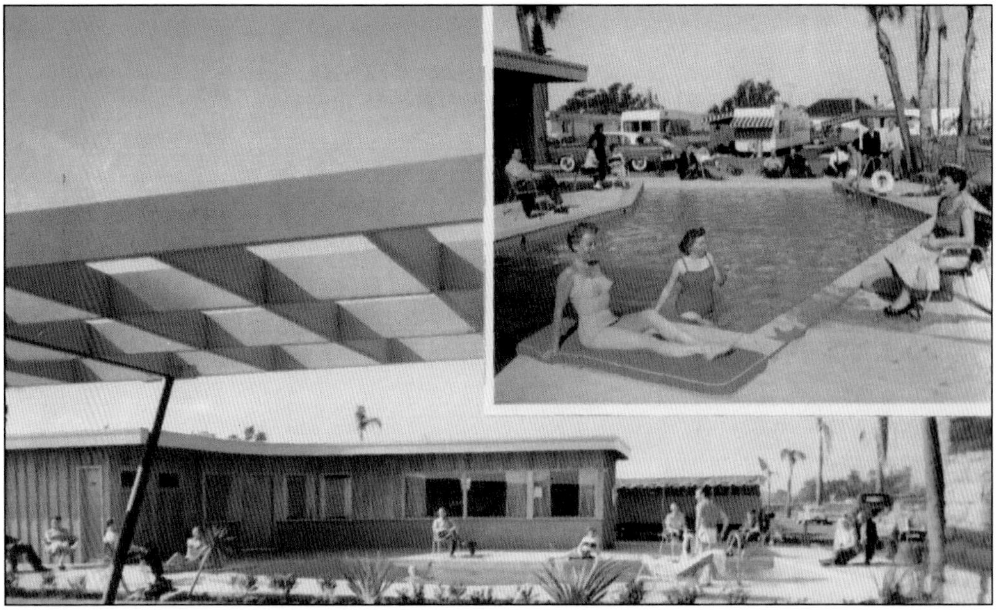

The Gardena Trailer Lodge proclaimed it was known "For Gracious Living." The caption on the reverse reads, "Enjoy California's finest 109 space park. Beautifully landscaped, spacious patios, heated swimming pool, recreation room, shuffle board, natural gas, sewer and phone connection to all spaces. 16949 South Western Avenue, Gardena, Calif." (Courtesy James Osborne; published by Dexter Press, Inc.)

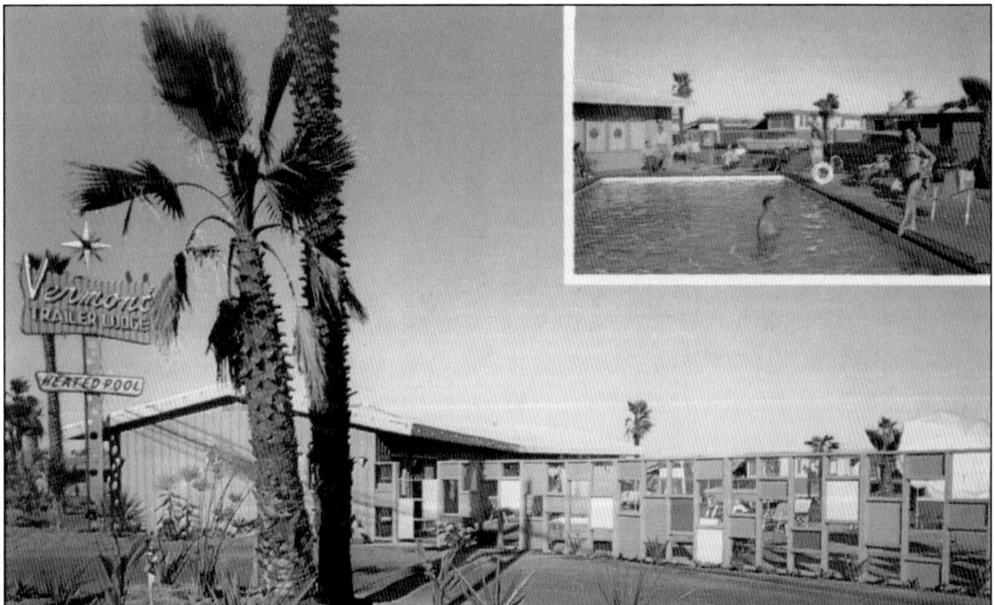

The Vermont Trailer Lodge proclaimed that it was known for "Luxurious Trailer Living." The caption on the reverse side elaborates, "Enjoy California's finest 128 space park. Beautifully landscaped, spacious patios, heated swimming pool, recreation room, natural gas, sewers and phone connection to all spaces. 18750 South Vermont Avenue, Gardena, Calif." (Courtesy James Osborne; published by Mellinger Studios.)

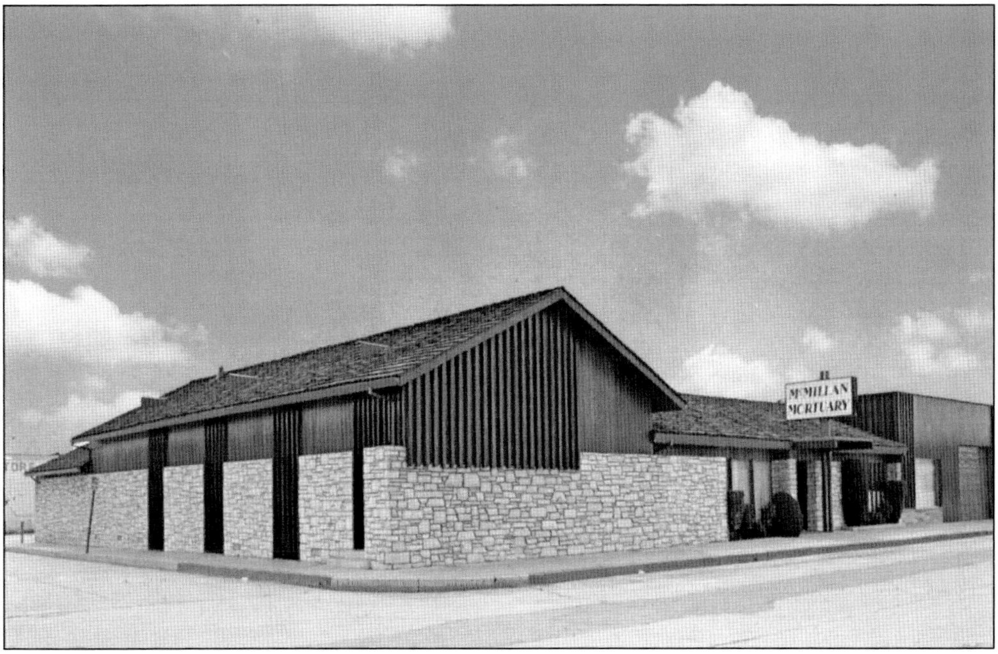

The McMillan Mortuary is located at the corner of Vermont Avenue and 164th Street. The reverse-side caption reads, "Gardena's preferred mortuary serving families of all faiths since 1912." McMillan continues to serve families to this day. (Courtesy James Osborne; published by Jasper Nutter.)

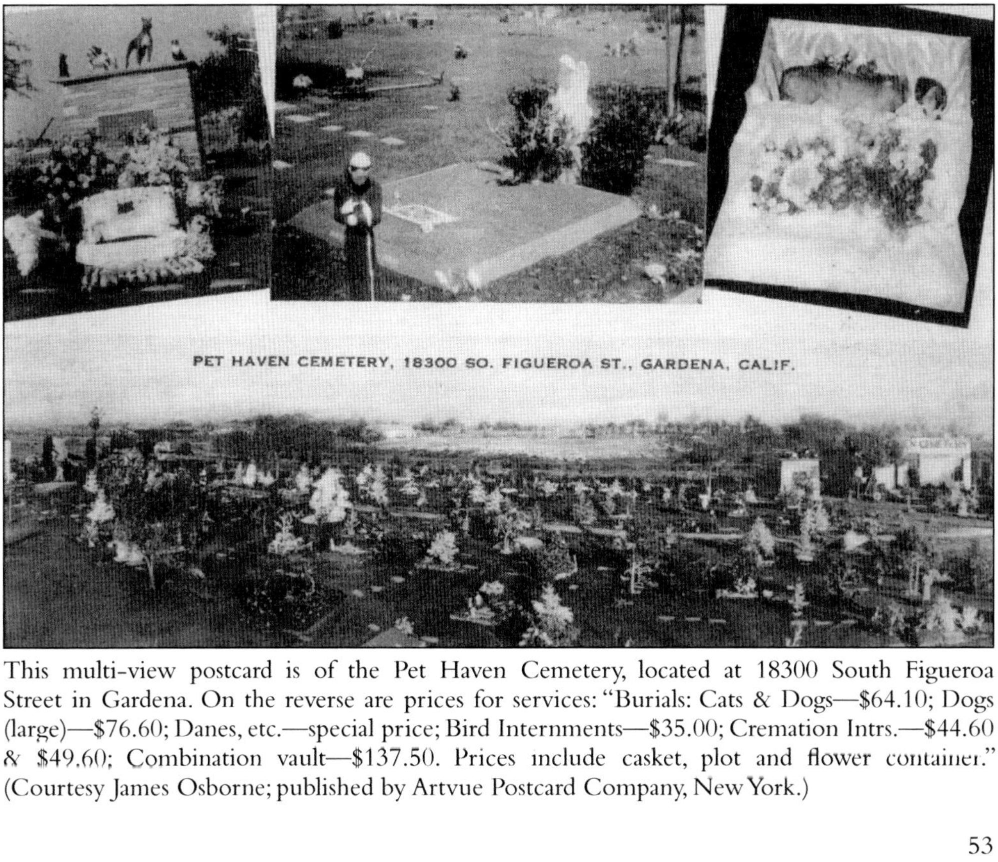

This multi-view postcard is of the Pet Haven Cemetery, located at 18300 South Figueroa Street in Gardena. On the reverse are prices for services: "Burials: Cats & Dogs—$64.10; Dogs (large)—$76.60; Danes, etc.—special price; Bird Internments—$35.00; Cremation Intrs.—$44.60 & $49.60; Combination vault—$137.50. Prices include casket, plot and flower container." (Courtesy James Osborne; published by Artvue Postcard Company, New York.)

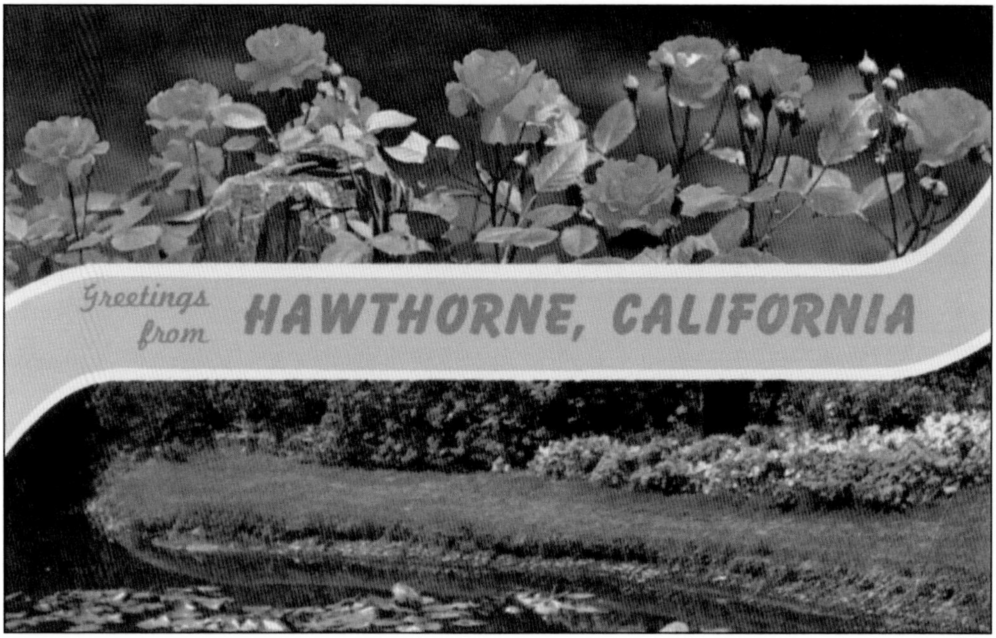

If the reader cares to look back to page 10, he or she will learn that the flowers and landscaping in old El Segundo bore a remarkable resemblance to the same in old Hawthorne, as depicted in these "Greetings from Hawthorne, California." (Courtesy James Osborne; published by Dexter Press, Inc., West Nyack, New York.)

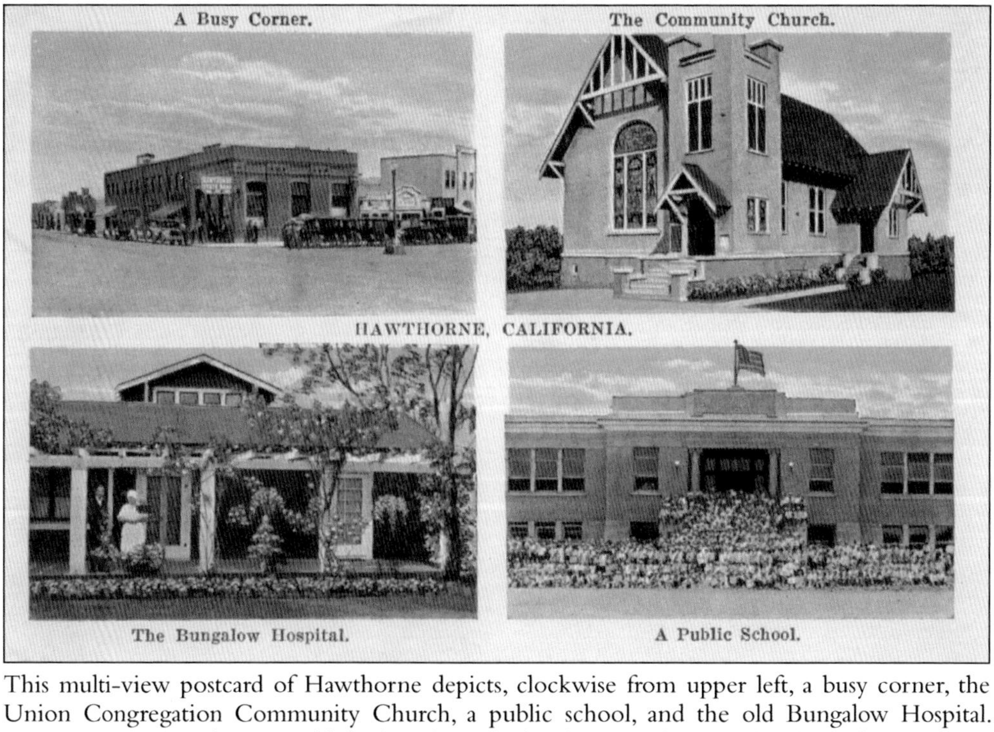

This multi-view postcard of Hawthorne depicts, clockwise from upper left, a busy corner, the Union Congregation Community Church, a public school, and the old Bungalow Hospital. (Courtesy James Osborne; published exclusively for the Hawthorne Chamber of Commerce, Hawthorne, California.)

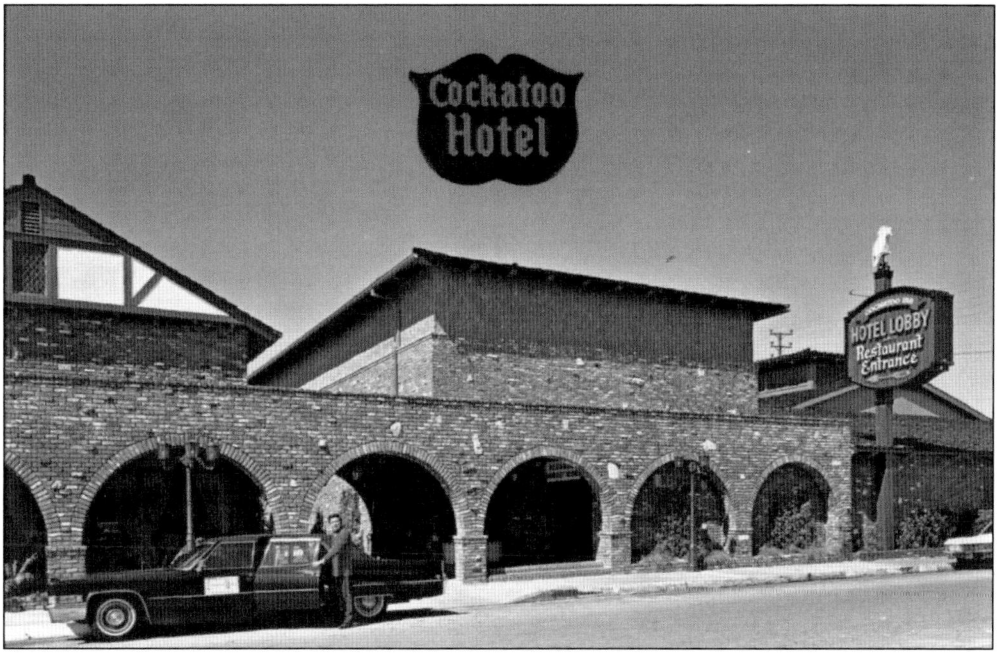

The Cockatoo Hotel and Restaurant was located at 4334 West Imperial Highway and was owned by Andrew Lococo. (Courtesy James Osborne; published by Schlendering.)

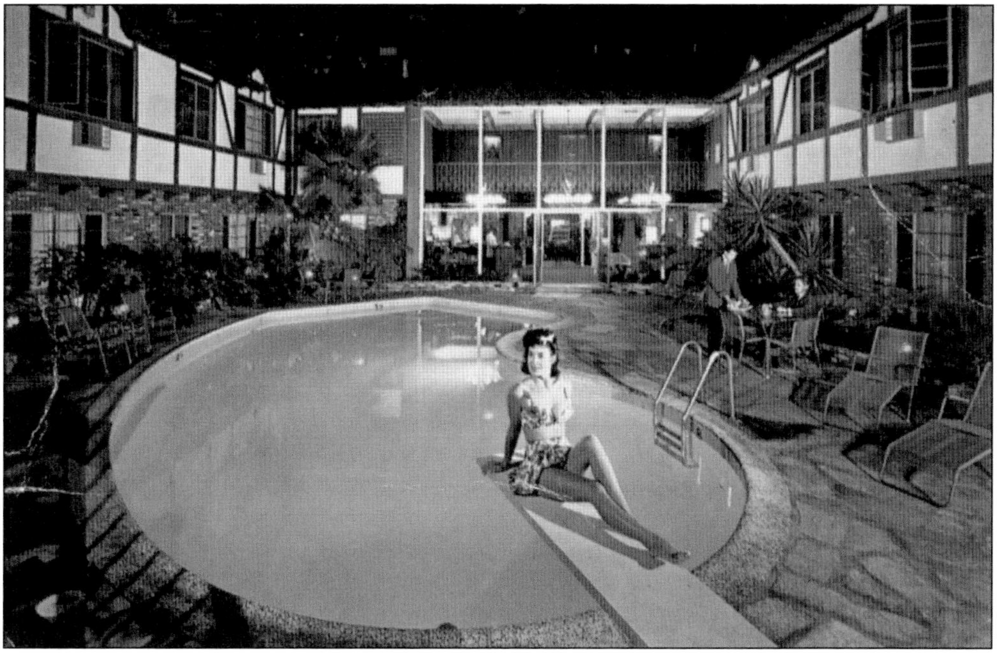

This is a night view of the pool at the Cockatoo Hotel, one of Hawthorne's most legendary hangouts, the bar of which was used as a filming location for Quentin Tarantino's *Jackie Brown* (1997) This postcard was postmarked on August 11, 1969. (Courtesy James Osborne; published by Schlendering.)

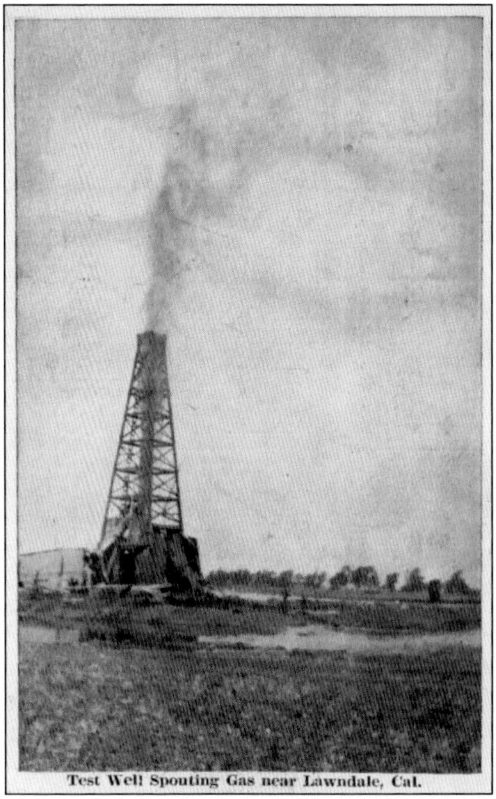

A test well spouting gas near Lawndale is depicted here. During the 1920s, oil was discovered in the western portion of Lawndale. By March 1929, more than 70 wells were drilled, which earned Lawndale the nickname "The Black Gold Village." By the early 1930s, the oil boom went bust and drilling ceased. (Courtesy James Osborne; published by Auburn Postcard Manufacturing Company, Auburn, Indiana.)

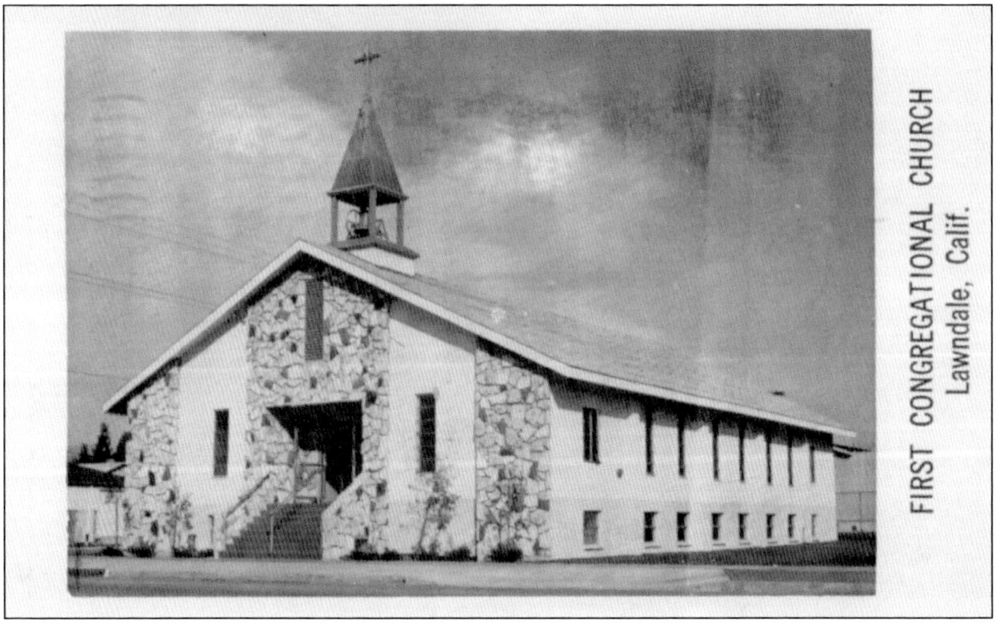

The Lawndale Congregational Church was founded on April 9, 1907. The original building was demolished on March 25, 1963, and the church seen in this postcard was constructed on the site in 1965. This church lasted until June 30, 2002, when the last service was held. This postcard has a postmark of September 12, 1967. (Courtesy James Osborne.)

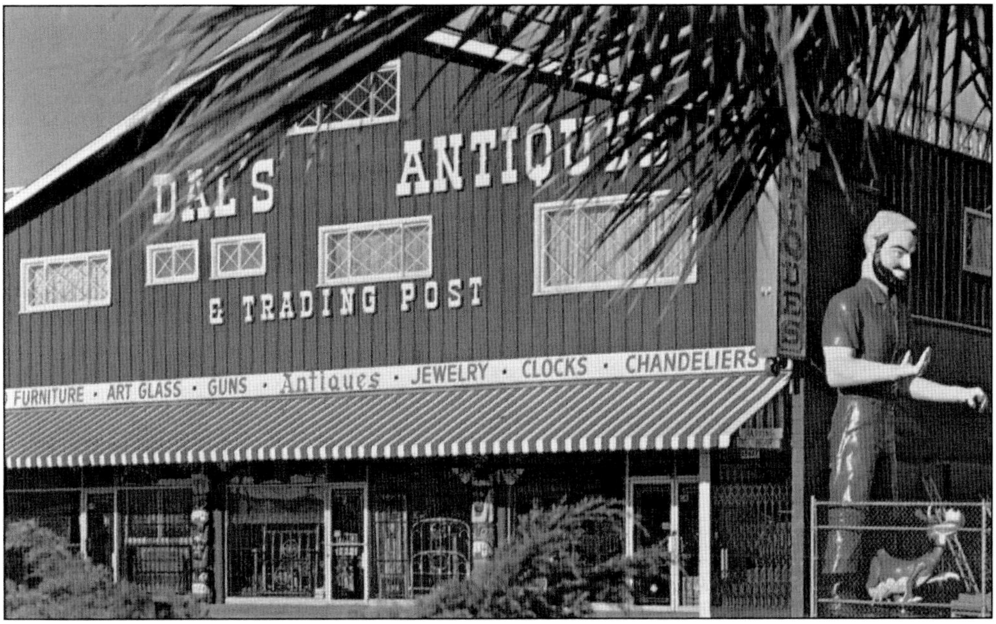

Seen here is Dal's Antiques and Trading Post, located at 15617 Hawthorne Boulevard, Lawndale. The caption on the reverse side reads, "Since 1953, Dal's has built their reputation and expanded facilities until now, with 6,600 square feet under one roof, they feature a fabulous collection, famous coast to coast, of elaborately carved furniture, objets d'art, jewelry, hardware, tools and household goods." (Courtesy James Osborne; published by Victor Baldwin, Costa Mesa, California.)

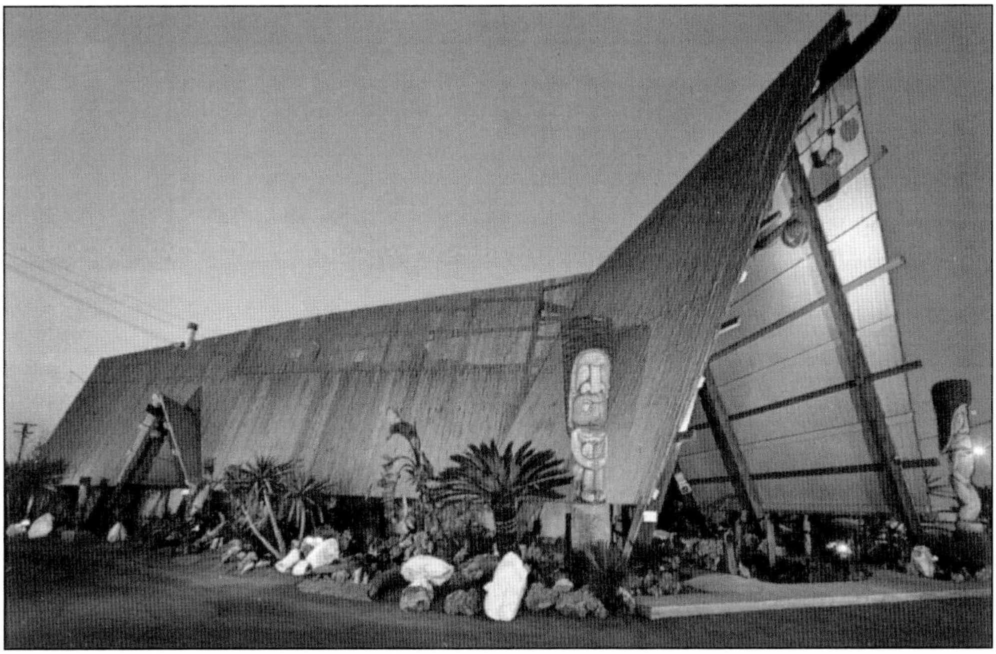

The Tiki-kai Restaurant, located at 4469 Redondo Beach Boulevard, in Lawndale, is seen here. The reverse-side caption reads, "Our purpose at this Paradise House is to serve you the finest Cantonese cuisine and exotic drinks carefully selected by South Seas travelers. The food and drink and prices will delight you. We are looking forward to seeing you soon." (Courtesy James Osborne.)

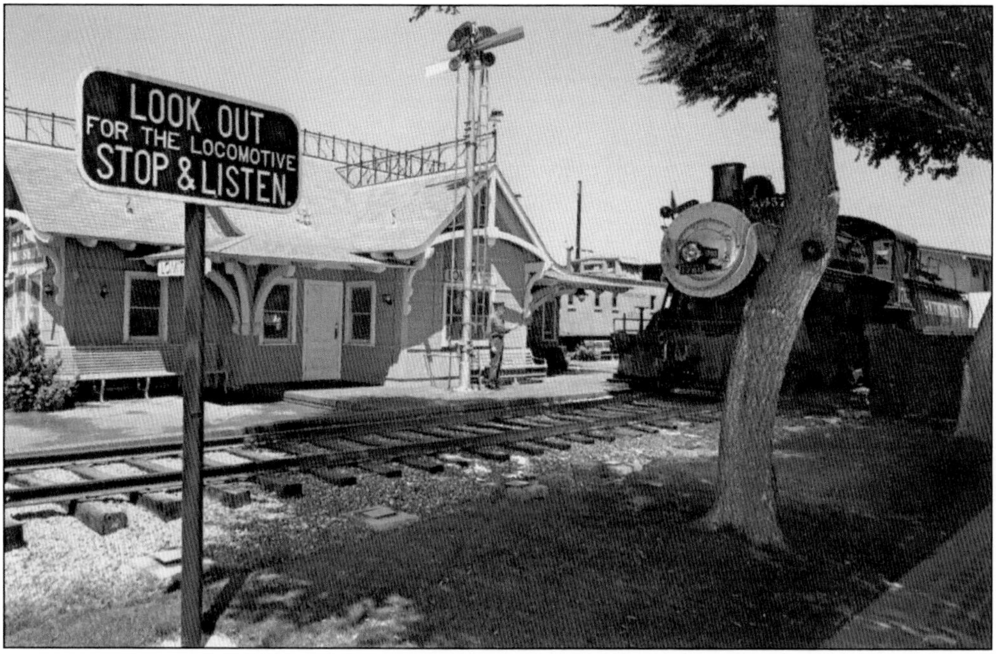

Perhaps Lomita's most notable landmark is the Lomita Railroad Museum. The reverse-side caption reads, "A Victorian Depot, built in 1966 by Irene Lewis and given to the city. Exact in every detail, it has hardwood interior and bricked-in yard. A #1765 Mogul built by Baldwin in 1902, and a U. P. caboose of 1910 are realistically exhibited in tracks. A unique display of railroadiana is housed here." (Courtesy James Osborne; published by Mitock and Sons, North Hollywood, California.)

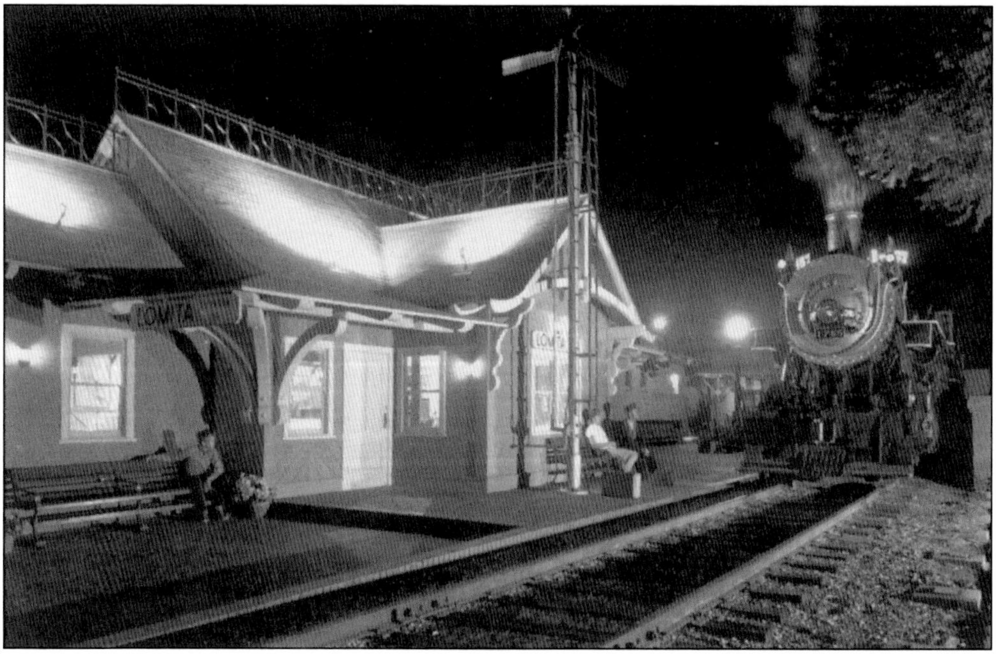

A night view of the museum is seen here at its location in a residential neighborhood on the corner of Woodward Avenue and 250th Street in Lomita. (Courtesy James Osborne; published by Mitock and Sons, North Hollywood, California.)

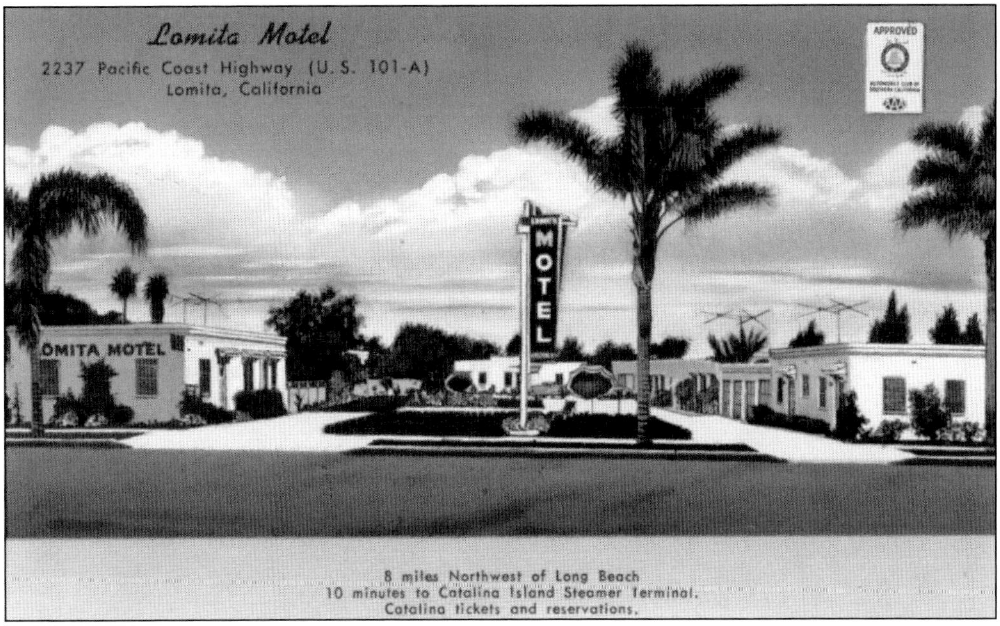

The Lomita Hotel is located at 2237 Pacific Coast Highway in Lomita. The reverse-side caption reads, "A very lovely 20 unit motel with furnace heat; tubs and full-tile showers; wall to wall carpets. TV and radios in units. Some complete kitchens. Mr. and Mrs. C. E. Hopkins, Managing Owners." (Courtesy James Osborne; published by Colourpicture, Boston, Massachusetts.)

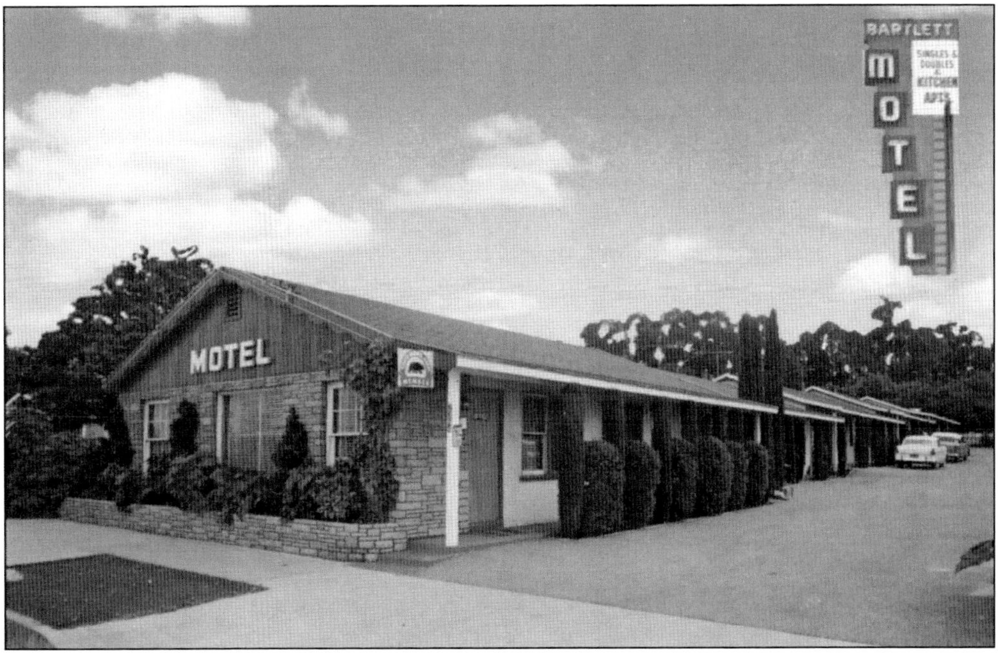

The Bartlett Motel was located at 2364 Pacific Coast Highway in Lomita. The reverse-side caption reads, "Your host—Ray and Betty Wertz. Centrally located for fine food, beaches, pier fishing and harbor, Near Disneyland, Marineland, and Knotts Berry Farm. Featuring singles and family units with or without kitchens. All rooms with TV. (Courtesy James Osborne; published by Mike Roberts, Berkeley, California.)

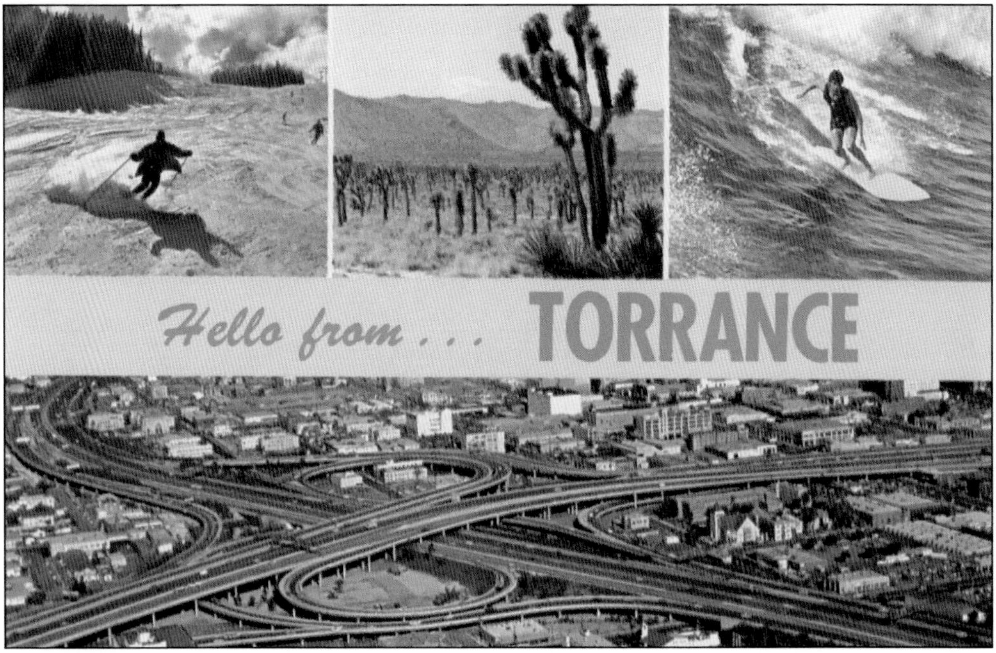

The reverse side of this "Hello from Torrance" postcard reads, "Southern California: A land of varied climates from the desert to the sea offers winter sports, desert scenery, surfing and boating, ALL within easy access of the freeways." (Courtesy James Osborne; published by Kolor View, Los Angeles, California.)

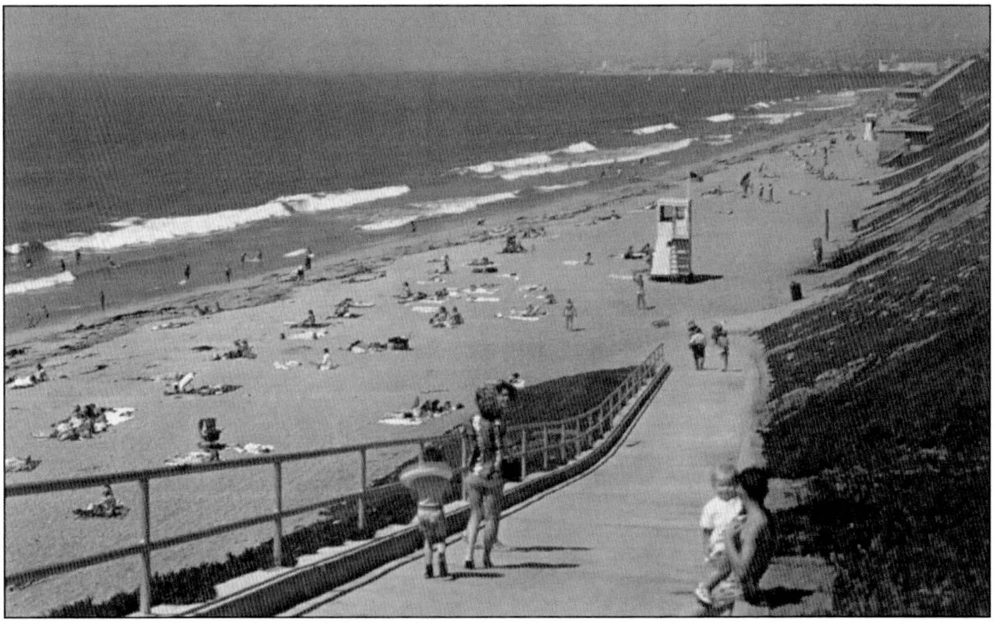

Although Torrance is primarily an inland city, it does contain a small section of beach between Palos Verdes Estates on the south and Redondo Beach on the north. The reverse side of the card identifies this scene as "Looking down a ramp leading from the Esplanade to Redondo Beach State Park near the road from Redondo Beach to Palos Verdes Estates." (Courtesy James Osborne; published by Golden West, Long Beach, California.)

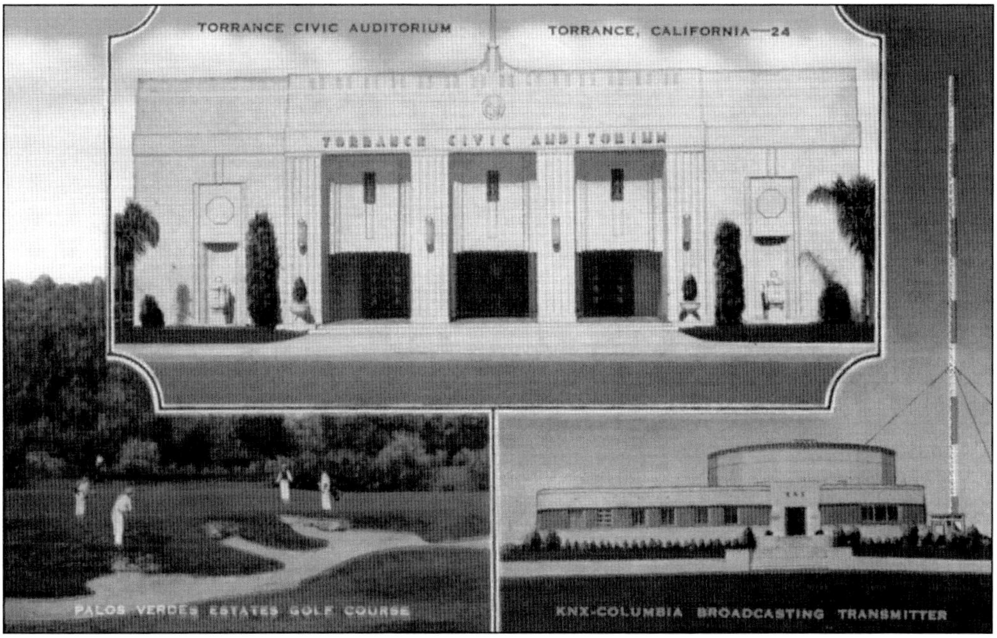

This multi-view postcard includes scenes of the Torrance Civic Auditorium, which was dedicated in 1937, and the KNX-Columbia Broadcasting Transmitter at the site of today's Columbia Park. The postcard's flip side reads, "Torrance—an outstanding industrial center. Home of the largest steel plant in the southwest U.S. and CBS-KNX transmitter station. Adjoins world-famous Palos Verdes 23-mile drive. Has noteworthy civic center. Golfing, bathing, beautiful parks. 15 miles south of Los Angeles. Population 10,000." (Courtesy James Osborne; published by E. C. Kropp Company, Milwaukee, Wisconsin.)

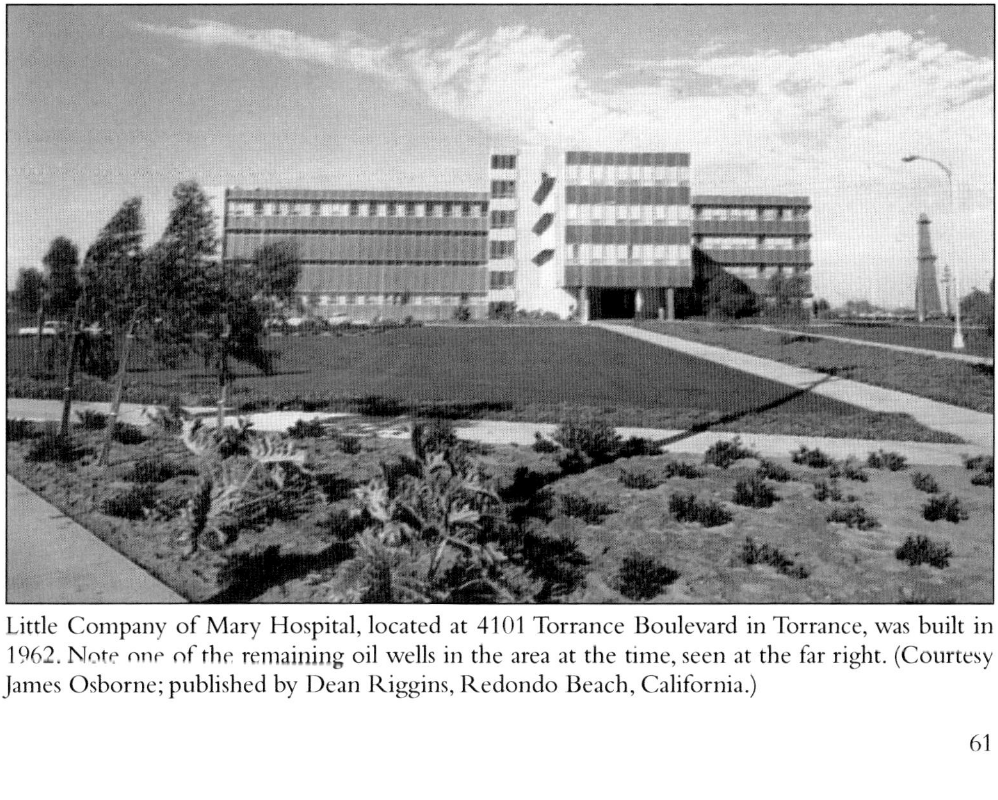

Little Company of Mary Hospital, located at 4101 Torrance Boulevard in Torrance, was built in 1962. Note one of the remaining oil wells in the area at the time, seen at the far right. (Courtesy James Osborne; published by Dean Riggins, Redondo Beach, California.)

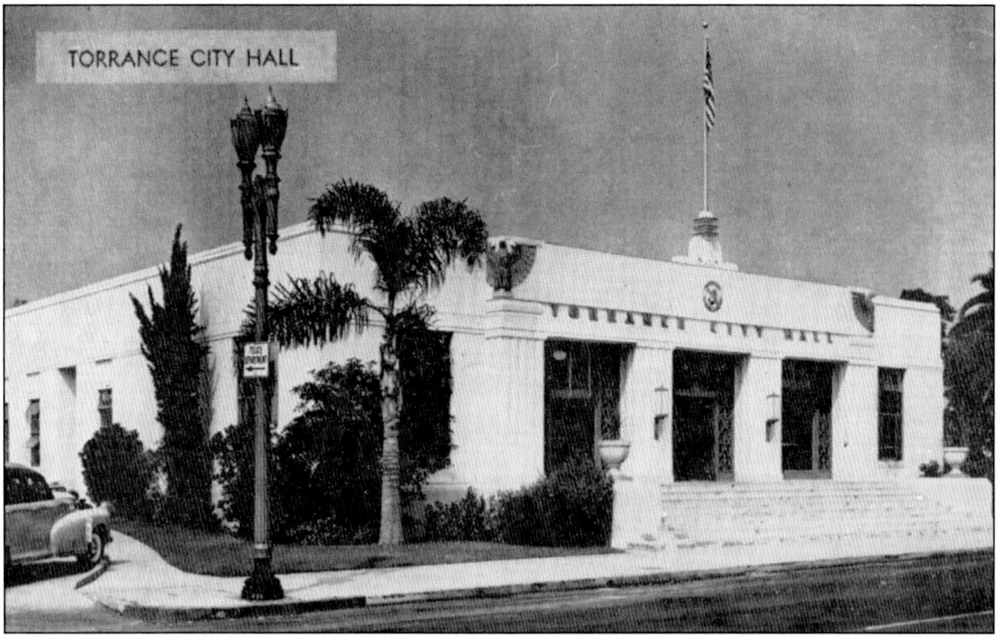

The old Torrance City Hall, located on Cravens Avenue, was designed by architects Walker and Eisen. It was constructed in 1936 and later served as cable television offices. (Courtesy James Osborne; published by the Torrance Chamber of Commerce.)

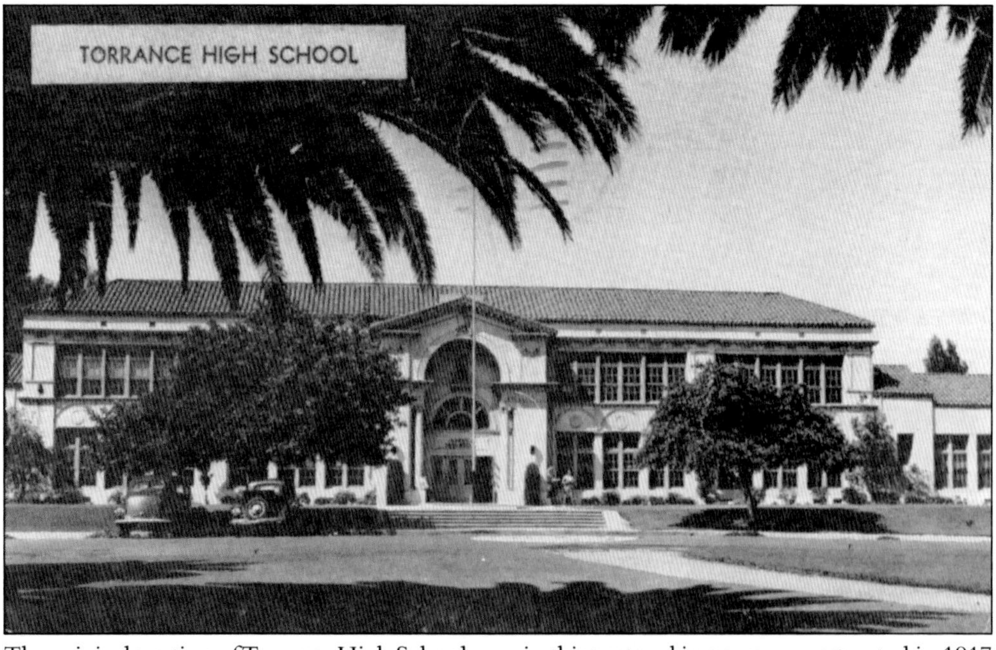

The original portion of Torrance High School seen in this postcard image was constructed in 1917 and became the first building in Torrance to be placed on the National Register of Historic Places. This postcard was postmarked November 9, 1948, with a message that reads, "This is the school Joe teaches in. All is fine this a.m. Love, T. K." (Courtesy James Osborne; published by the Torrance Chamber of Commerce.)

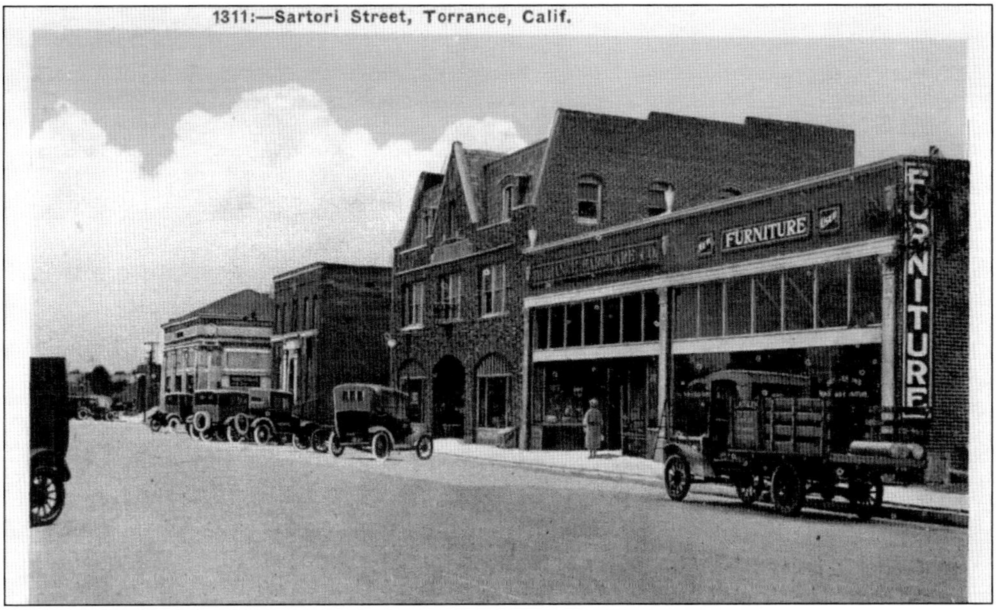

The Torrance downtown business district is seen here in the 1920s. Although labeled "Sartori Street," this thoroughfare is correctly known as Sartori Avenue—named for Joseph Sartori, founder and president of the Security Savings Bank in Los Angeles. Sartori was one of Jared Sidney Torrance's partners in the creation of the City of Torrance. (Courtesy James Osborne; published by M. Kashower Company, Los Angeles, California.)

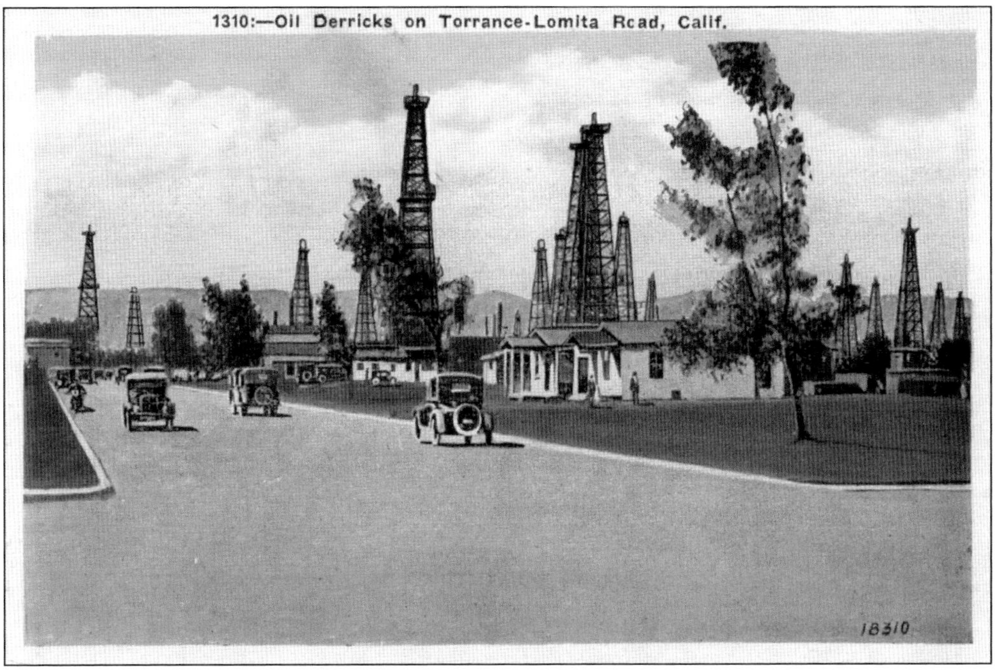

Some of the derricks that were a regular site in Torrance during the oil boom of the 1920s are seen here. Despite this postcard indicating a "Torrance-Lomita Road," today Torrance Boulevard and Lomita Boulevard are separate east-west thoroughfares. (Courtesy James Osborne; published by M. Kashower Company, Los Angeles, California.)

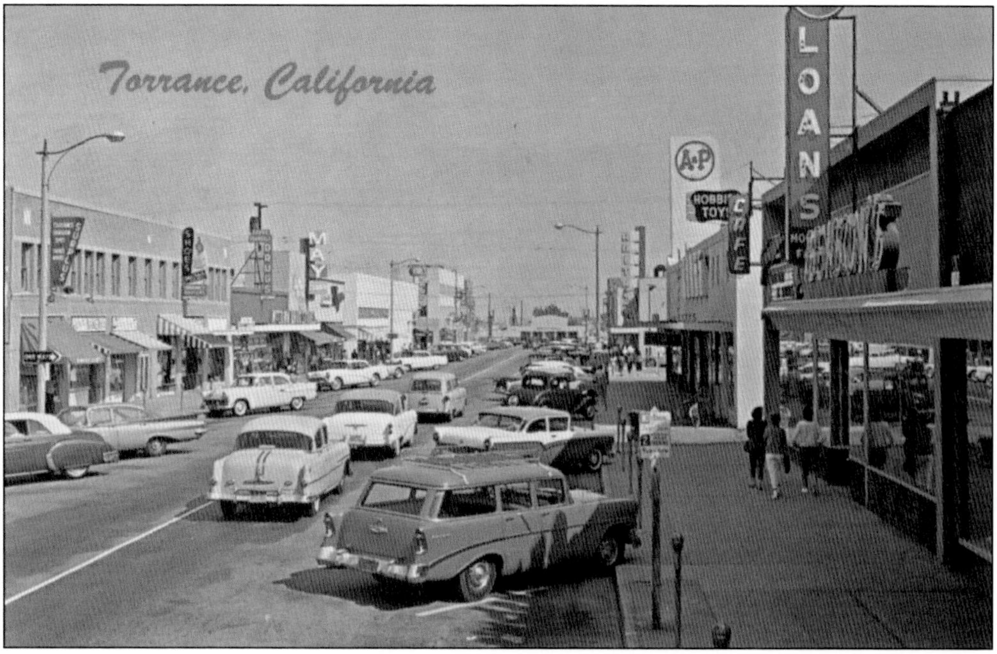

The caption on the reverse side of this postcard reads, "Greetings from Torrance, California: Looking northeast on El Prado from [the] vicinity of Cravens Avenue in the downtown shopping district." (Courtesy James Osborne; published by Golden West, Long Beach, California.)

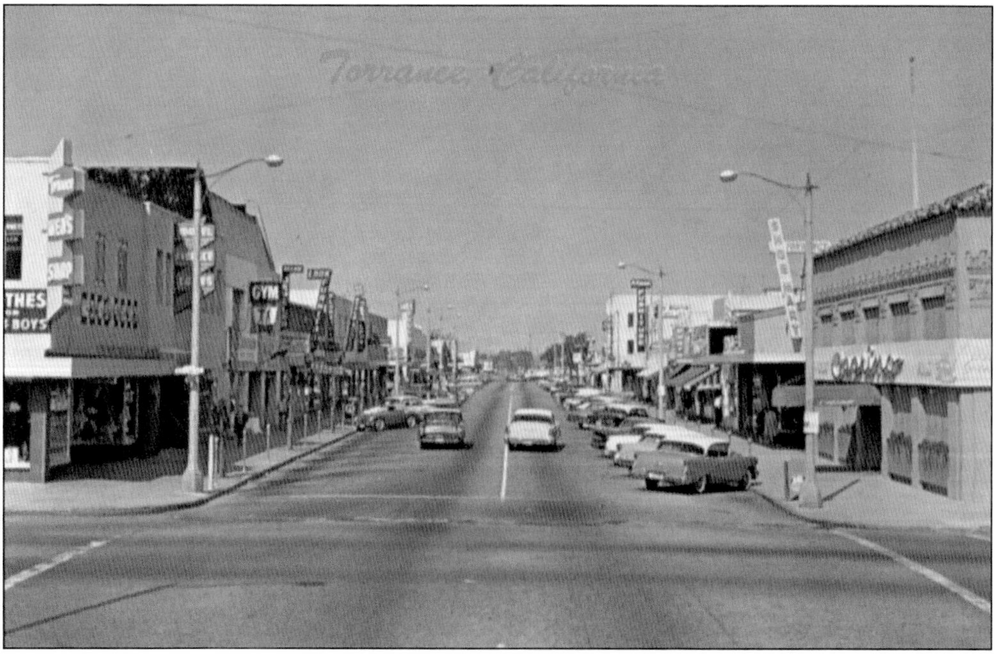

The view here looks northwest on Sartori Avenue, from Marcelina Avenue in the downtown shopping district of Torrance—today an area known as Old Torrance. (Courtesy James Osborne; published by Golden West, Long Beach, California.)

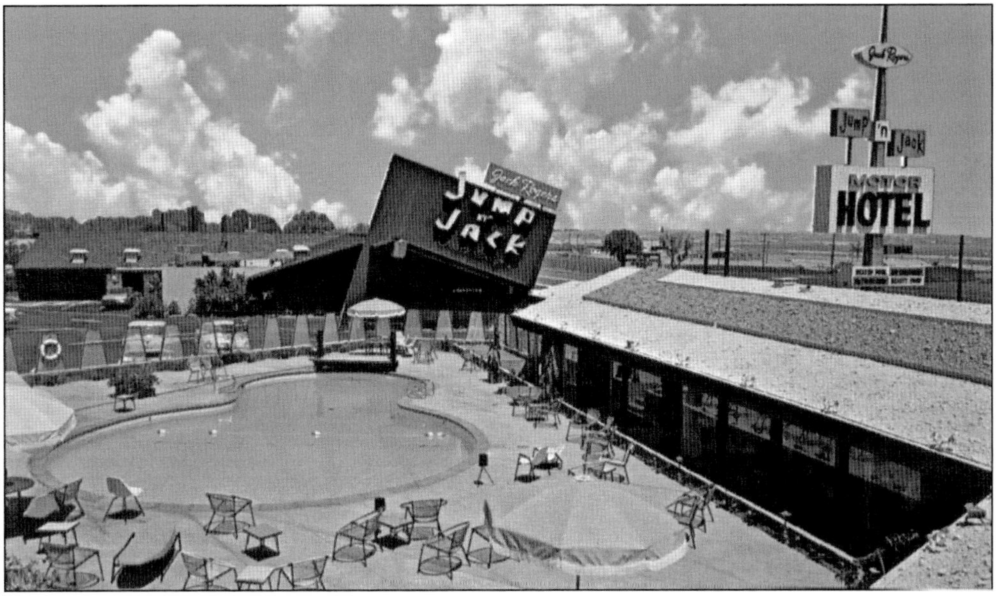

The caption on this card's reverse reads: "Jack Rogers—Jump N' Jack Hotel, 2880 Pacific Coast Hwy., Torrance, California. Heated pool, 88 individually air conditioned rooms and suites. Accommodations for business gatherings and conventions. Centrally located for vacationers. Switchboard service, restaurant, cocktail lounge, coffee shop, barber shop, water beds, king-size beds, efficiency apartments, South Bay area's newest and finest." (Courtesy James Osborne; published by Edward G. Wheeler, Tustin, California.)

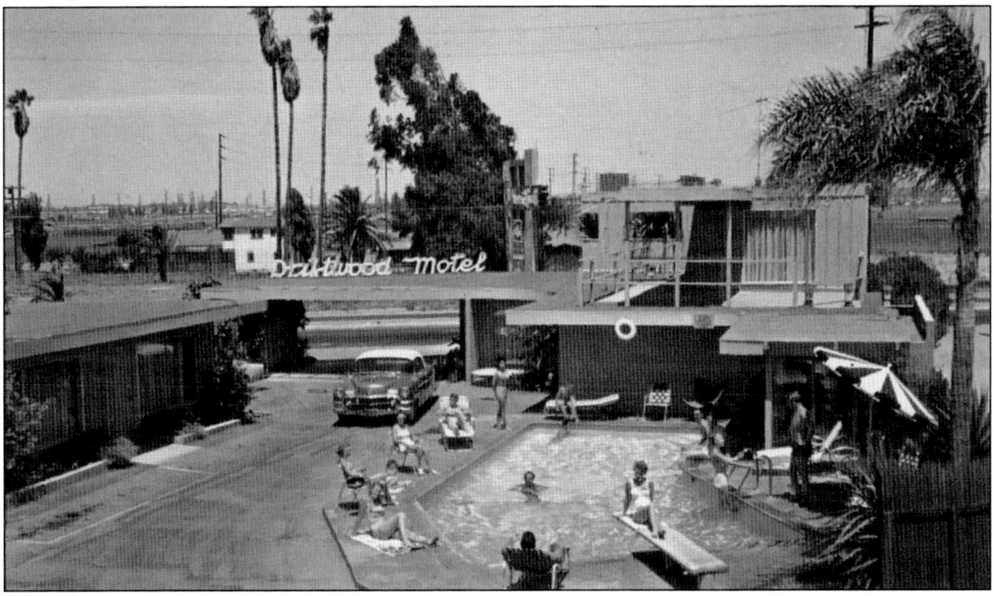

The reverse-side caption reads: "Driftwood Motel, 3960 Pacific Coast Highway, Torrance California. New, tropical modern, out of smog area. Relax in deluxe accommodations. Lounge, heated pool, suites, bridal suite, snack bars. Enjoy complimentary coffee, private phones, TV. Adjacent to fine restaurants. Centrally located for beaches, Marineland, Catalina, Hollywood, Knotts Berry Farm, Disneyland, Hollywood Park races, and International Airport." (Courtesy James Osborne; published by Forest Mathews, Pasadena, California.)

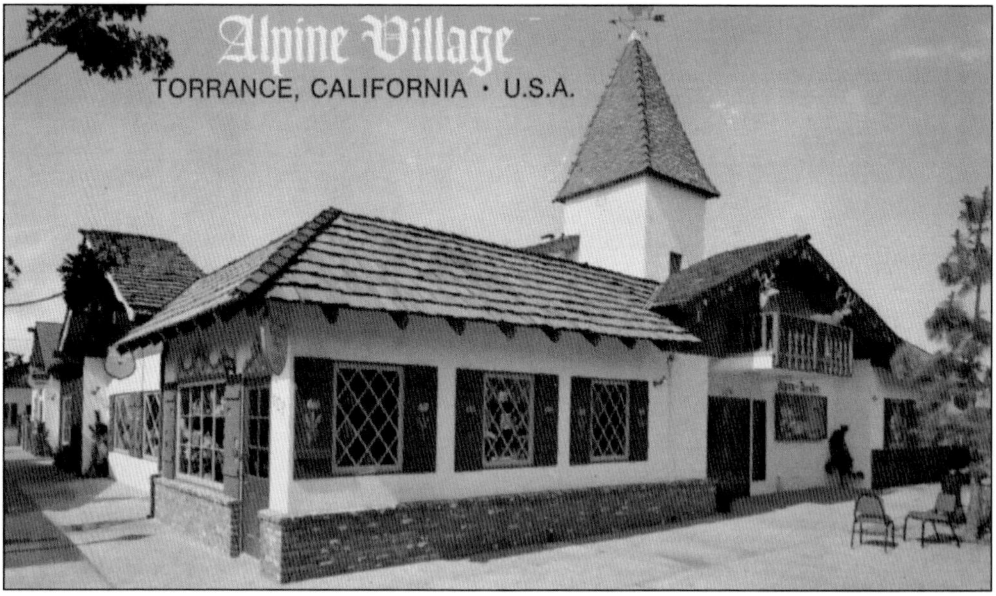

Alpine Village was actually built outside Torrance's eastern border in 1965 in the Harbor Gateway strip section of the city of Los Angeles. "With authentic Bavarian Alps Décor, chalet-type shops at the Alpine Village offer imports from many European countries," reads the postcard's reverse side. "A foreign-language movie, restaurant and biergarten, soccer field and picnic area are also here—at Vermont [Avenue] and Torrance [Boulevard], just west of the Harbor Freeway between Los Angeles and San Pedro." (Courtesy James Osborne; published by Golden West, Long Beach, California.)

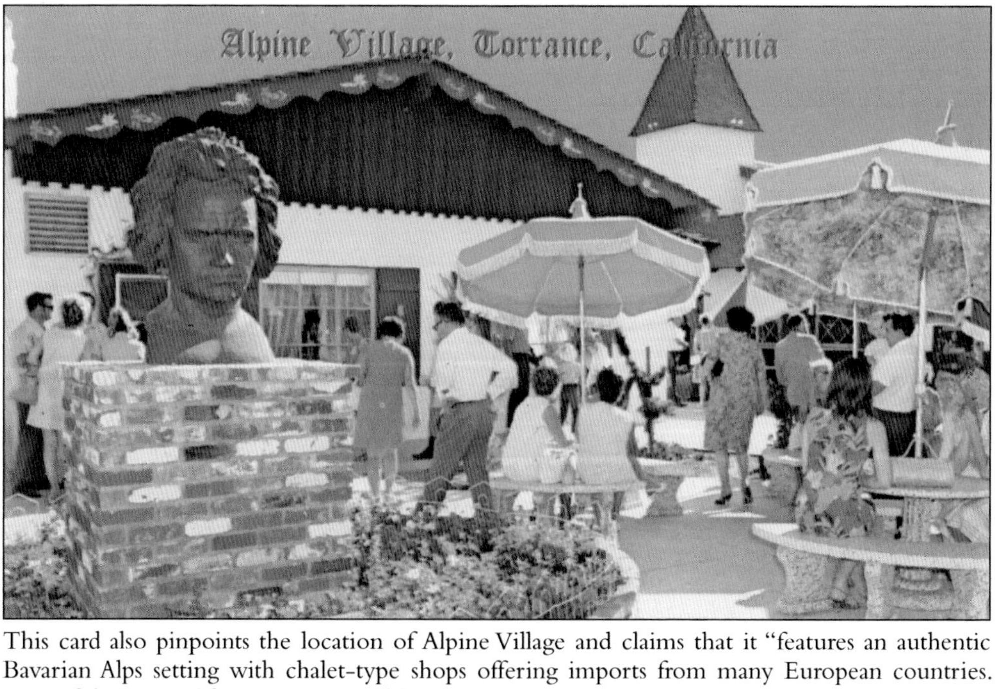

This card also pinpoints the location of Alpine Village and claims that it "features an authentic Bavarian Alps setting with chalet-type shops offering imports from many European countries. One of the visitors' favorites is the 'Olde Legende Candies and Toys.'" (Courtesy James Osborne; published by Mitock and Sons, North Hollywood, California.)

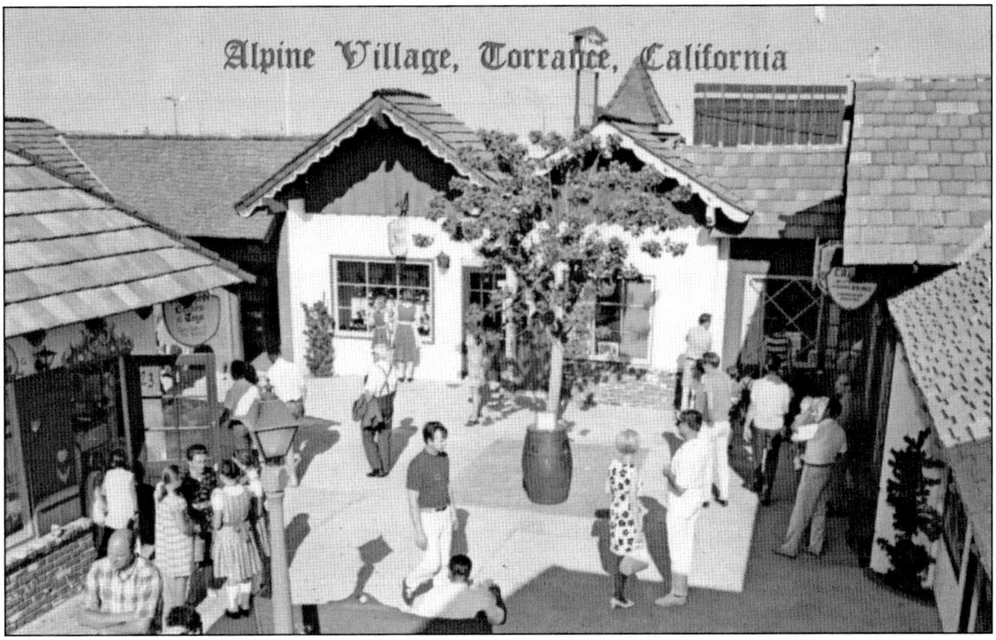

Visitors to Alpine Village on Torrance Boulevard are seen walking about in this view. (Courtesy James Osborne; published by Mitock and Sons, North Hollywood, California.)

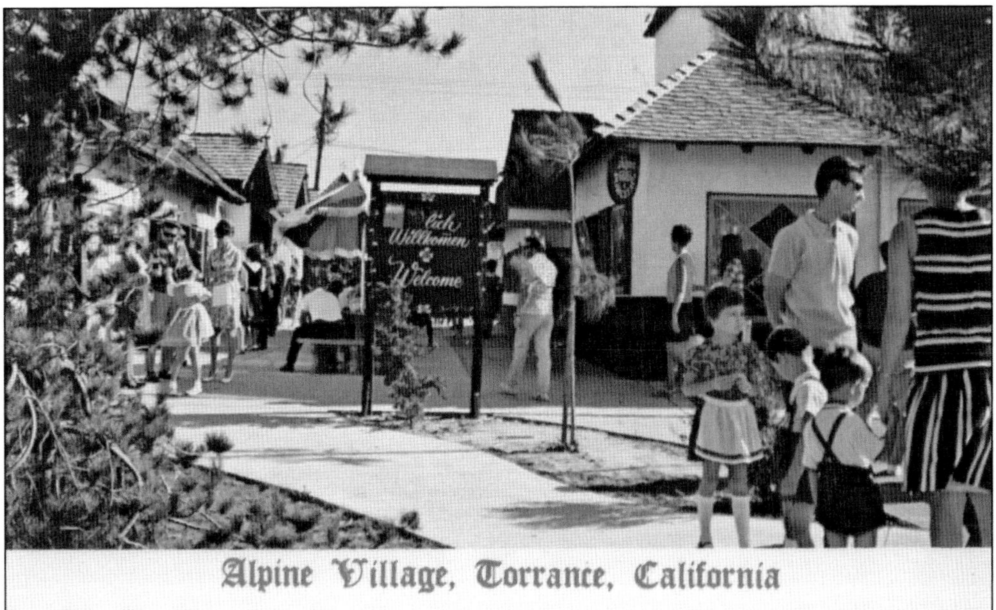

Another view of Alpine Village is seen here, with children in German costumes. Alpine Village has been the site over the years of large swap meets as well as its well-advertised Oktoberfest celebration. (Courtesy James Osborne; published by Mitock and Sons, North Hollywood, California.)

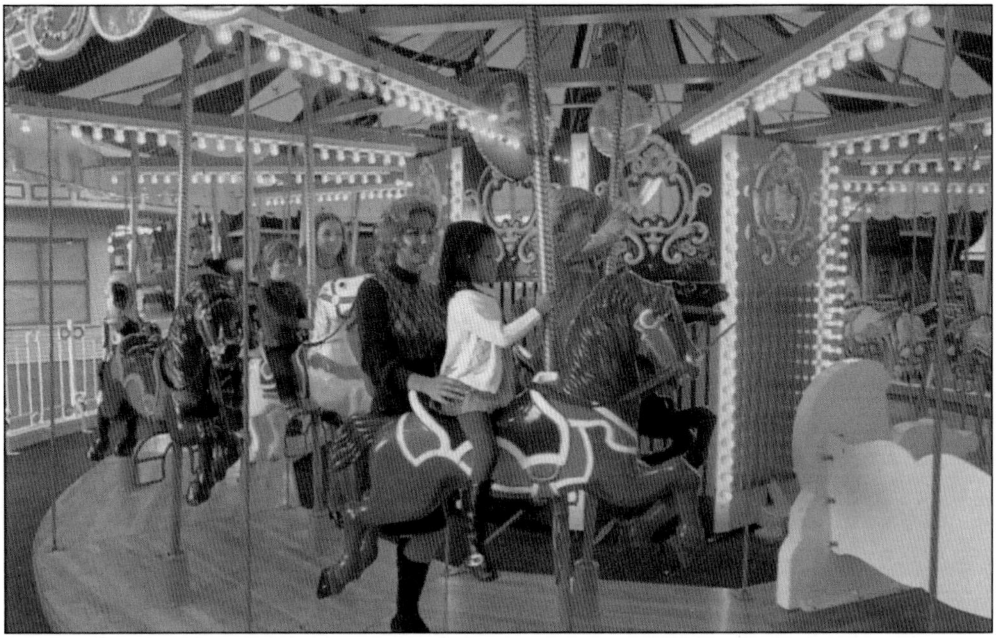

During the early 1970s, Torrance shoppers could enjoy the experience of stepping back in time when they visited the Old Towne Mall that once existed at 19800 Hawthorne Boulevard. "The $50,000 antique carousel is Old Towne's pride and joy," reads the reverse side. "It has become a favorite for the very young and the young at heart. It is located in the main entrance to the $30 million shopping and entertainment attraction." (Courtesy James Osborne; published by Mike Roberts, Berkeley, California.)

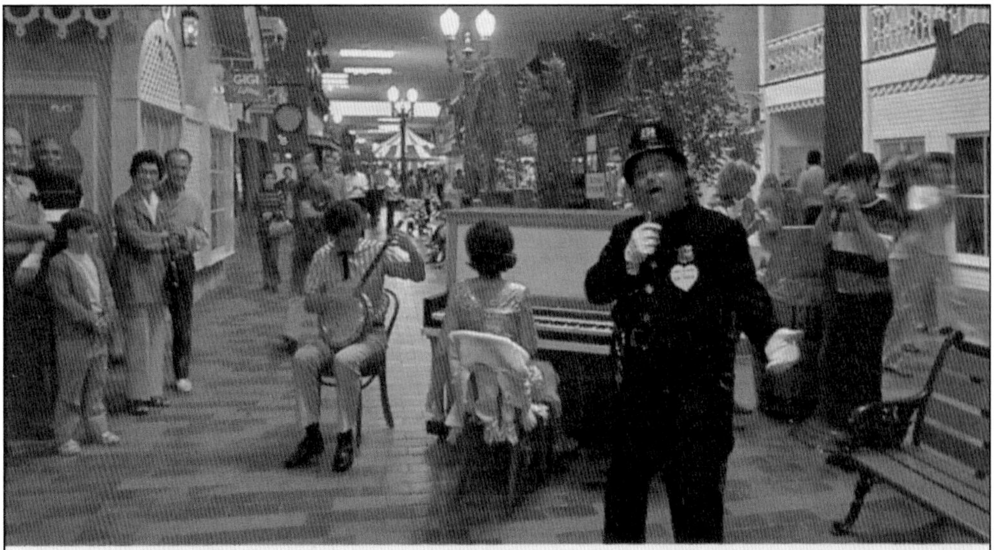

"One of Old Towne's lovable residents is its Keystone Kop, Bruce Bishop, who patrols Old Towne Lane and belts out delightful songs of yesterday and today as he works his beat," reads the back-side caption. "Old Towne is a turn-of-the-century shopping and entertainment attraction in Torrance, California." (Courtesy James Osborne; published by Mitock and Sons, North Hollywood, California.)

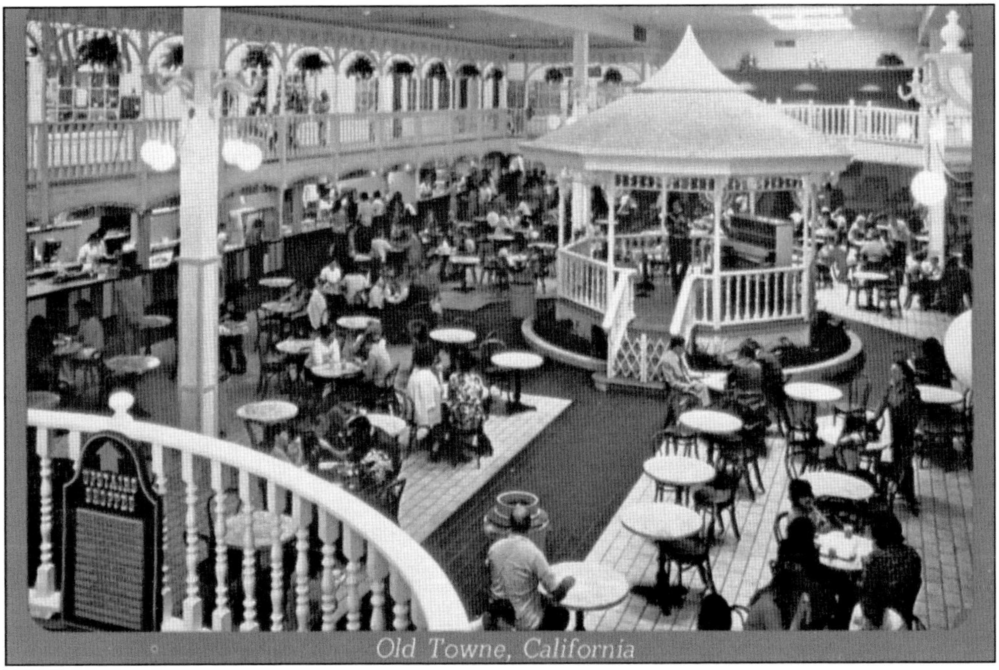

The reverse-side caption reads, "Old Towne, California: relaxed dining with early century musical accompaniment at 'Old Towne Mall,' Torrance, California." (Courtesy James Osborne; published by Mitock and Sons, North Hollywood, California.)

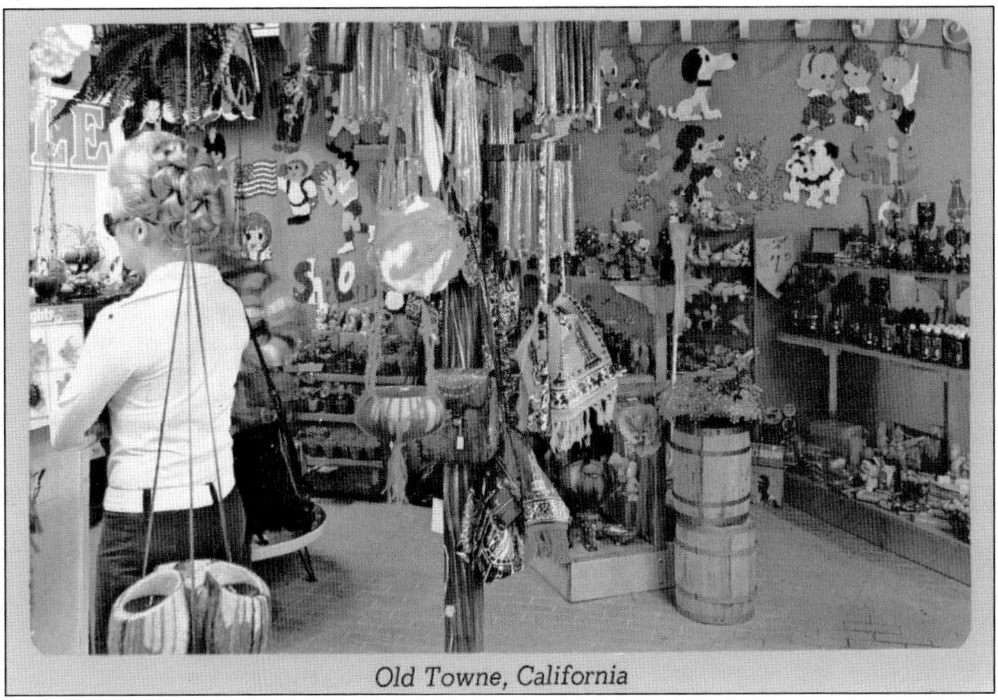

The identifying caption on the reverse of this postcard reads, "Old Towne, California: Shopping in the relaxed manner of times gone by." (Courtesy James Osborne; published by Mitock and Sons, North Hollywood, California.)

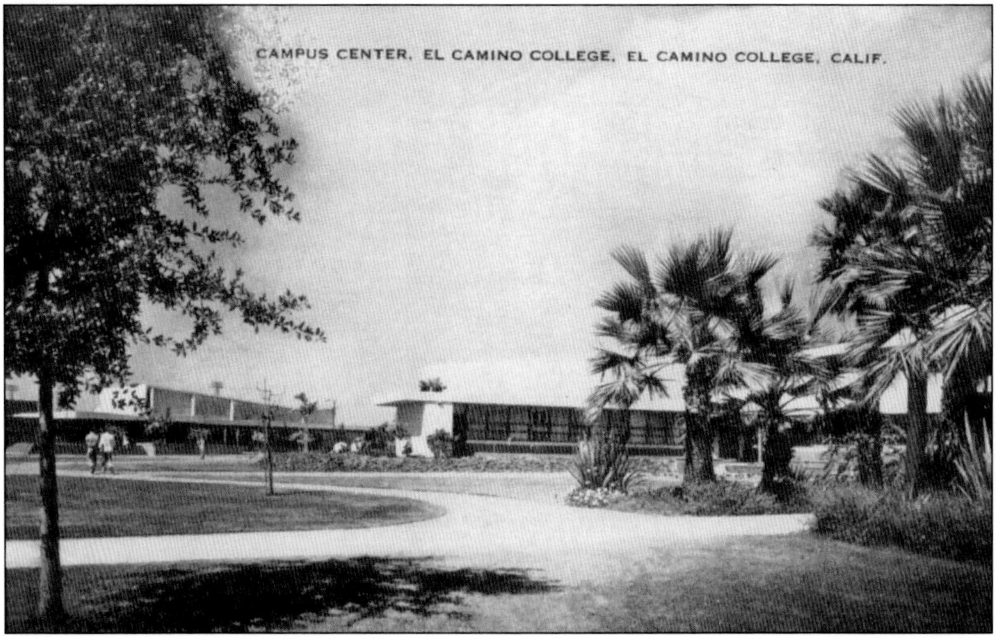

Although it is located in the unincorporated area of Los Angeles County between Torrance and Gardena, El Camino College maintains a Torrance mailing address. The college was founded in 1946, offers two-year associate degrees, and also prepares students for transfers to four-year universities. This postcard illustrated the campus center and lawn area. (Courtesy James Osborne; published by Artvue Postcard Company, New York.)

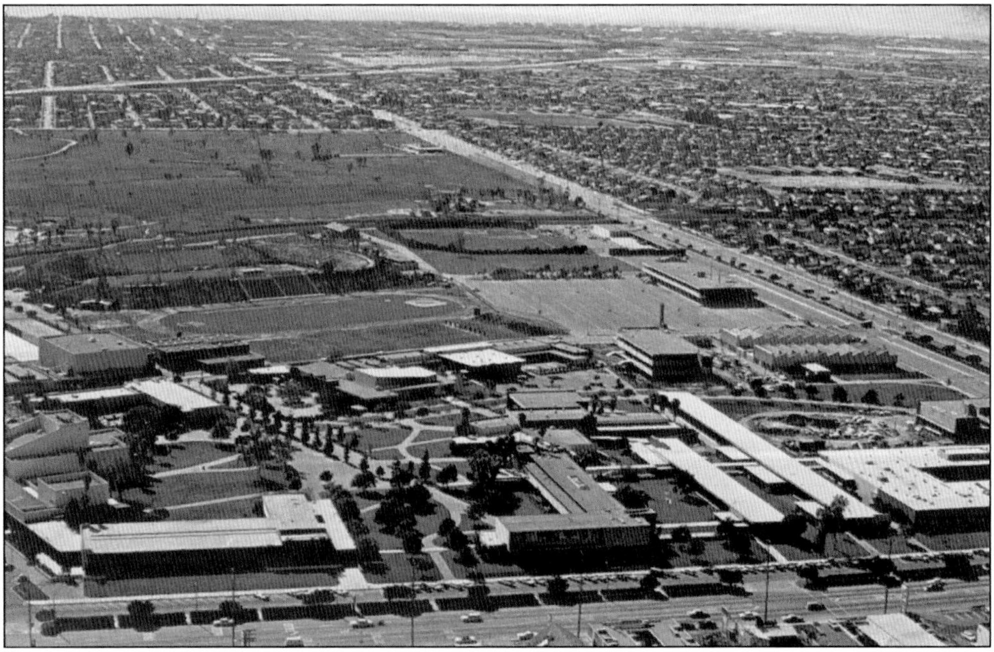

"El Camino College, Crenshaw and Manhattan Beach Blvds., Los Angeles County, California," reads the reverse side. A pencil note on the back indicates "1964." (Courtesy James Osborne; published by Audio Visual Association, Redondo Beach, California.)

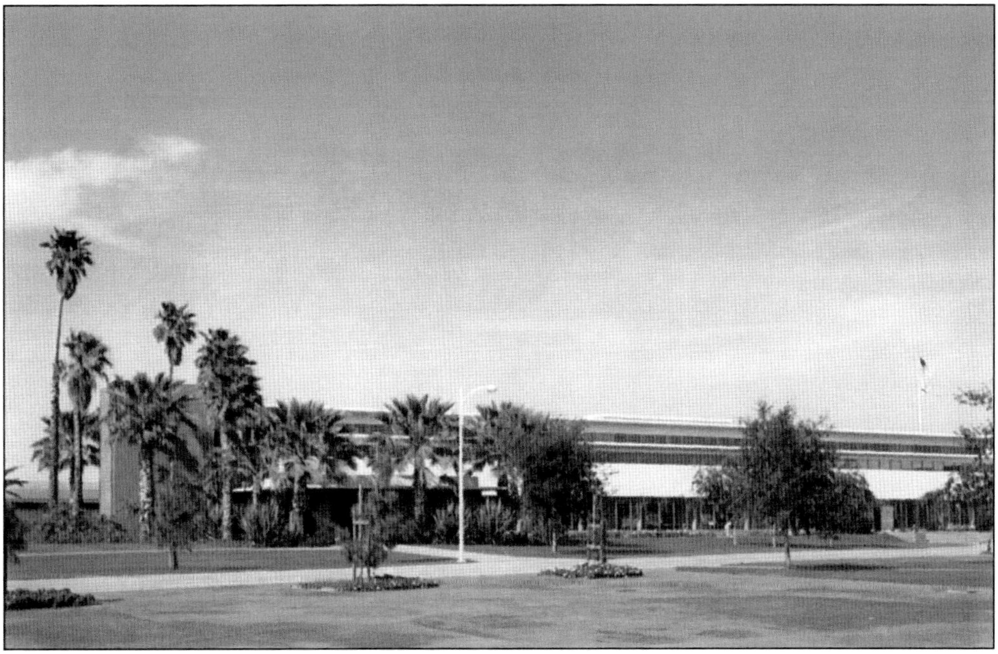

The Administration Building on the campus of El Camino College is depicted on this postcard. (Courtesy James Osborne; published by Dexter Press, Inc., West Nyack, New York, and Chase's Studio, Scottsdale, Arizona.)

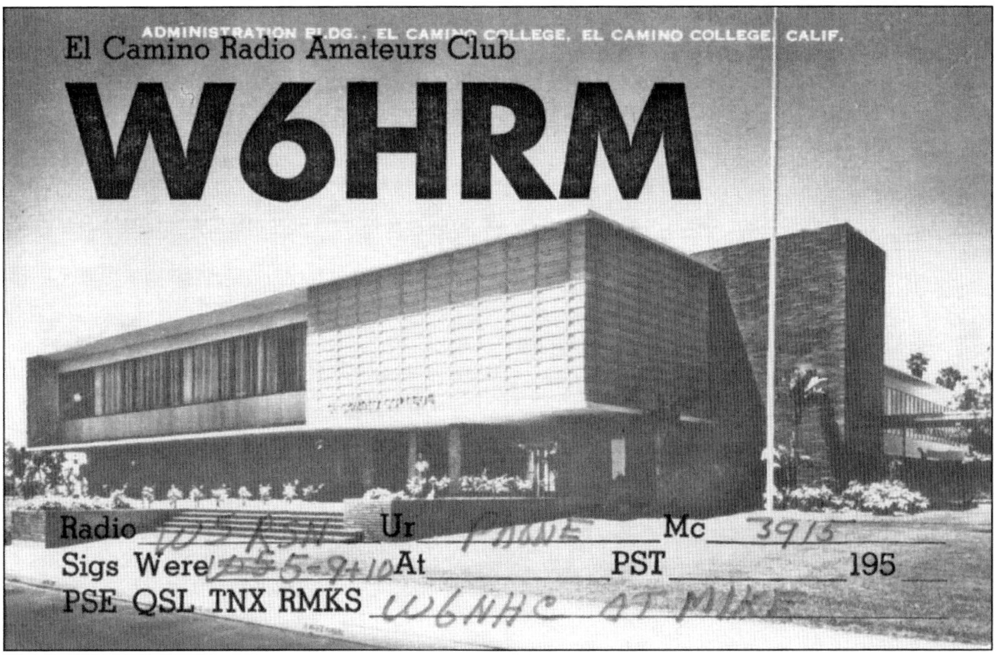

Produced for the El Camino Radio Amateurs Club, this postcard depicts the Administration Building and is postmarked December 7, 1954. (Courtesy James Osborne; published by Artvue Postcard Company, New York.)

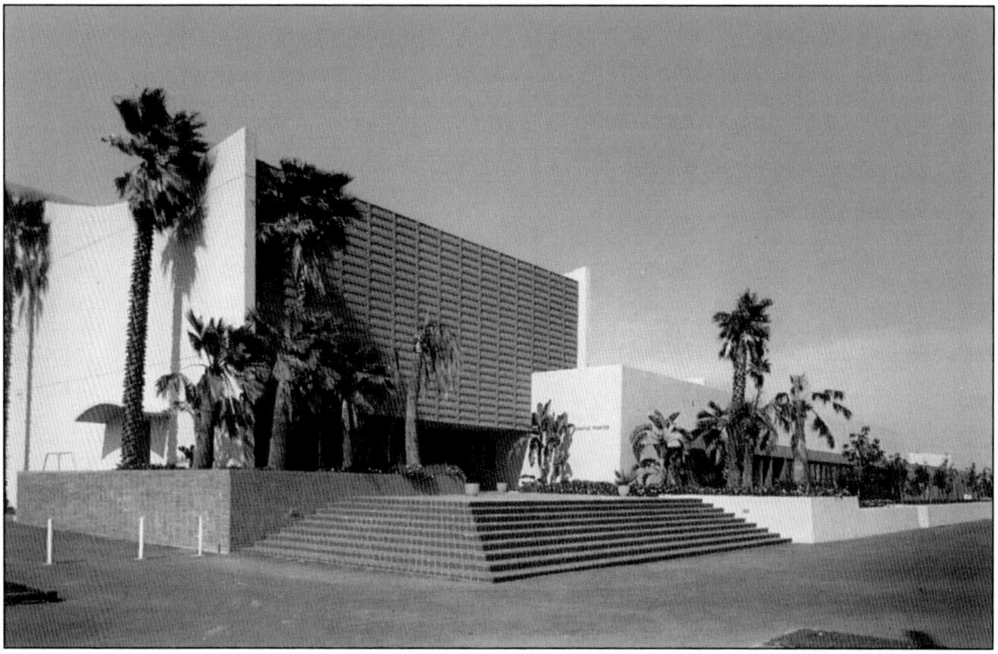

The Campus Theater at El Camino College is depicted here. The school's theater arts and dance departments have made optimum use of the intimate space. (Courtesy James Osborne; published by Dexter Press, Inc., West Nyack, New York, and Chase's Studio, Scottsdale, Arizona.)

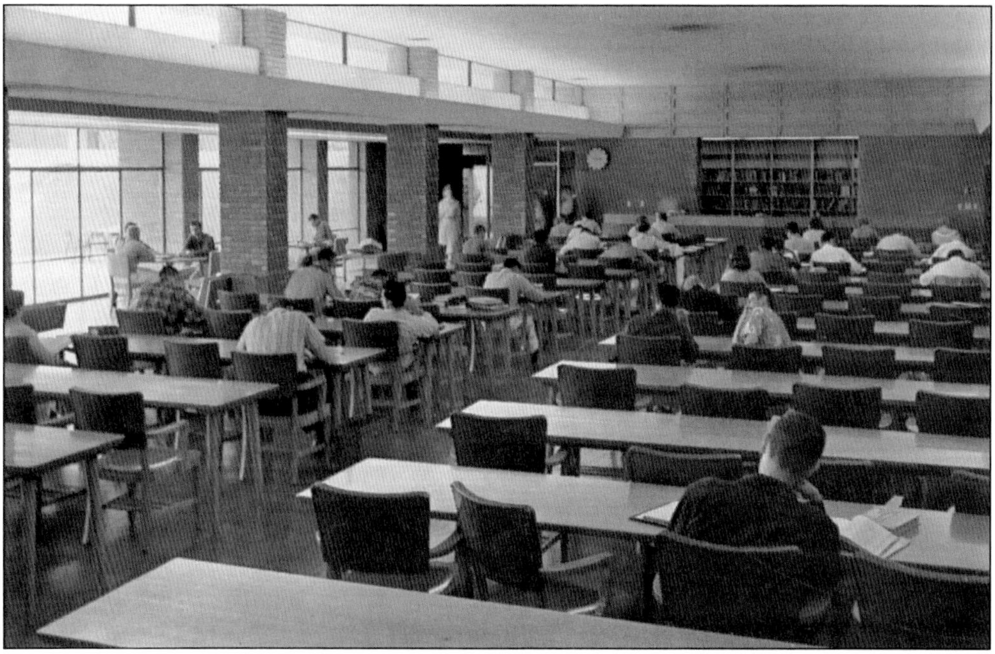

The reserve reading room in the campus library at El Camino College is depicted on this postcard. (Courtesy James Osborne; published by Dexter Press, Inc., West Nyack, New York, and Chase's Studio, Scottsdale, Arizona.)

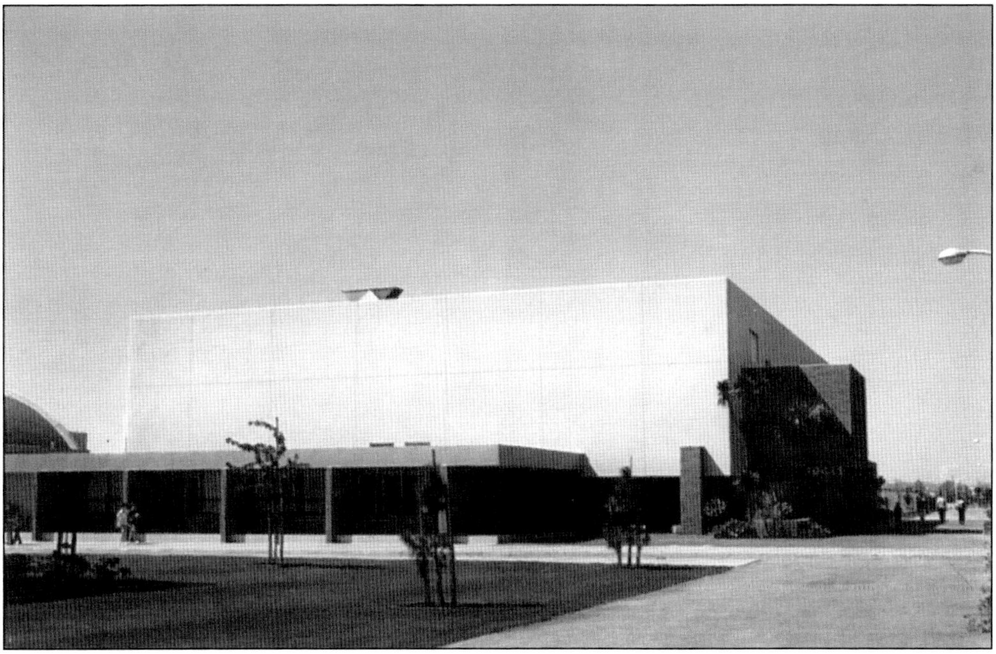

The exterior of El Camino College's Pool Building and Health Center are depicted here. (Courtesy James Osborne; published by Dexter Press, Inc., West Nyack, New York, and Chase's Studio, Scottsdale, Arizona.)

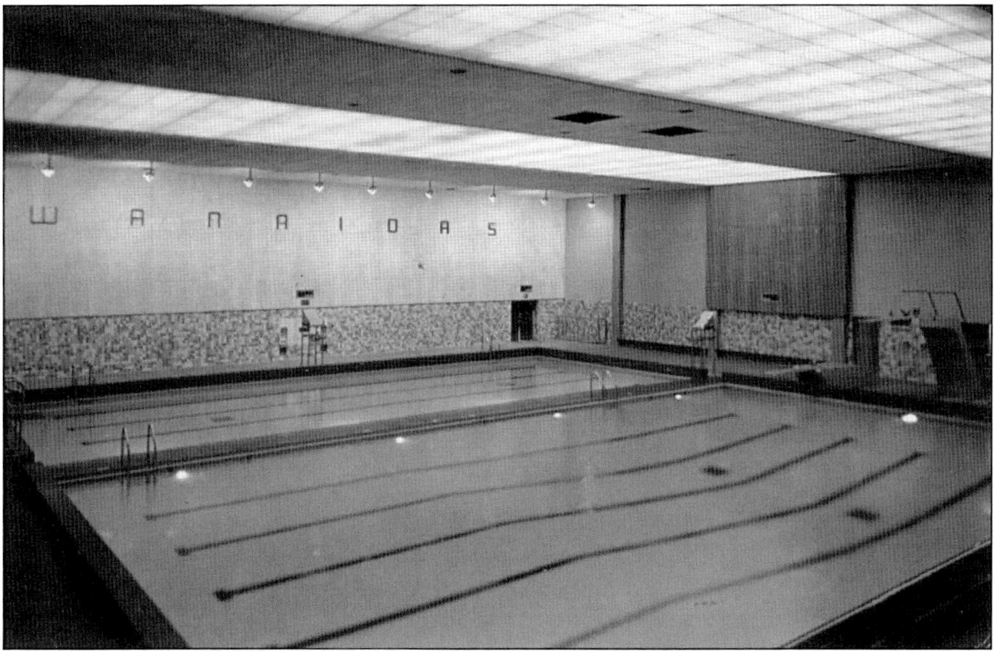

This is an interior view of El Camino College's Olympic-size swimming pool. (Courtesy James Osborne; published by Dexter Press, Inc., West Nyack, New York, and Chase's Studio, Scottsdale, Arizona.)

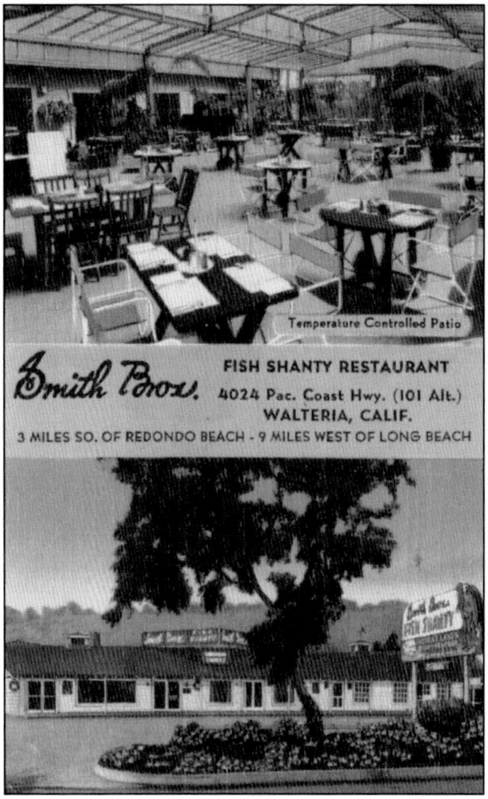

The Walteria section of Torrance is believed to have been named after Captain Walters, who at one time maintained a lodge in the area. Walteria is generally the areas east and southeast of Torrance's Hollywood Riviera section between the cities of Palos Verdes Estates and Rolling Hills Estates to the west and Lomita to the east. This postcard depicts the Smith Brothers Fish Shanty Restaurant, once located in Walteria at 4024 Pacific Coast Highway. (Courtesy James Osborne; published by Colourpicture, Boston, Massachusetts.)

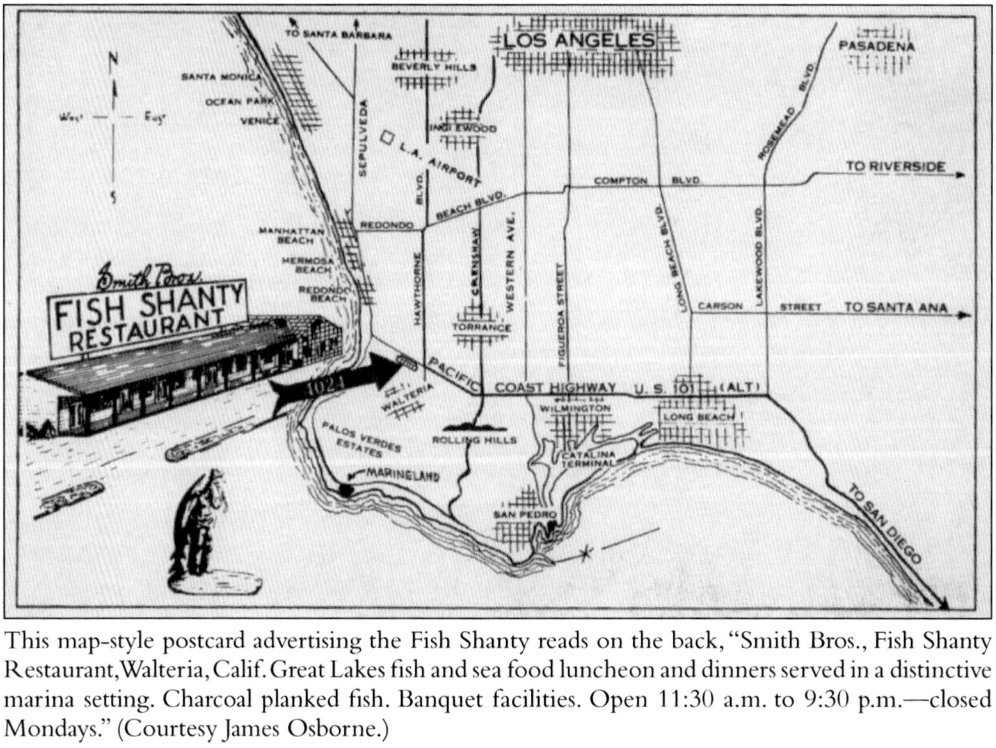

This map-style postcard advertising the Fish Shanty reads on the back, "Smith Bros., Fish Shanty Restaurant, Walteria, Calif. Great Lakes fish and sea food luncheon and dinners served in a distinctive marina setting. Charcoal planked fish. Banquet facilities. Open 11:30 a.m. to 9:30 p.m.—closed Mondays." (Courtesy James Osborne.)

Three

Inglewood

Inglewood was on the national radar frequently for decades as the locale of the Great Western Forum, longtime home of the National Basketball Association's Los Angeles Lakers, for several of the team's World Championships. Inglewood also remains the home of Hollywood Park Race Track.

The northernmost city in the South Bay Council of Governments, Inglewood is also one of the main support communities for Los Angeles International Airport (LAX) and its ancillary businesses.

The history of this community, which boasted nearly 130,000 residents by 2000, began with one of the settlers of Los Angeles in 1781, the Spanish soldier Jose Manuel Orchado Machado. He was described as a 23-year-old muleteer from Los Alamos in Sinaloa, Mexico. Ordered by the San Gabriel Mission to graze their animals on the ocean side of Los Angeles, the soldiers drove cattle to the green pastures near Centinela Springs. The initial building was completed by Ignacio Avila, who built a corral and hut for his vaqueros in 1822, according to historian Gladys Waddington.

Avila eventually built a three-room adobe on a rise overlooking the creek that ran from Centinela Springs to the Pacific Ocean. This adobe no longer exists. However, in 1834, Ignacio Machado, a son of Jose Machado, built the Centinela Adobe. Today this structure is a museum and historical library that sits on a small bluff above I-405, the San Diego Freeway. Settlements began as early as 1873, leading to the Centinela-Inglewood Land Company platting a community in 1887.

Inglewood was one of the communities in suburban Los Angeles that experienced a cultural transformation in the decades after World War II. Like Huntington Park, Compton, Carson, and several other L.A. County communities, Inglewood became a truly racial and ethnic polyglot into the 21st century.

Hollywood Park Race Track, located about 9 miles from the Hollywood community limits, got its appropriate name in a direct manner. The track's first chairman was Jack Warner, the driving force of Warner Brothers, and its 600 shareholders included Al Jolson and director Raoul Walsh.

And speaking of Hollywood in Inglewood, jazzman Zoot Sims noodled here, Esther Williams swam here, Carol Burnett's sidekick Vicki Lawrence wisecracked here, and Olympic volleyball great Flo Hyman spiked here.

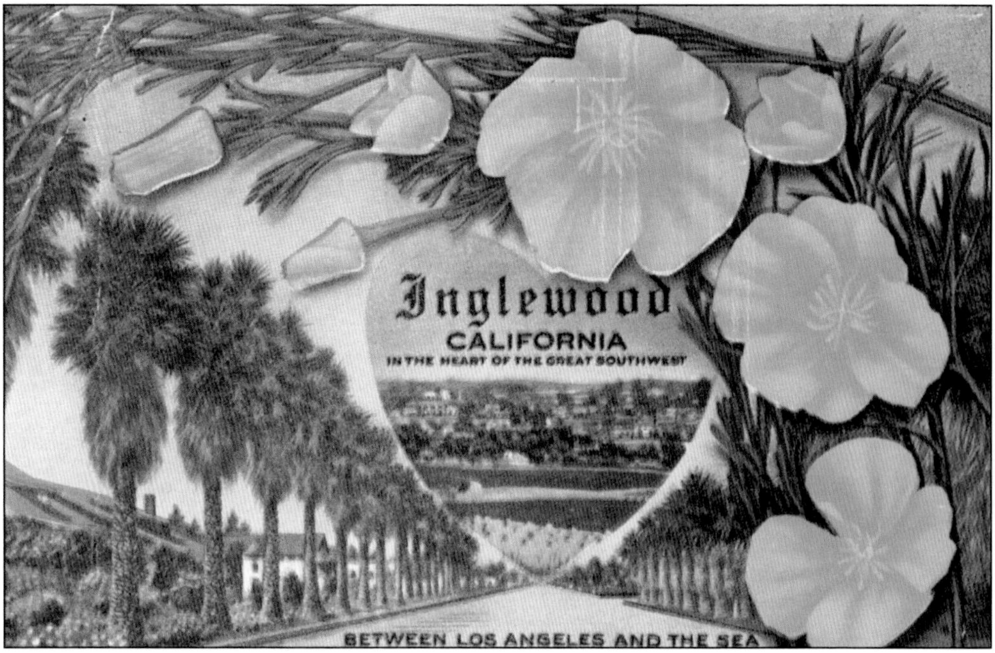

This postcard, framed with California poppies, declares, "Inglewood, California, in the heart of the great southwest." The reverse-side caption notes that the area was known for its pure water from the Centinela Springs. (Courtesy James Osborne; published by the Inglewood Chamber of Commerce.)

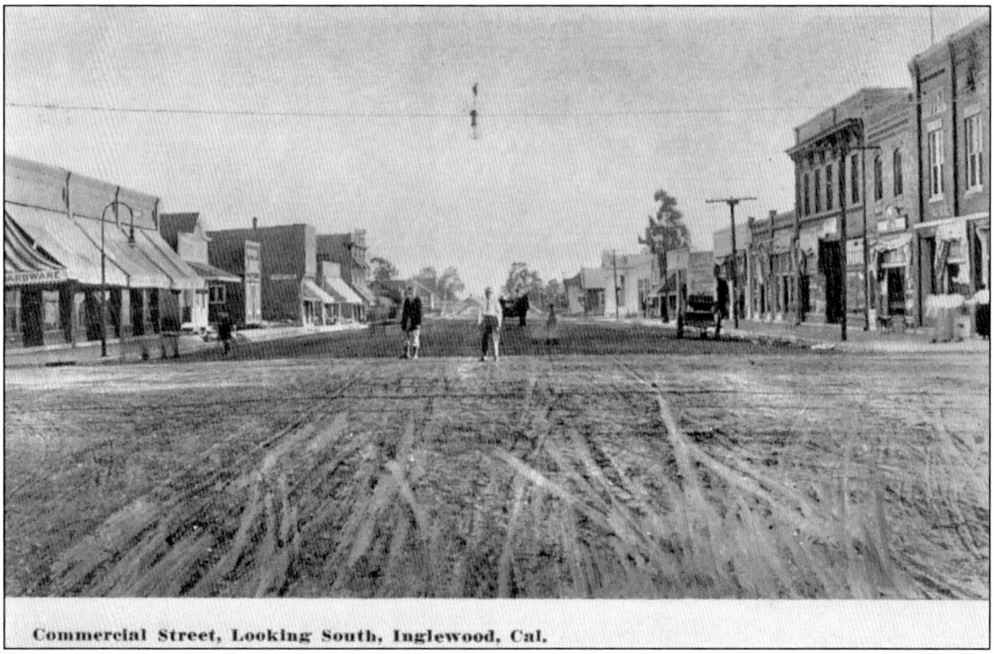

This view of Commercial Street in Inglewood looks south, back in the days of dirt streets. (Courtesy James Osborne.)

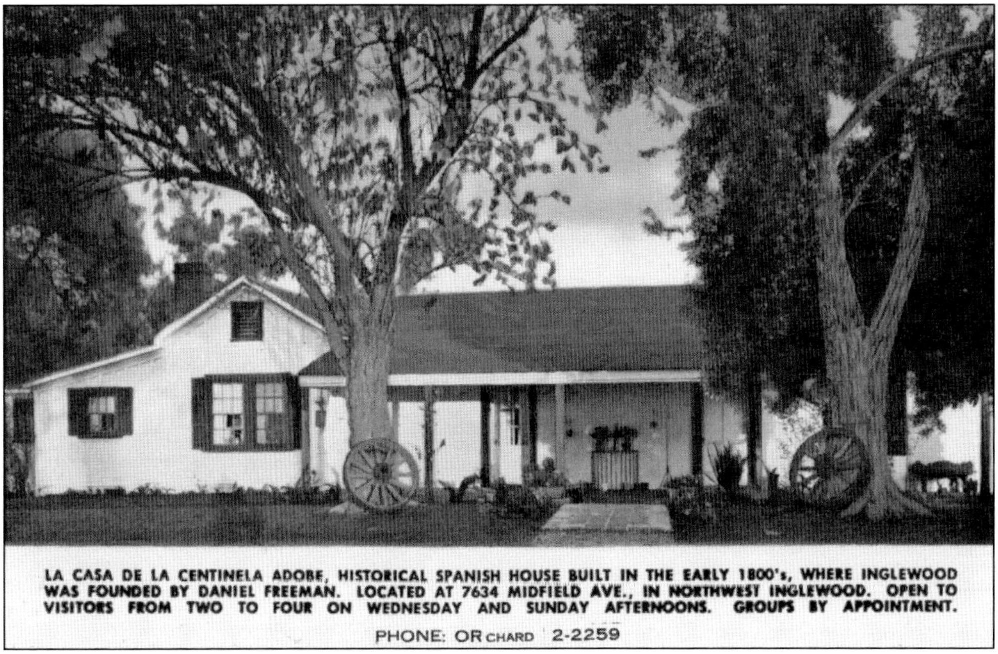

Inglewood's oldest home, the Centinela Adobe, is depicted here. It was built in 1834 by Ygnacio Machado. Today the adobe serves as the museum of the Historical Society of Centinela Valley. (Courtesy James Osborne; published by E. M. Thomas, Hamstead, New Hampshire.)

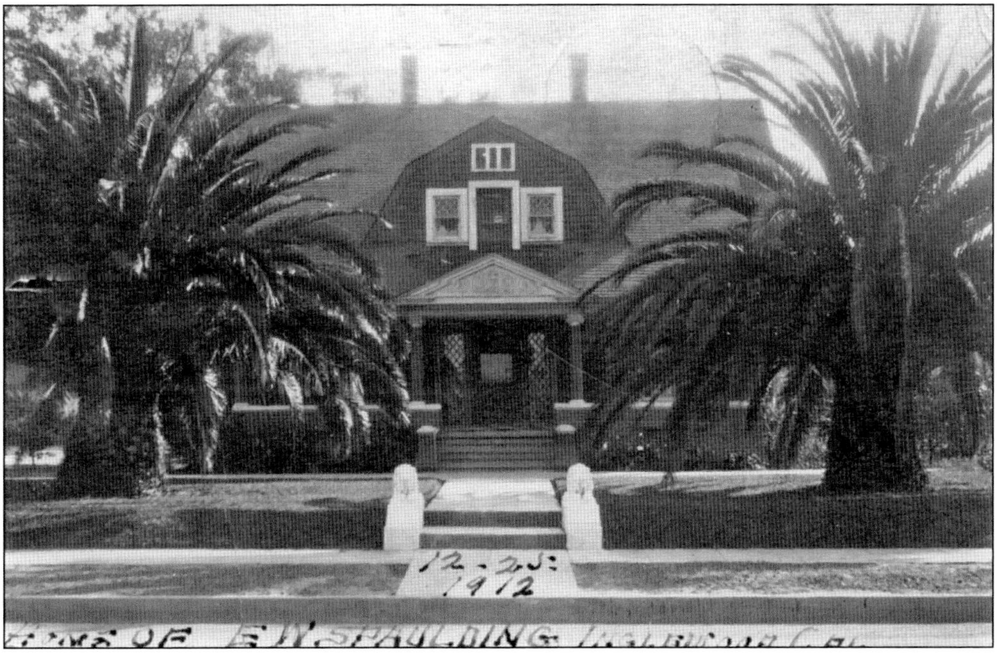

This real-photo postcard depicts the home of E. W. Spaulding, a pioneer Inglewood realtor, and is dated December 25, 1912. The caption on the reverse reads, "All are pretty well in Inglewood, Calif. Why don't you come out? Fine weather; not any sleighing yet. Picture taken Christmas. Let us hear from you. Yours truly, Ed Spaulding." This home was inhabited by four generations of Spauldings and was demolished in 1962. (Courtesy James Osborne.)

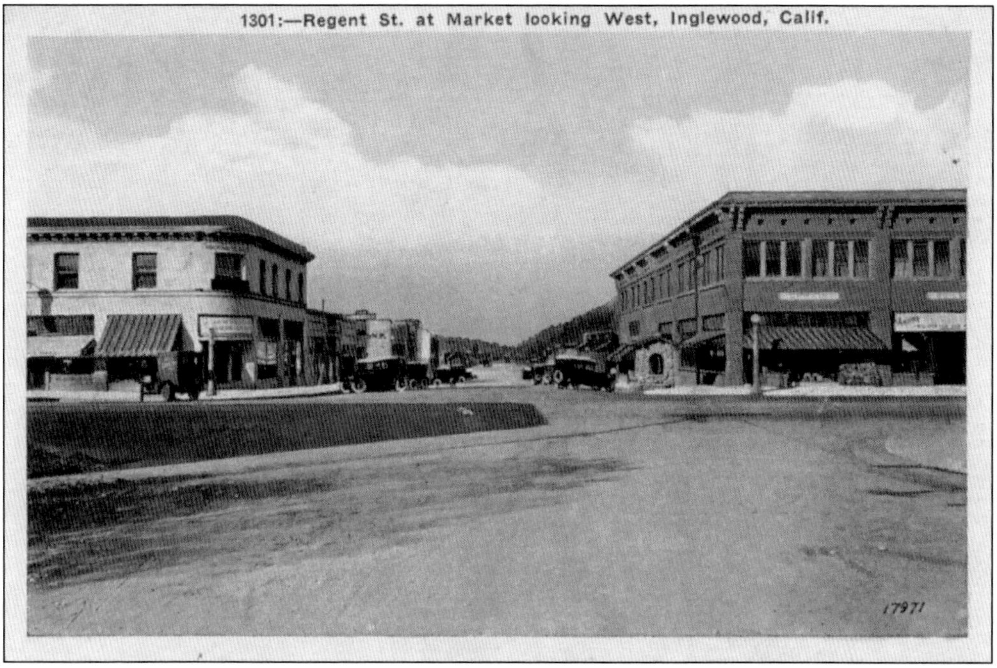

This view depicts the intersection of Regent and Market Streets looking west. (Courtesy James Osborne; published by M. Kashower, Los Angeles, California.)

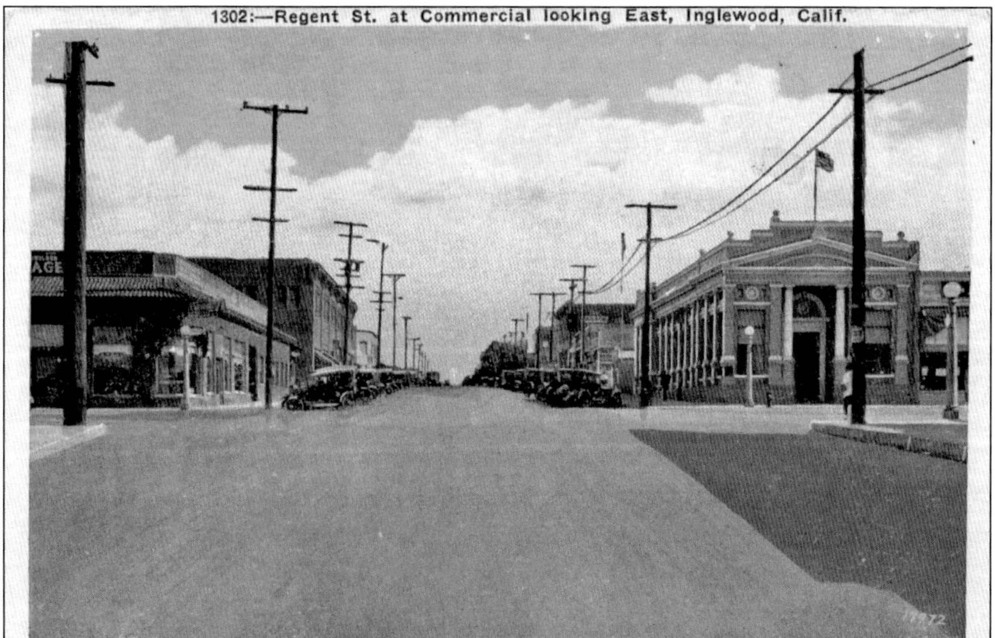

This 1920s view of Regent and Commercial Streets looks west. (Courtesy James Osborne; published by M. Kashower, Los Angeles, California.)

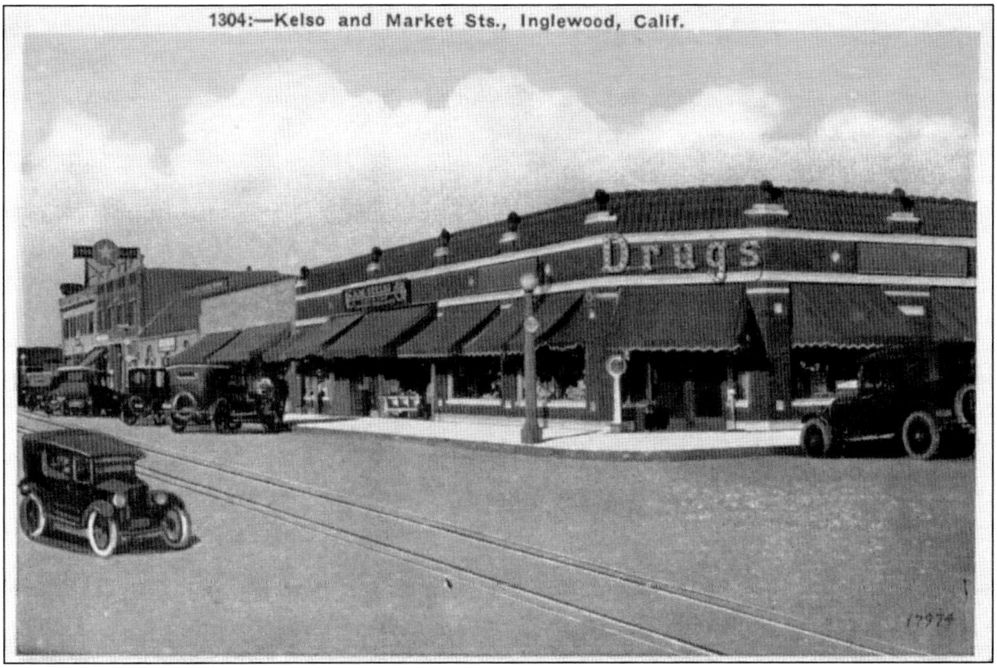

Kelso Street was named after William Kelso, a Pasadena realtor who purchased 60 acres soon after arriving in Inglewood. This view shows the drugstore at the corner of Kelso and Market Streets. (Courtesy James Osborne; published by M. Kashower, Los Angeles, California.)

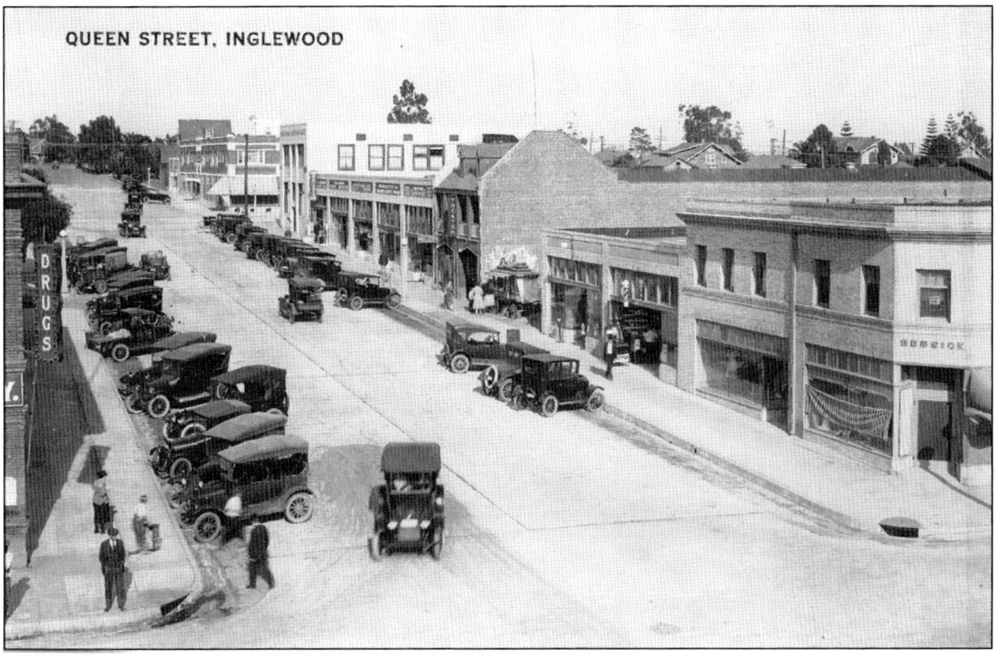

This RPPC depicts Queen Street in Inglewood. (Courtesy James Osborne.)

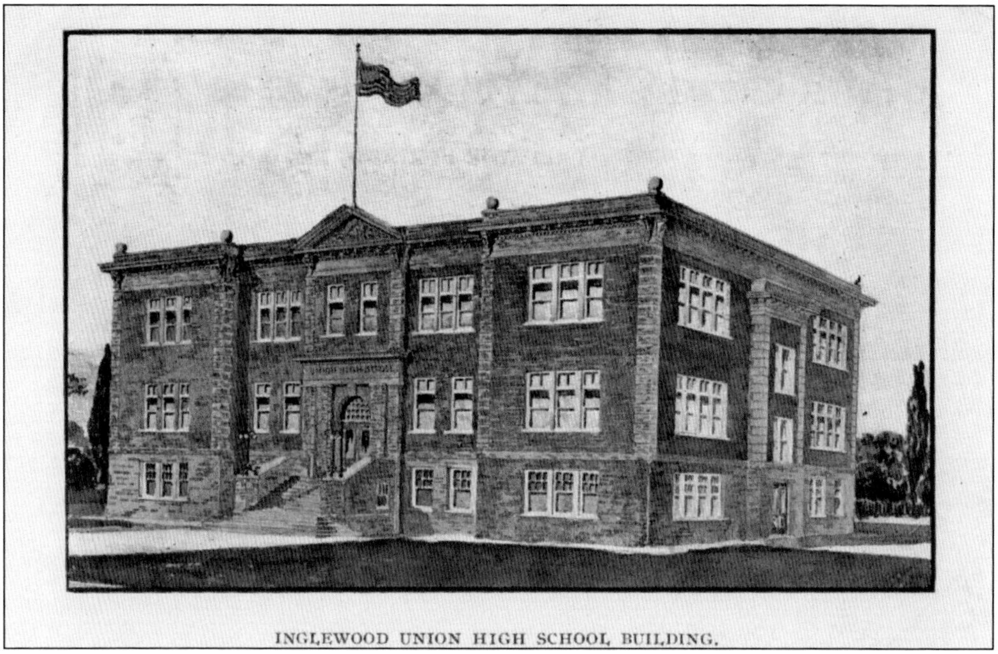

The Inglewood Union High School building was completed in 1908 and had one boy and four girls in the first graduating class. The message written on the reverse of this postcard reads, "Dear Louise, Our play will be Saturday evening, March 10. Be sure and come early Saturday. Come right to the house and you will find someone there. Get off at Kelso. Muriel." (Courtesy James Osborne.)

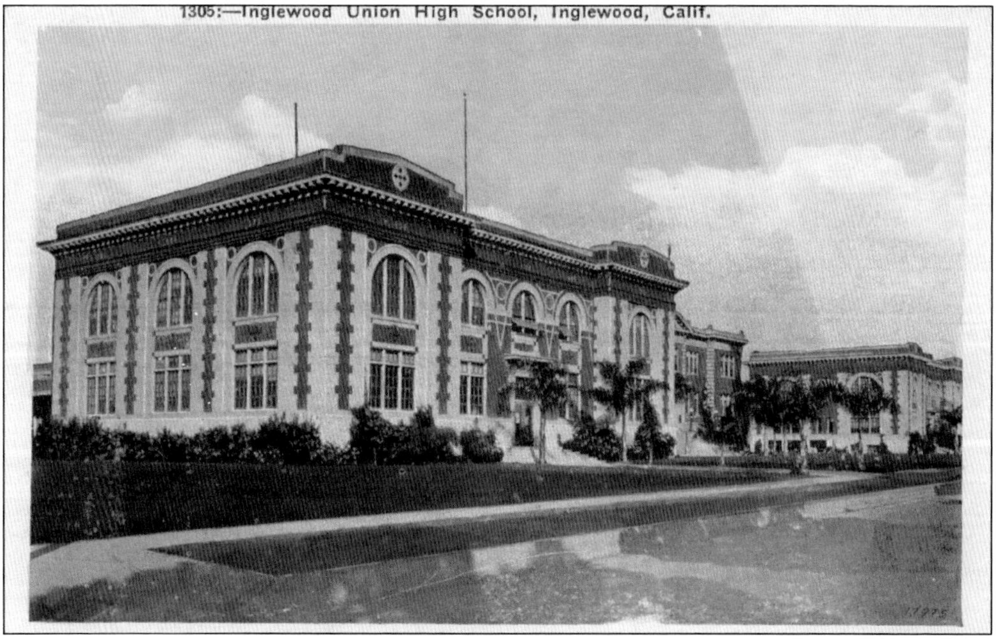

Seen here is another view of the additional Inglewood High School buildings, which were dedicated on February 28, 1916. (Courtesy James Osborne; published by M. Kashower, Los Angeles, California.)

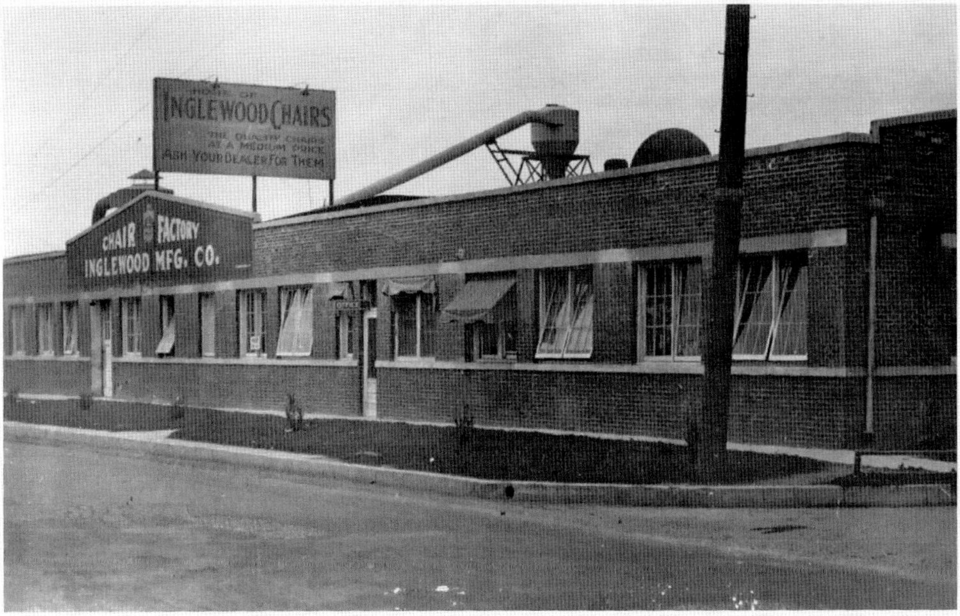

This RPPC depicts the Inglewood Chair Factory. It was partly owned by newspaperman Sam Greene, who moved to Inglewood in 1912 and purchased the *Inglewood News* for $4,500. He crawled through a window to save this building from a fire in 1926. (Courtesy James Osborne.)

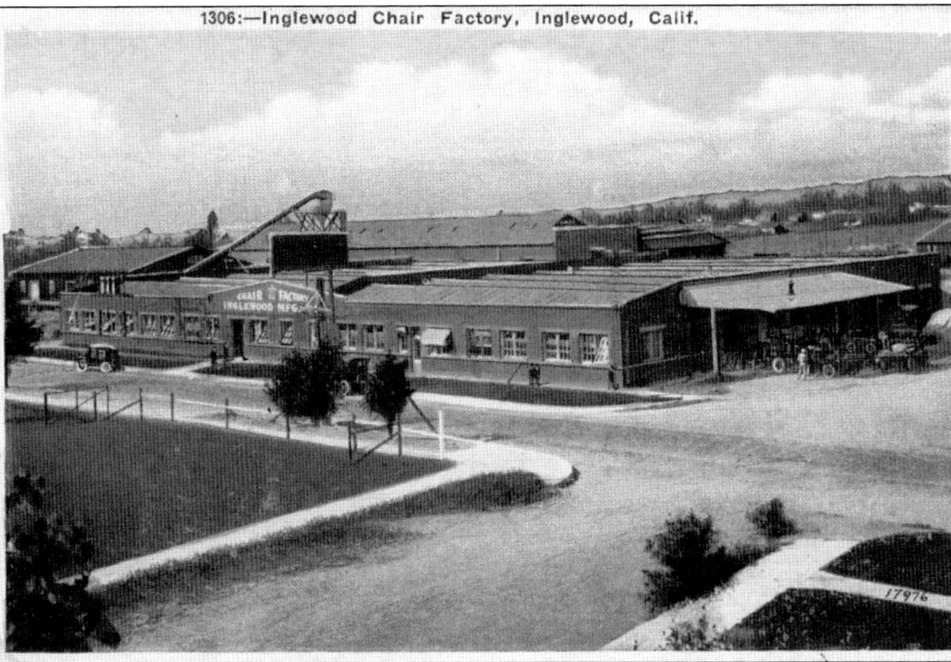

Seen here is another view of the Inglewood Chair Factory. (Courtesy James Osborne; published by M. Kashower, Los Angeles, California.)

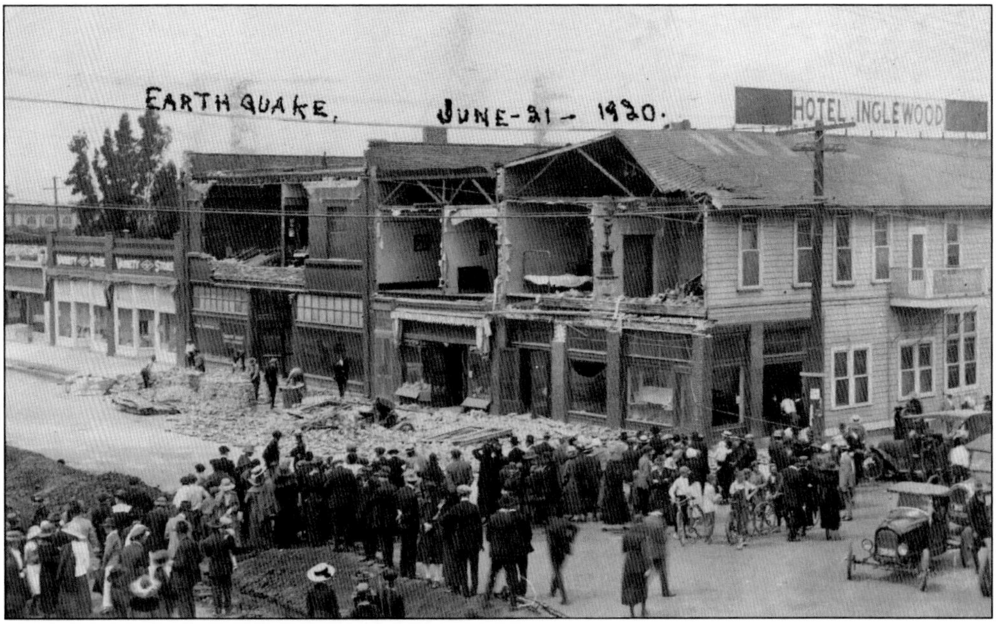

On the evening of June 21, 1920, right after most Inglewood residents were finishing dinner, an earthquake struck. This RPPC depicts a crowd of onlookers surveying the damage the earthquake caused to the Hotel Inglewood and other buildings. The message written on the reverse of this card reads, "Dear Emma, You no doubt read of the earthquake we had out here last Monday evening and most all of the damage done was in this little town of Inglewood. This is the worst part of it although not many chimneys are left on any houses and plate glass windows are out all over the town. It was some shake. Sarah." (Courtesy James Osborne.)

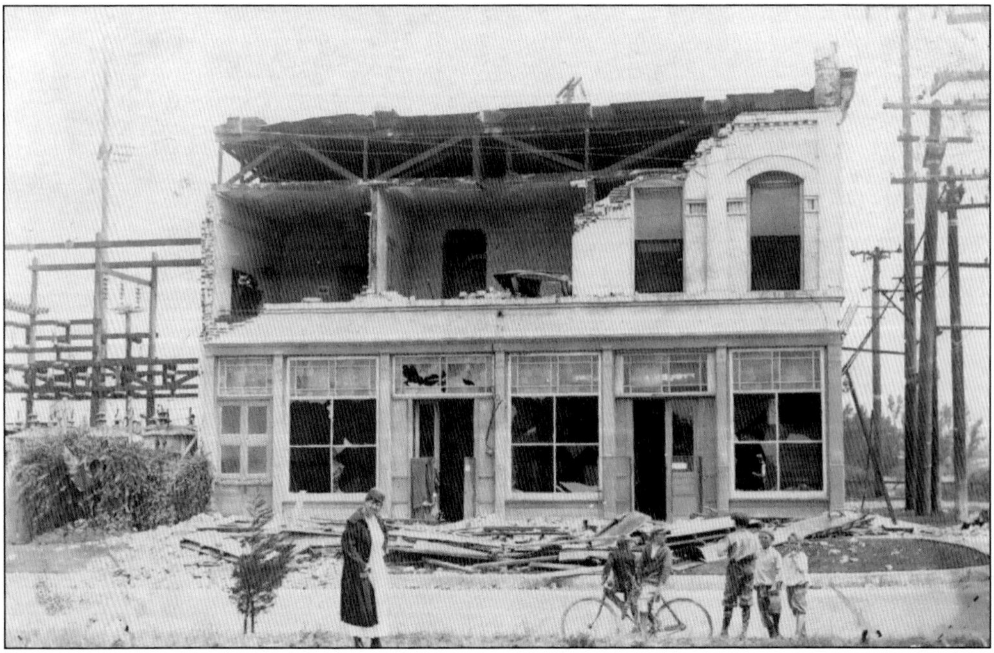

This RPPC shows the damage the Inglewood earthquake caused to the Edison substation located at Florence and Fir Avenues. (Courtesy James Osborne.)

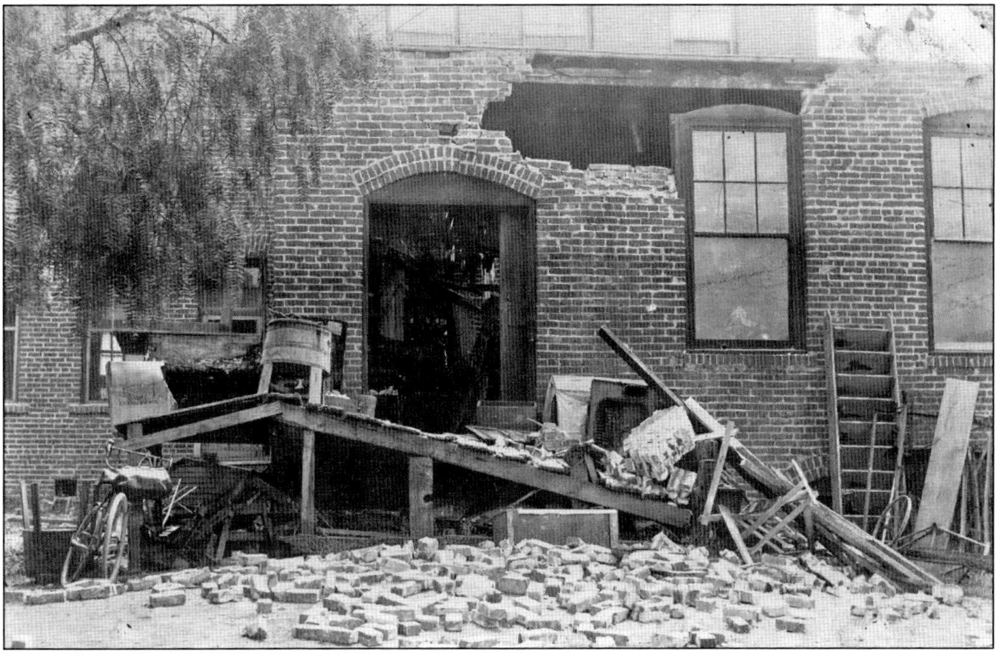

More of the earthquake damage can be seen in this real-photo postcard. The disturbance was due to a small displacement of the rocks on the Inglewood–Newport–San Onofre fault or fault zone, which parallels the Baldwin Hills–Los Cerritos ridge, according to Stephen Taber, writing in the *Bulletin of the Seismological Society of America.* (Courtesy James Osborne.)

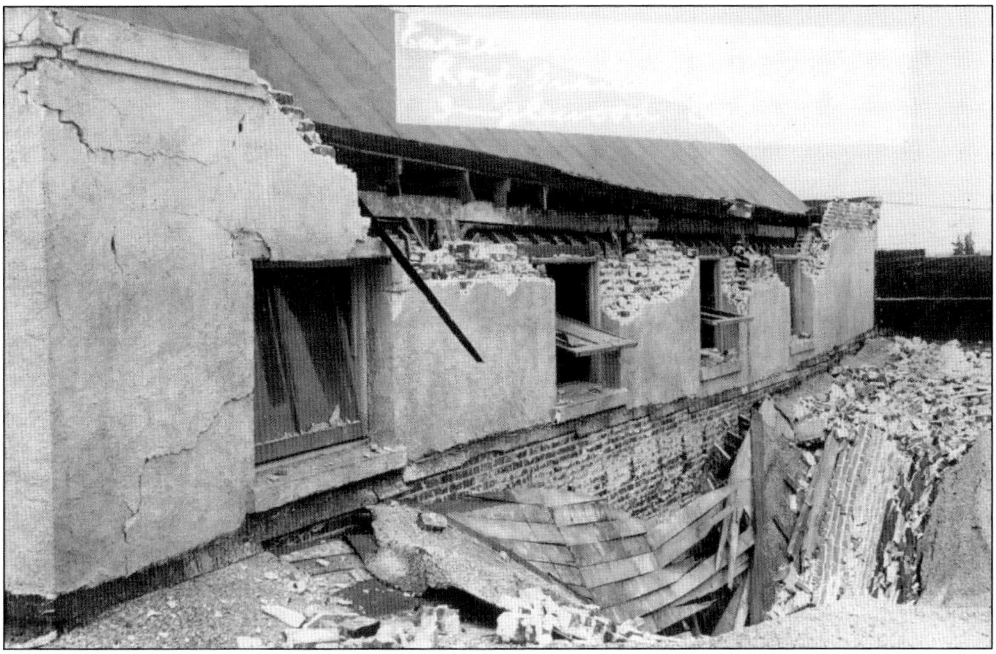

Some of the devastation wrought upon the grammar school building by the quake is seen here. It was fortunate that the quake struck in the evening, when no students were present. (Courtesy James Osborne.)

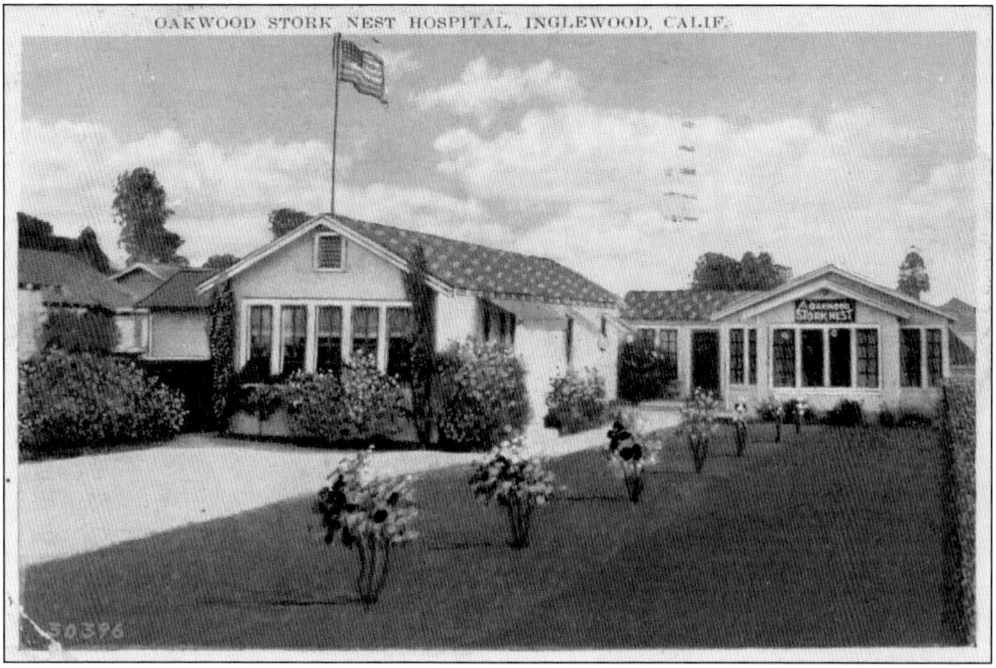

The Oakwood Stork Nest Hospital is depicted here. The message on the back of this card, postmarked January 22, 1932, reads, "Dear Georgia, At the hospital Bertha wants me to write this for her. Both doing fine. Some girl. She will write in a few days. She will be here 10 days. Kenneth." (Courtesy James Osborne; published by M. Kashower, Los Angeles, California.)

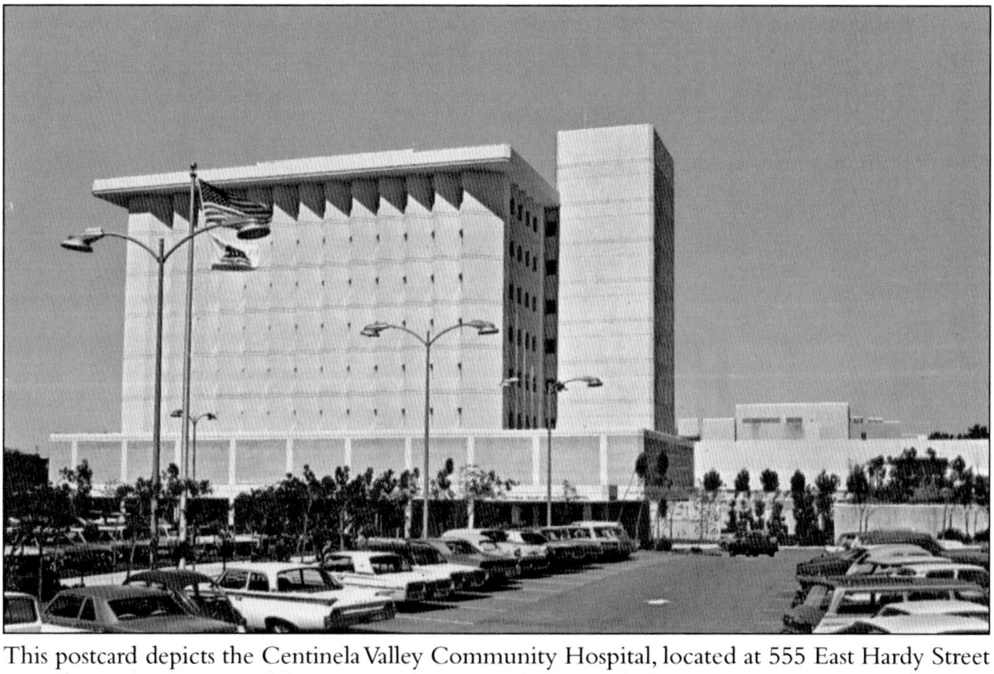

This postcard depicts the Centinela Valley Community Hospital, located at 555 East Hardy Street in Inglewood. In 1968, California governor Ronald Reagan helped dedicate the new eight-story tower. This hospital was the first in the nation to offer private rooms for its patients. (Courtesy James Osborne; published by Kolor View, Los Angeles, California.)

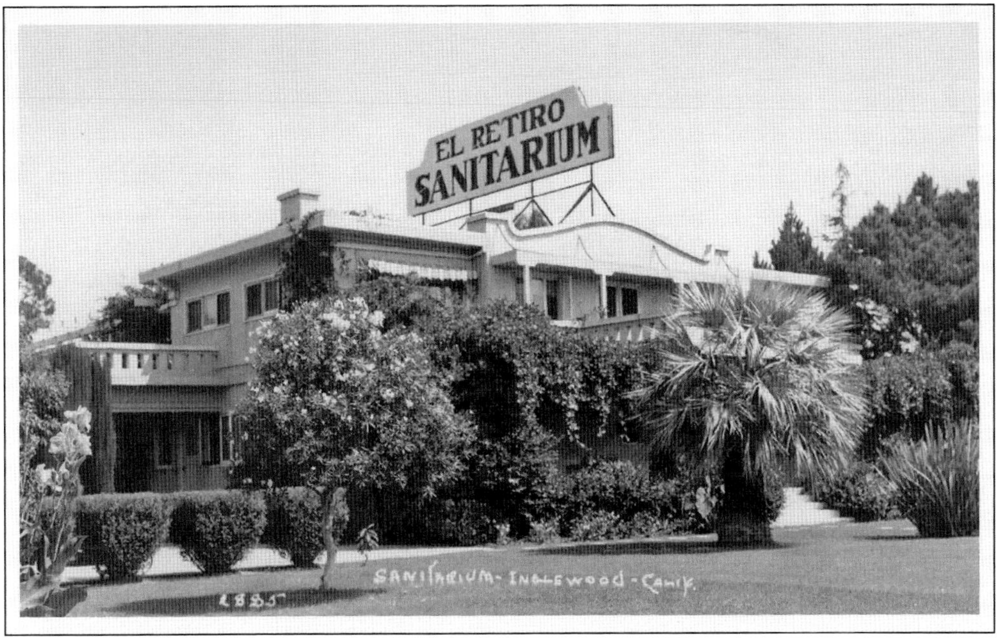

Depicted here is the El Retiro Sanitarium in Inglewood. (Courtesy James Osborne.)

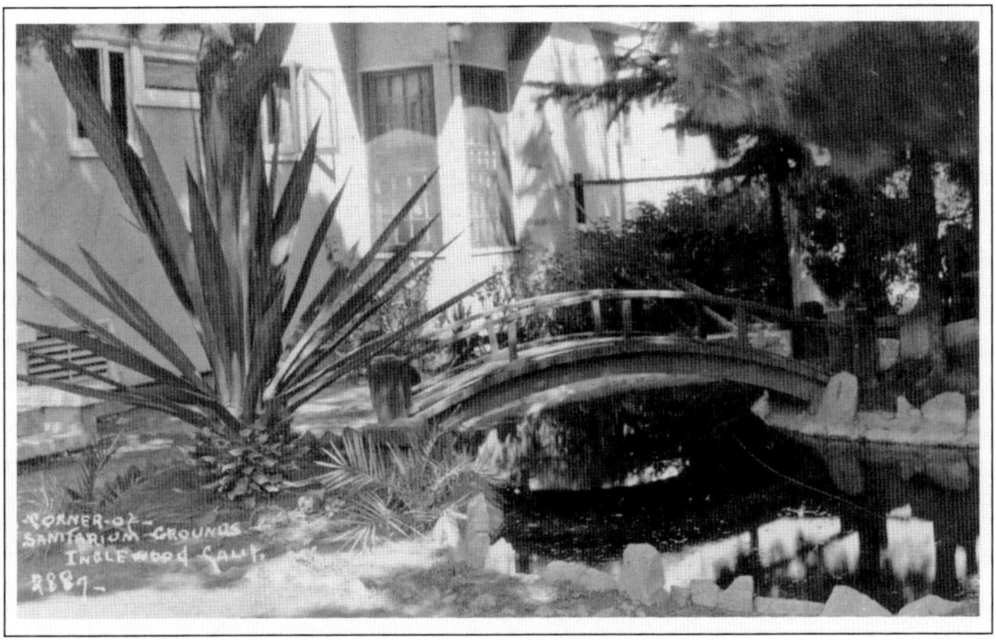

Another view of El Retiro Sanitarium shows a portion of the garden and pond. (Courtesy James Osborne.)

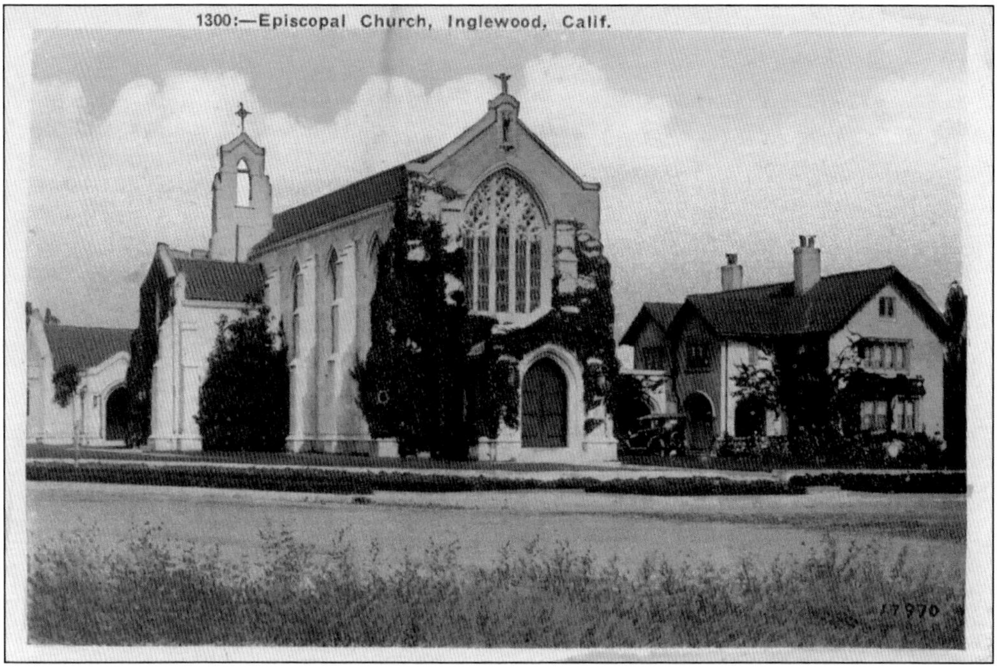

In 1907, the first group of Inglewood Episcopalians began meeting in a member's home. In 1913, the cornerstone of the Holy Faith Episcopal Church was laid, and construction was paid for by Grace and Charles Howland in memory of their mothers. (Courtesy James Osborne; published by M. Kashower, Los Angeles, California.)

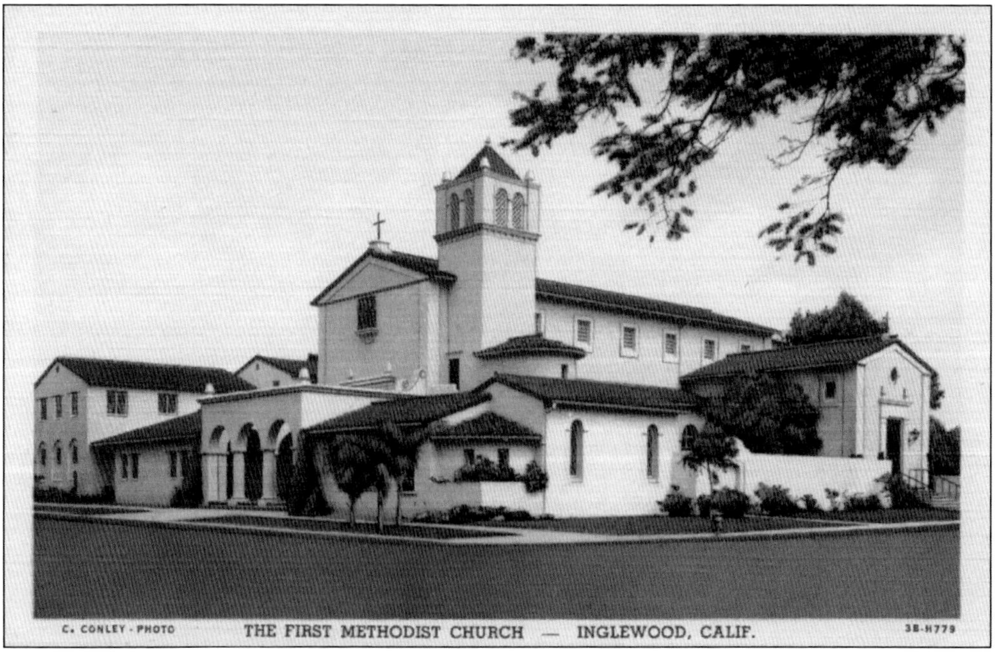

Inglewood's First Methodist Church was organized in 1905 with seven charter members. Seen here is the second church building on the corner of Kelso Street and Spruce Avenue. (Courtesy James Osborne; published by C.T. Art-Colortone.)

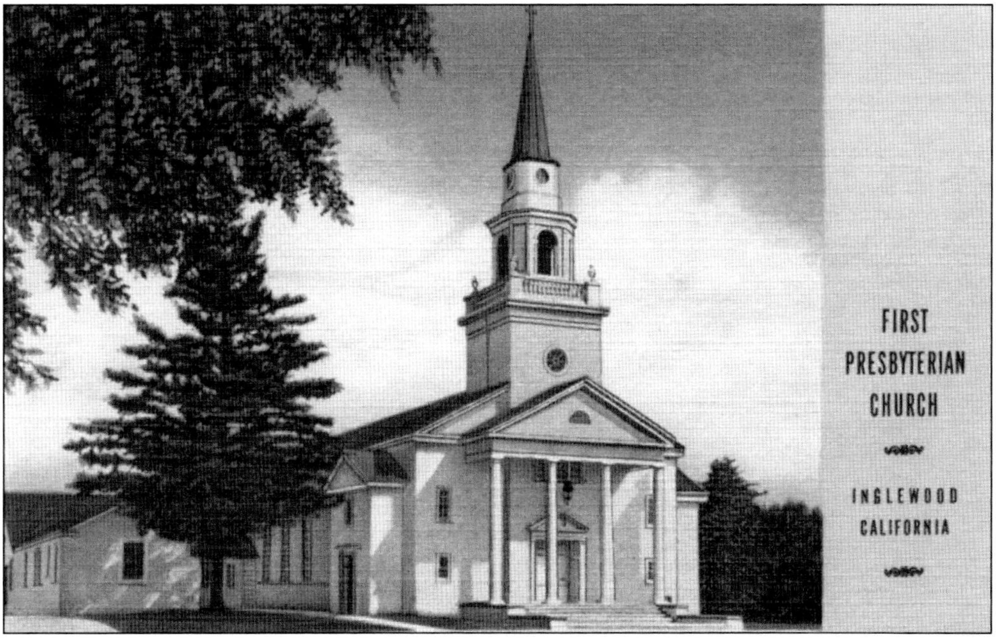

Inglewood's First Presbyterian Church was originally set to be organized on December 8, 1889, but stormy weather caused it to be postponed until January 19, 1890. Seen here is the third church building, which was dedicated in 1947. (Courtesy James Osborne; published by C. T. Art-Colortone.)

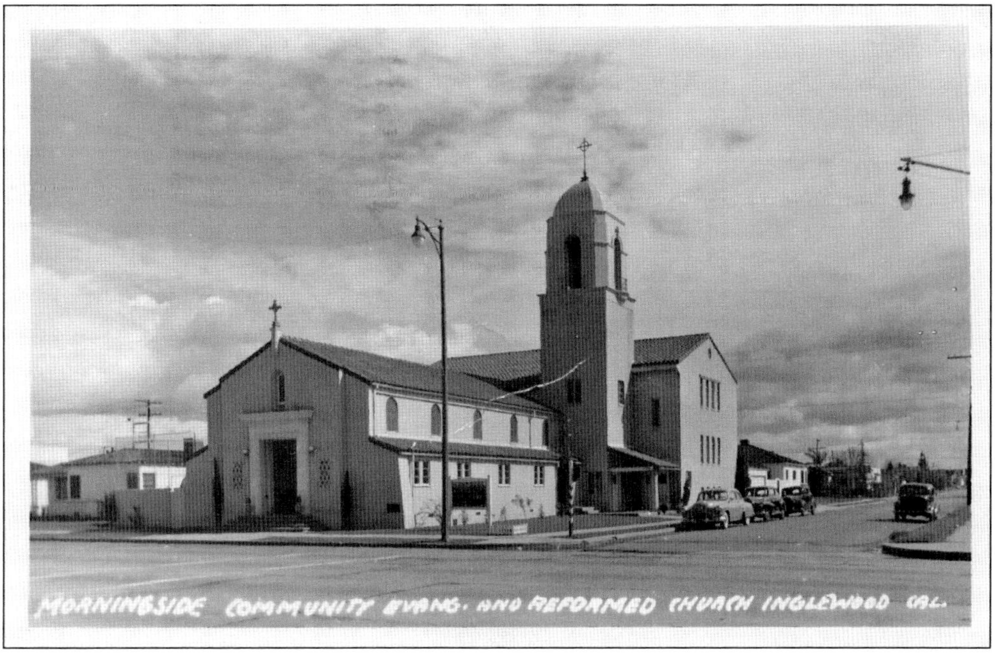

This RPPC shows the Morningside Community Evangelical and Reformed Church of Inglewood. (Courtesy James Osborne.)

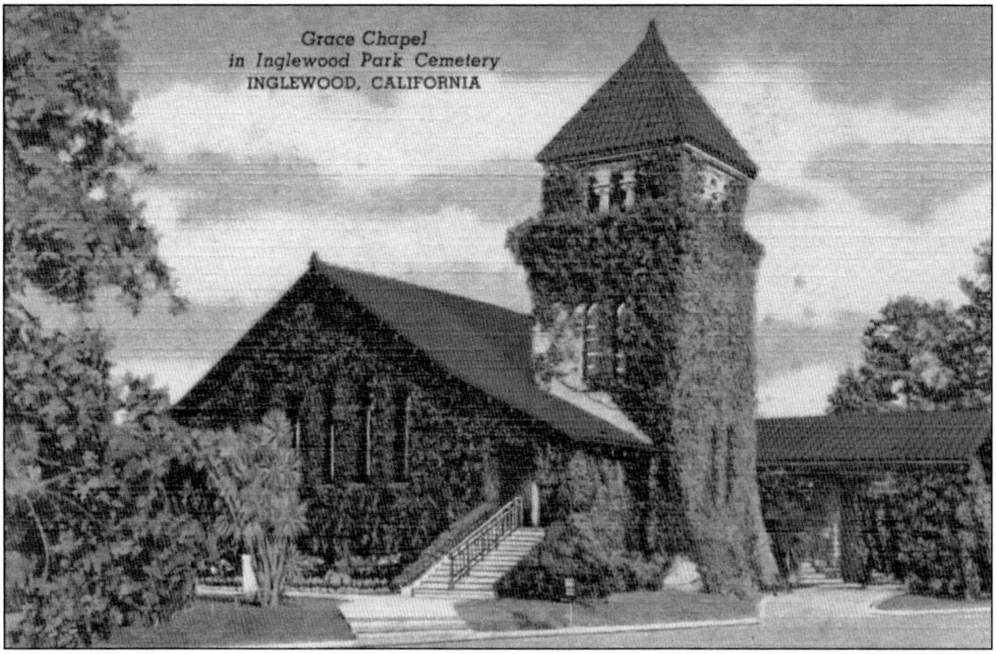

The Inglewood Park Cemetery was founded in 1905 by a group of businessmen who included Charles B. Hopper, the founder of Lawndale. Seen here is the ivy-covered Grace Chapel, which was built in 1925 as a replica of Grace Chapel in London. (Courtesy James Osborne; published by C. T. Art-Colortone.)

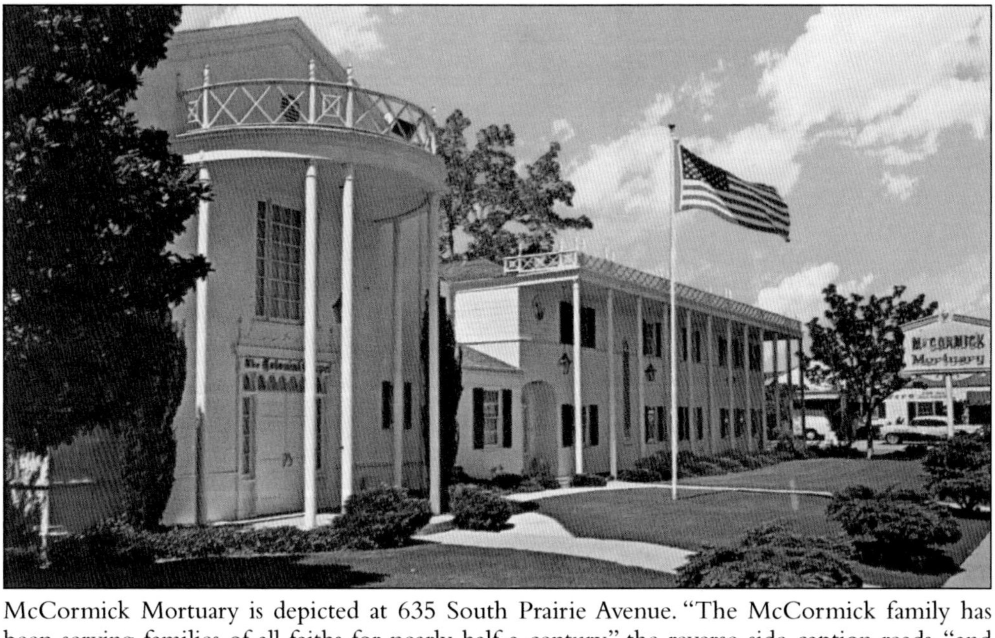

McCormick Mortuary is depicted at 635 South Prairie Avenue. "The McCormick family has been serving families of all faiths for nearly half a century," the reverse-side caption reads, "and now have chapels in Inglewood, Westchester, Hawthorne, Redondo Beach, Manhattan Beach, Gardena, Whittier, and Lake Tahoe to serve the entire Southwest. This view shows their Inglewood establishment, which is one of California's finest mortuaries." (Courtesy James Osborne; published by Bill Brunk.)

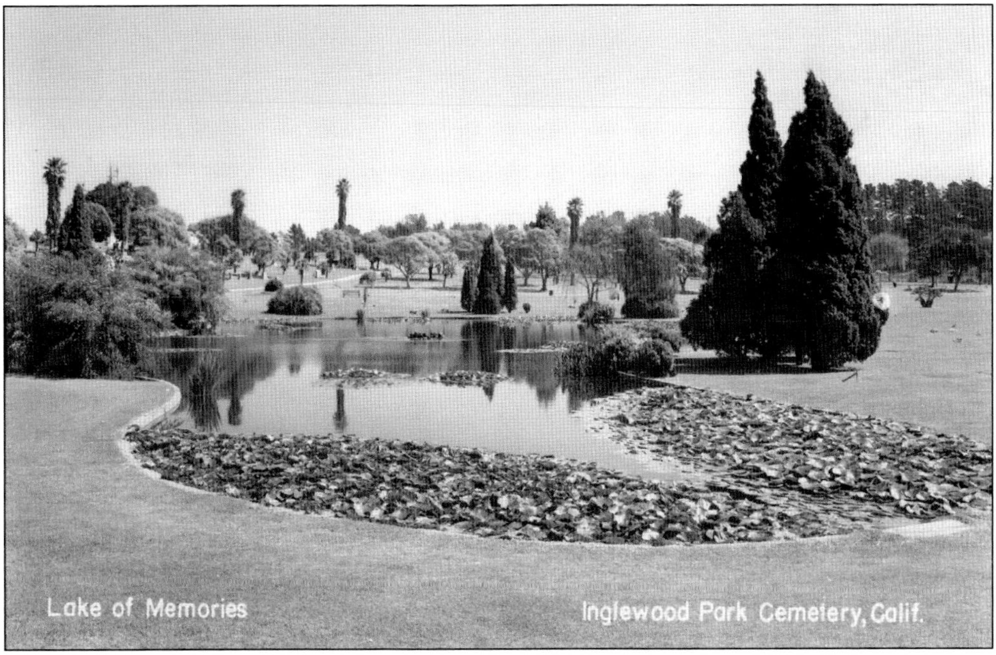

The "Lake of Memories" at Inglewood Park Cemetery is seen here. Some of the notables interred in this cemetery include Ella Fitzgerald, Ray Charles, Betty Grable, Cesar Romero, Edgar Bergen, and former Los Angeles mayor Tom Bradley. (Courtesy James Osborne.)

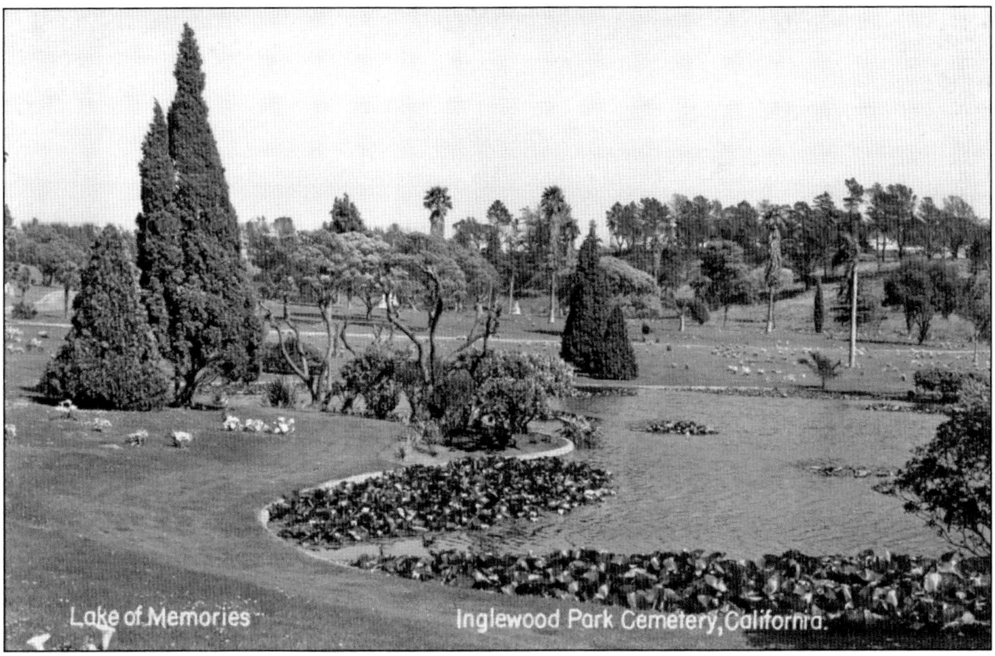

Another view of the "Lake of Memories" is seen here. Buried under the lawn in the middle of the park are the famous stripper Gypsy Rose Lee and the great prizefighter Sugar Ray Robinson, the subject of the biography *Sweet Thunder* by Wil Haygood. (Courtesy James Osborne.)

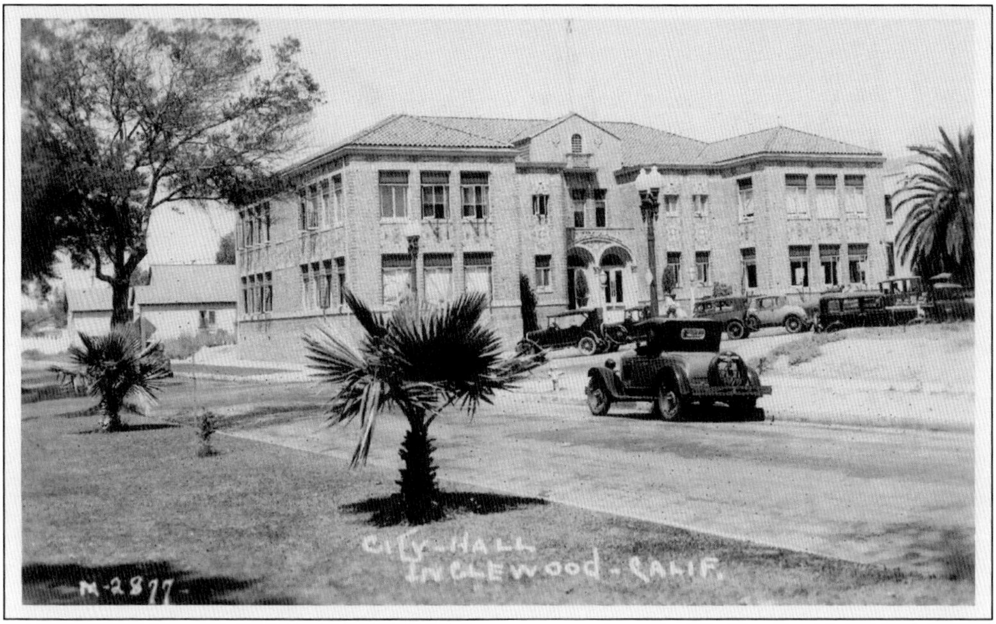

This real-photo postcard depicts the second Inglewood City Hall, which was dedicated in 1923. (Courtesy James Osborne.)

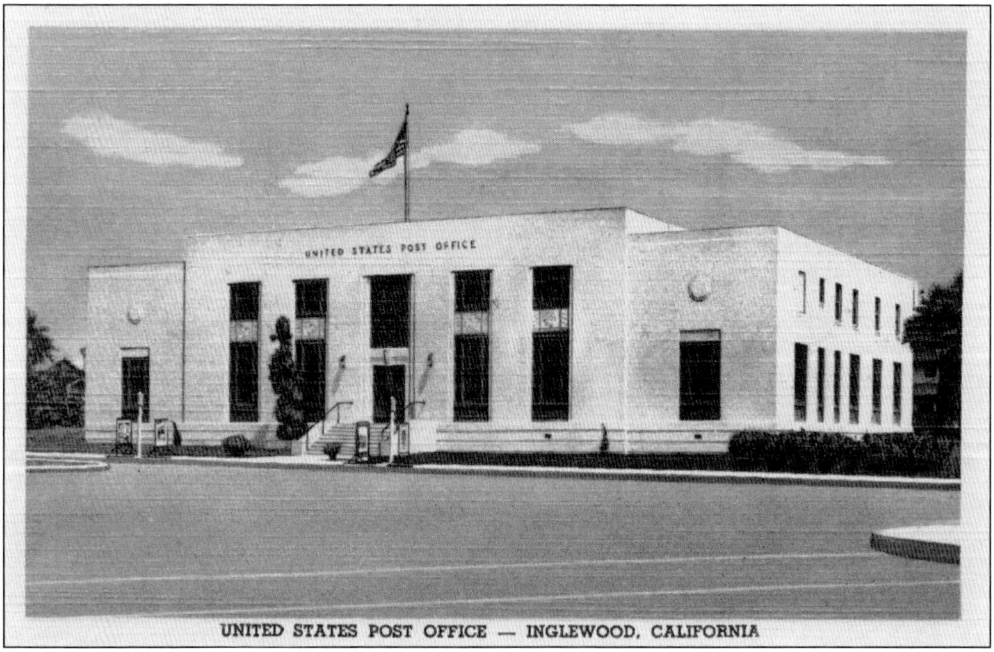

"The Inglewood Post Office is a two division plan first class post office with mailing and finance departments," imparts the reverse side of this card. (Courtesy James Osborne; published by C.T. Art-Colortone.)

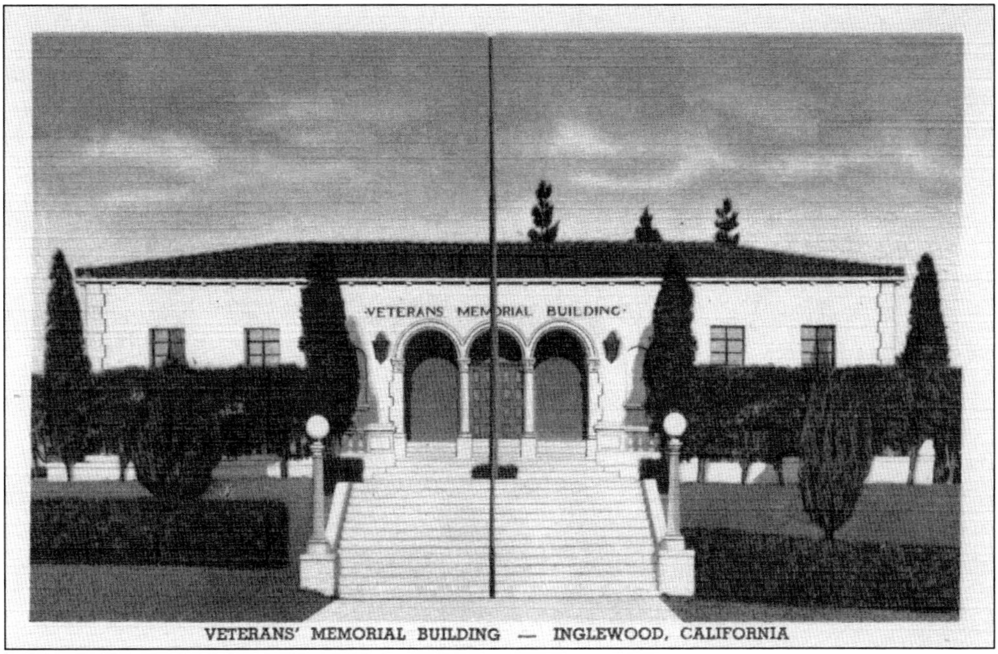

The Veterans Memorial Building was constructed by the Works Progress Administration. The caption on the opposite side of this card reads, "Veterans Memorial Building built after World War I as a memorial. This building is now used by veterans organizations. Located on the west side of Centinela Park, it stands as a beautiful monument to Inglewood's war heroes." (Courtesy James Osborne; published by C.T. Colortone.)

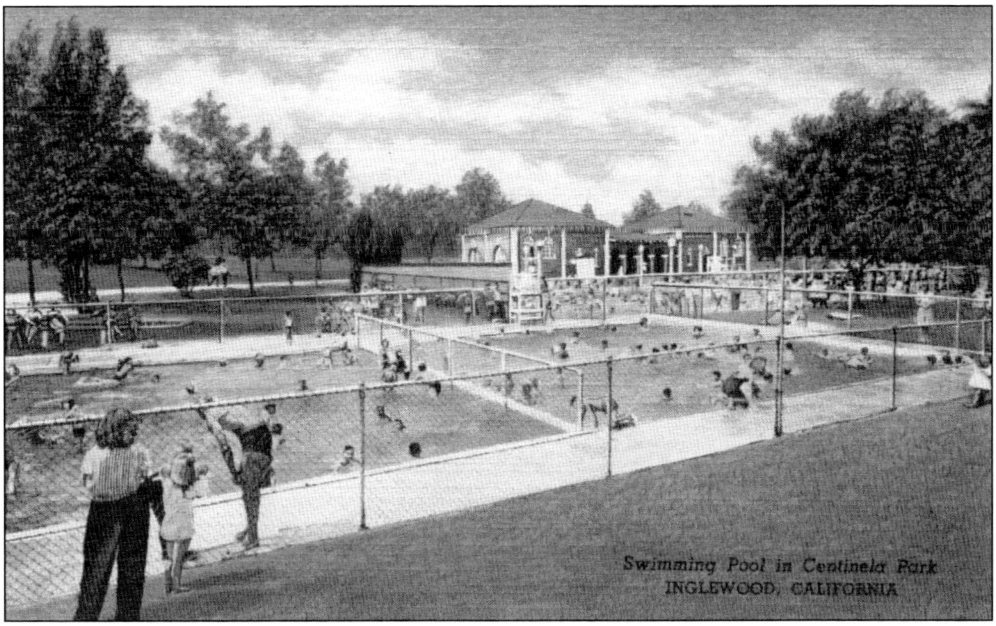

The swimming pool located in Centinela Park was also built by the Works Progress Administration. This postcard was postmarked in Lawndale on December 1, 1949. The message on the flip side reads, "Thought you would like postmarked *[sic]*; first day opening of a small-town post office." (Courtesy James Osborne; published by C.T. Colortone.)

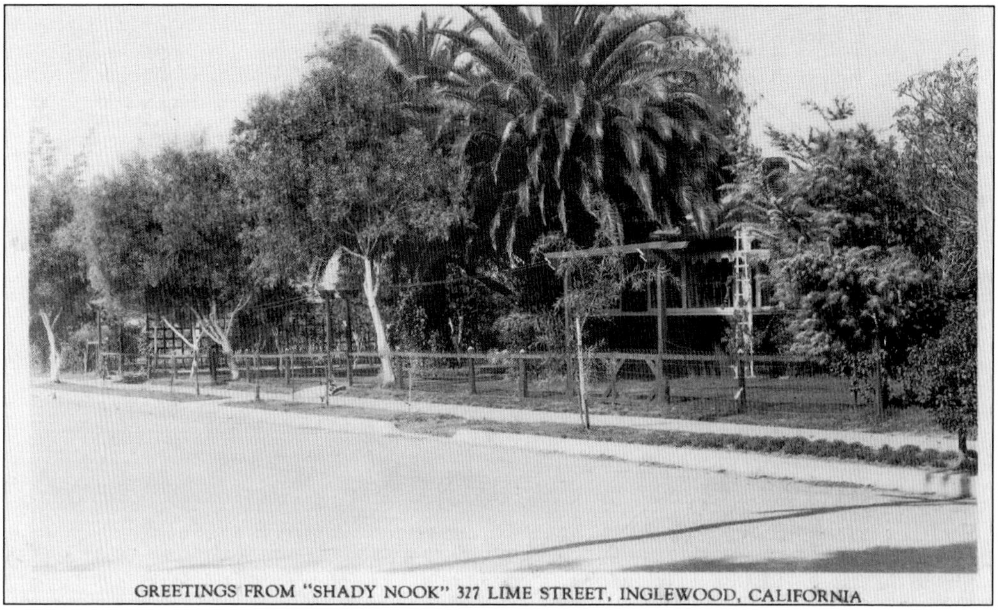

This RPPC depicts Shady Nook at 327 Lime Street in Inglewood. The handwritten message on the card's reverse reads, "Friend Eddy, This is where I stay while Charles is at Trona [in San Bernardino County]. It is a very pretty place. All kinds of trees—palm, pepper, oranges, lemon. We have a [*sic*] aviary with about 150 birds. Also all kinds of beautiful flowers. So you throw snowballs for me and I'll pick oranges for you. Best wishes to your mother. Olga Hogan." (Courtesy James Osborne.)

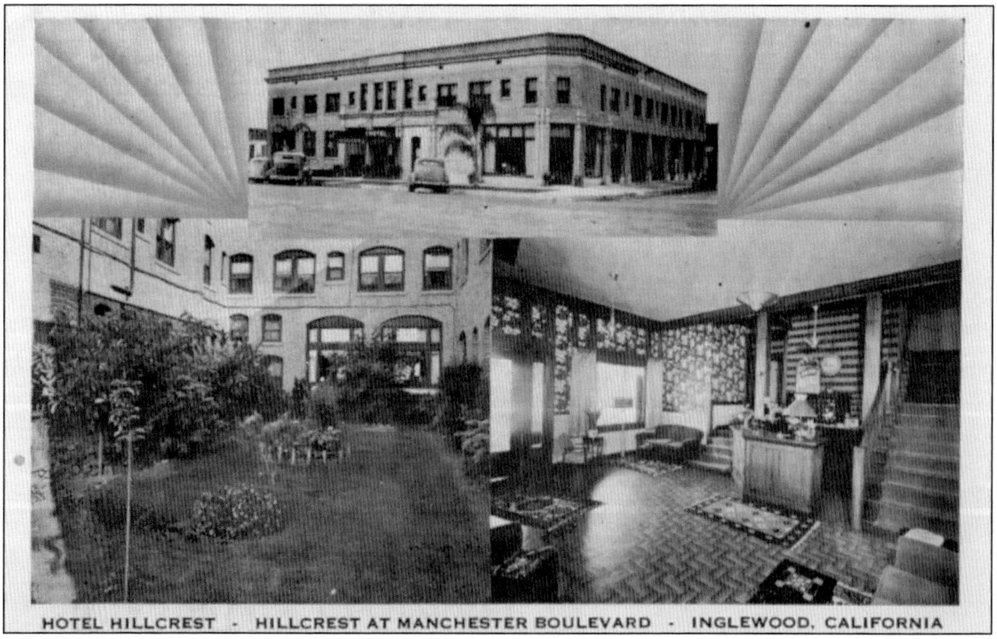

The Hotel Hillcrest was located at Hillcrest and Manchester Boulevards in Inglewood. The accommodations were described on the back: "Quiet, modern and convenient. Inglewood's leading hotel, Hillcrest at Manchester Boulevard. Close to Los Angeles International Airport and Hollywood Park Race Track." (Courtesy James Osborne; published by Nationwide Advertising Company, Arlington, Texas.)

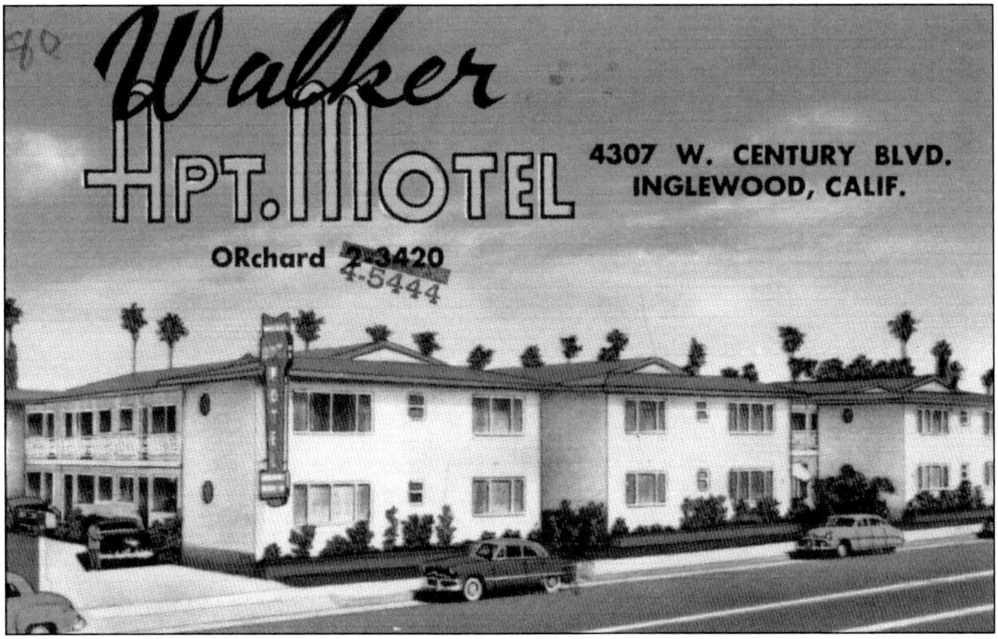

The Walker Apartment Motel was located at 4307 West Century Boulevard. The reverse-side caption reads, "Walker Apt. Motel, 44 units beautifully and completely furnished. Heated swimming pool, T.V. and radio, kitchens, maid service, near International Airport and Hollywood Race Track. In the center of everything. Privately owned." (Courtesy James Osborne; published by Nationwide Postcard Company, Arlington, Texas.)

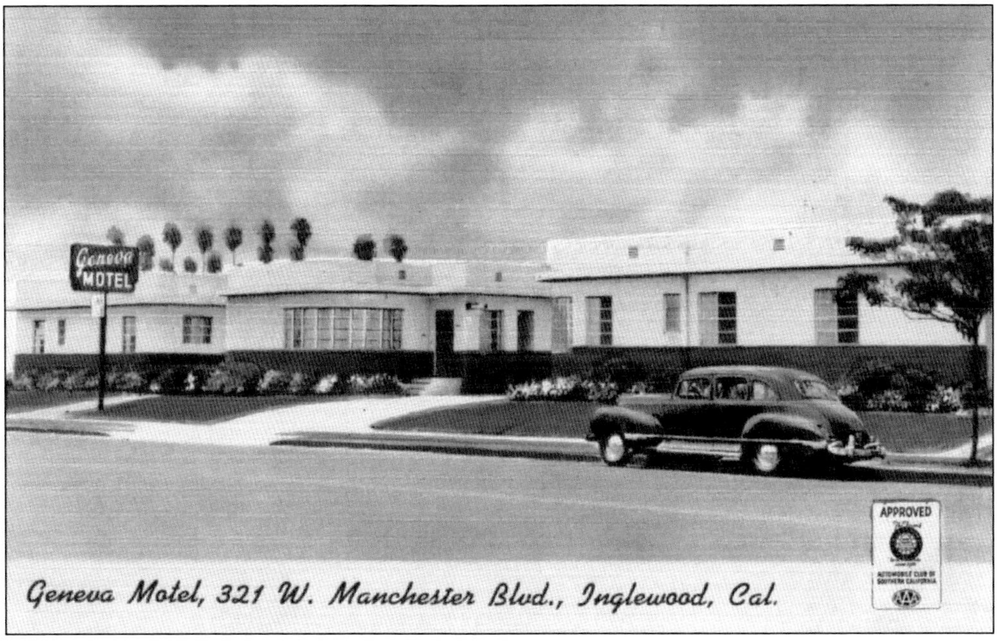

The Geneva Motel was located at 321 West Manchester Boulevard. Postmarked on July 24, 1950, this postcard's handwritten message reads, "Hello Sandy, I arrived here Saturday night. Quite a nice place. Seeing some interesting sights. Some of the ones I missed when I was here before. Ron." (Courtesy James Osborne; published by Colourpicture Publications, Boston, Massachusetts.)

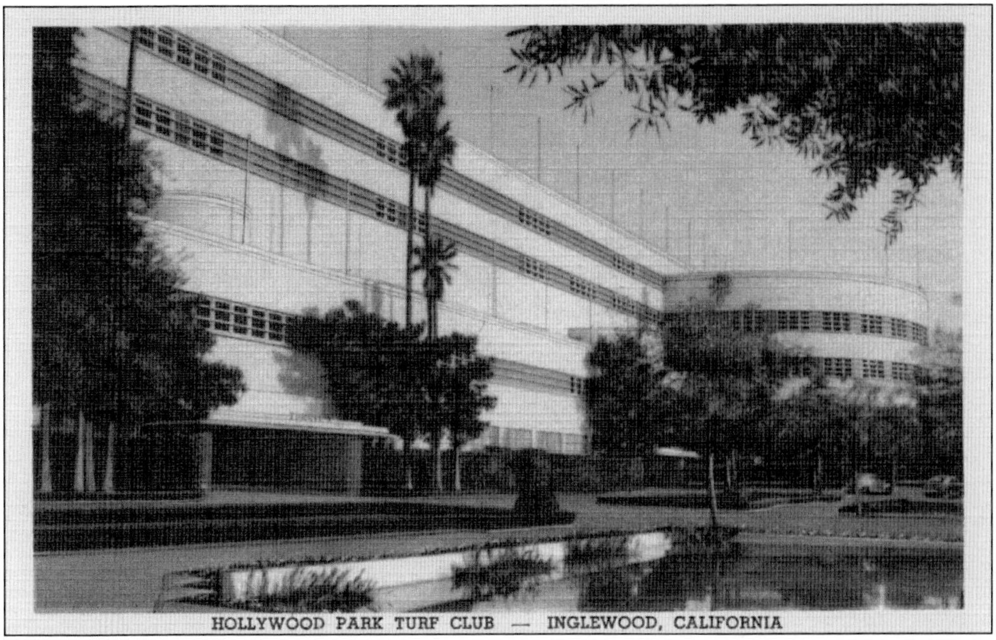

The Hollywood Park Turf Club was formed under the chairmanship of Jack L. Warner of Warner Brothers movie studio. Opening day was June 10, 1938. The caption on the back of this postcard reads, "Hollywood Park Turf Club is America's most modern race track. Its attractive lawns and colorful flowers add much to its beauty." (Courtesy James Osborne; published by C.T. Art-Colortone.)

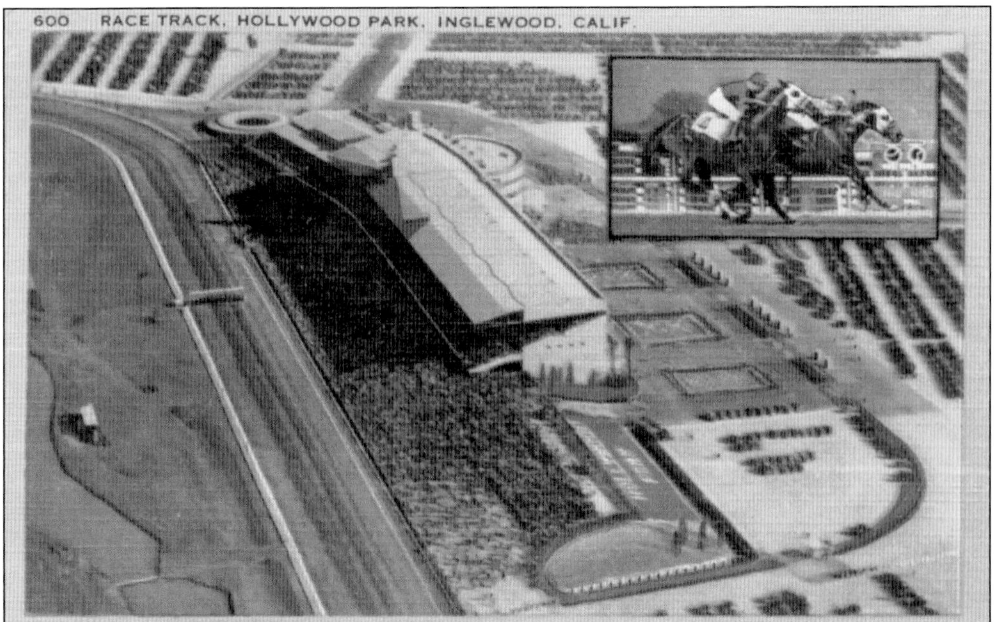

This postcard portrays the racetrack at Hollywood Park, which was frequented by many of the movie studios' biggest stars. However, Hollywood Park was not a park, and it was not in Hollywood. (Courtesy James Osborne; published by Longshaw Card Company, Los Angeles, California.)

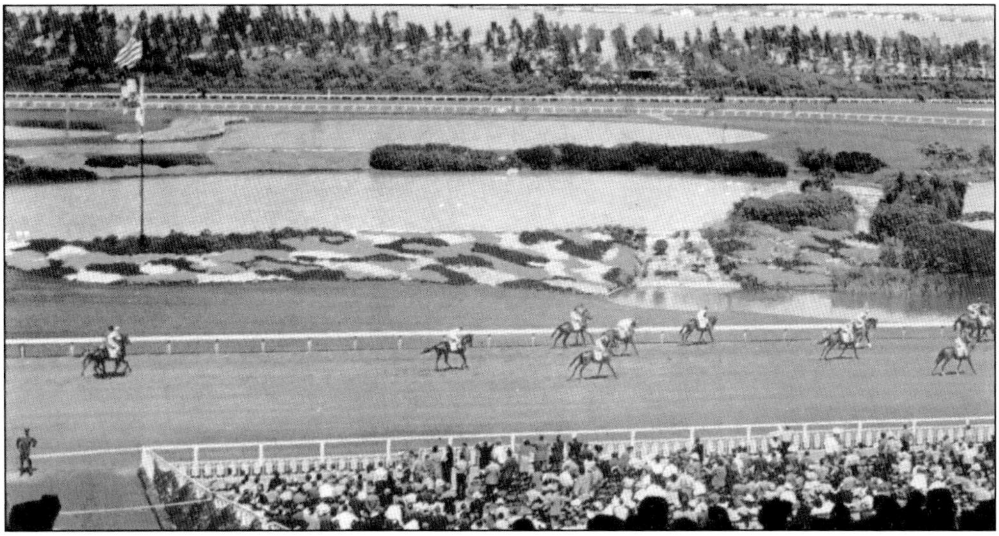

The reverse-side caption on this postcard claims, "Hollywood Park is one of the world's most beautiful homes of thoroughbred racing with its broad expanses of lakes, flowers, lawn, and semitropical shrubs, located close to the heart of Los Angeles, Hollywood, Beverly Hills, and the Santa Monica Bay district." The card also claims, "Cooled by breezes from the nearby Pacific, Hollywood Park is favored by ideal racing conditions. Its extensive racing program is climaxed each year by the $100,000 Hollywood Gold Cup, one of America's greatest racing classics." (Courtesy James Osborne.)

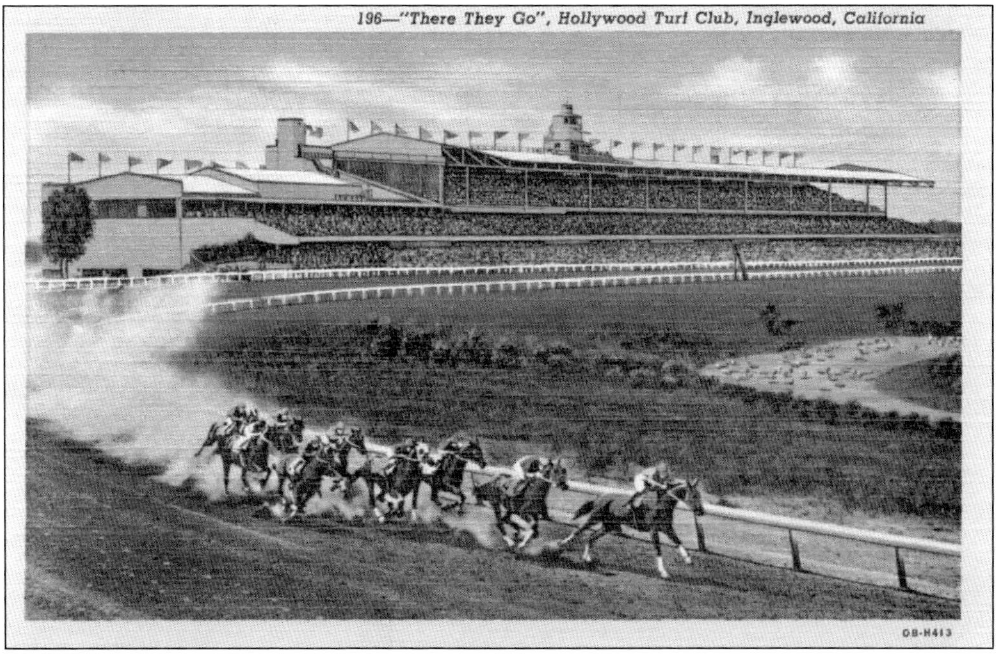

This card claims, "Hollywood Park, one of America's most beautiful race tracks, is situated in Inglewood, California, a short distance from Los Angeles. Here the summer visitor to Southern California may experience the double thrill of viewing the 'sport of kings' and mingle with Movieland's most glamorous personalities." (Courtesy James Osborne; published by Western Publishing and Novelty Company, Los Angeles, California.)

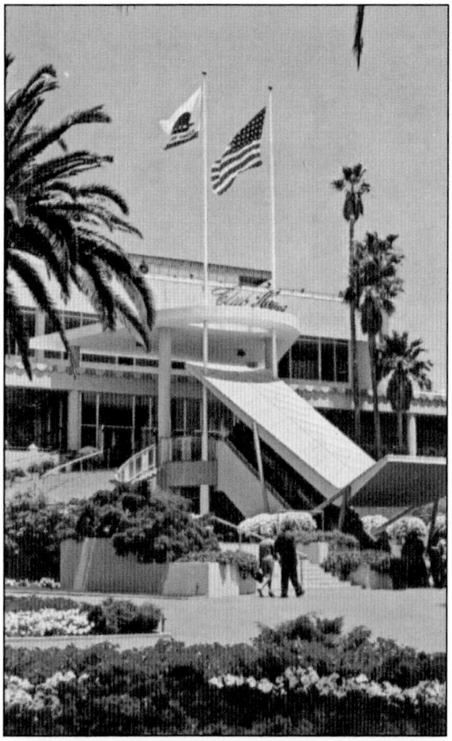

The back side of this postcard reads, "Hollywood Park, Inglewood, Calif. Acres of gardens line the stands of Hollywood park, America's leading race track in attendance and purse for many years. This flower-bedecked entrance leads to the commodious and glamorous Clubhouse section of the huge Grandstand-Clubhouse, Turf Club building, which is more than a quarter-mile long." (Courtesy James Osborne; published by Bob Plunkett, Los Angeles, California.)

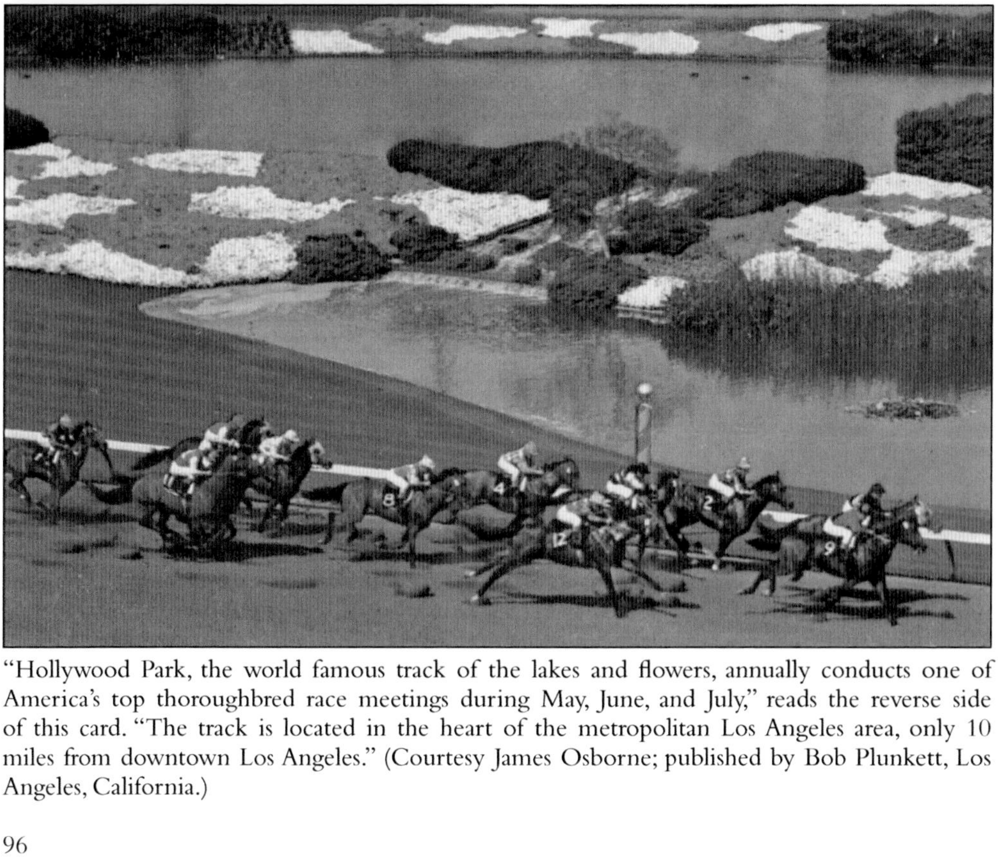

"Hollywood Park, the world famous track of the lakes and flowers, annually conducts one of America's top thoroughbred race meetings during May, June, and July," reads the reverse side of this card. "The track is located in the heart of the metropolitan Los Angeles area, only 10 miles from downtown Los Angeles." (Courtesy James Osborne; published by Bob Plunkett, Los Angeles, California.)

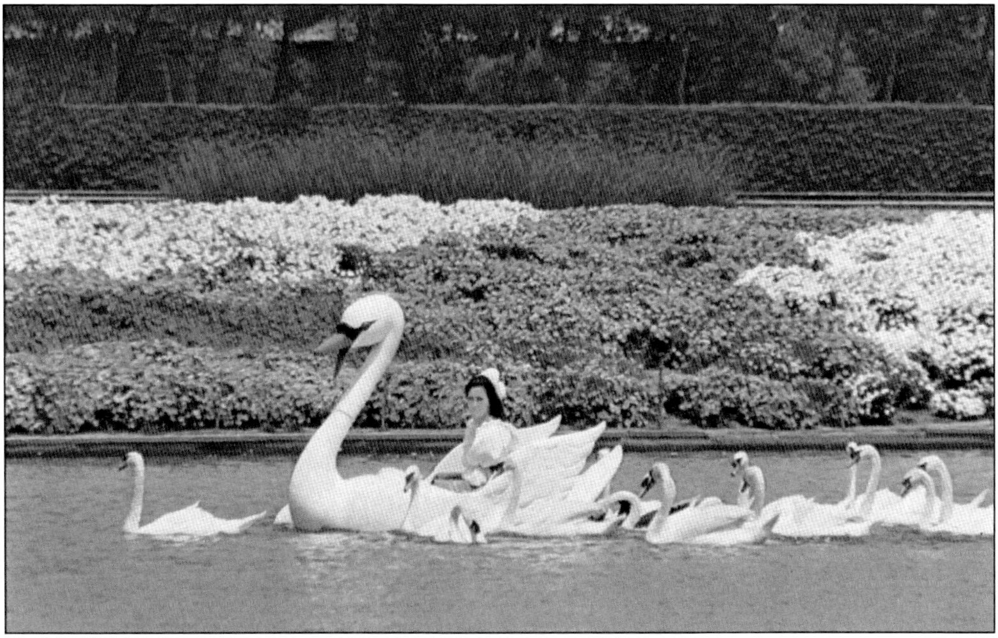

"Queen of the infield with its colorful gardens and 500 swans and geese is the lovely Goose Girl," reads this card's flip side, "elected before each race meeting in a beauty and personality contest. In this scene, she is riding in her electric swanboat, surrounded by some of Hollywood Park's stately waterfowl." (Courtesy James Osborne; published by Homer H. Boelter, Hollywood, California.)

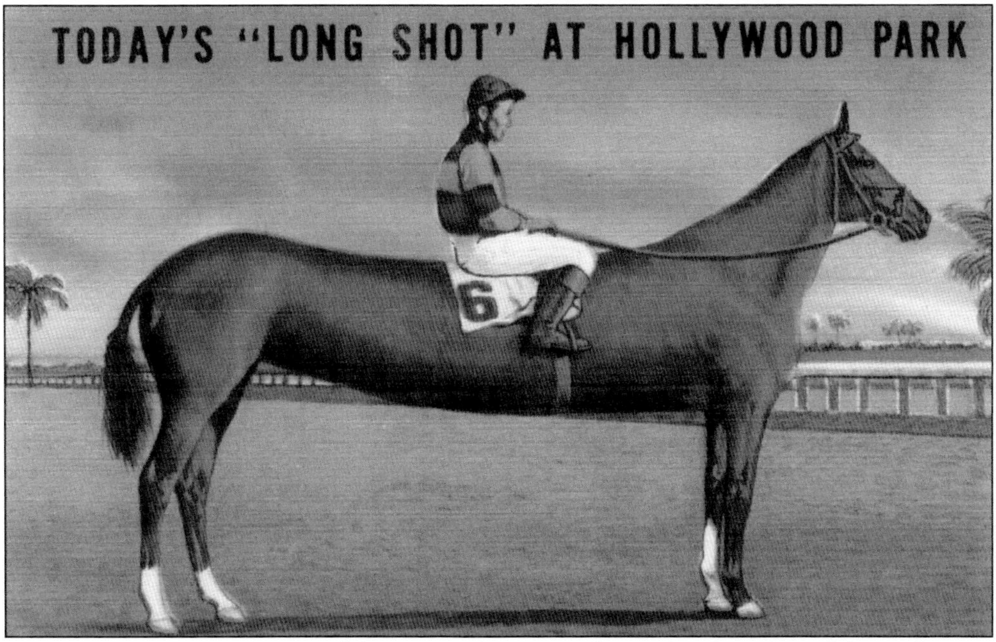

Seen here is a whimsical view of the "Long Shot" at Hollywood Park. A few of the Hollywood Park habitués included Bing Crosby, Walt Disney, Wallace Beery, Irene Dunne, Darryl F. Zanuck, Sam Goldwyn, Ronald Colman, George Jessel, Merv Griffin, Cary Grant, Omar Bradley, Fred Astaire, and many, many others. (Courtesy James Osborne; published by Western Publishing and Novelty Company, Los Angeles, California.)

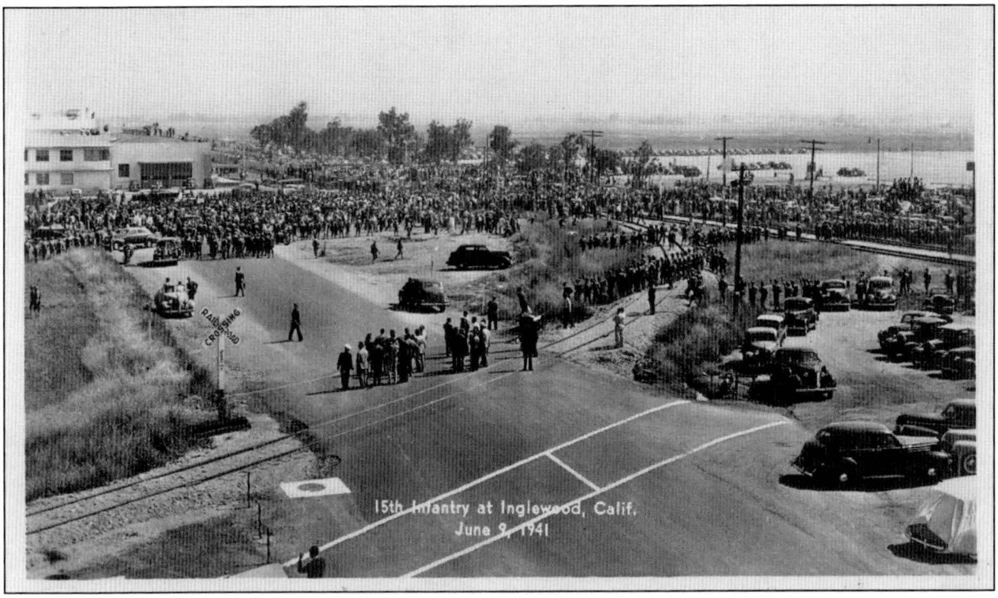

This real-photo postcard depicts the strike in June 1941 of 11,000 production workers at the North American Aviation Corporation in Inglewood. Pres. Franklin D. Roosevelt ordered the union to remove itself from the area, but the rank and file refused. Roosevelt then ordered in a battalion of the 15th Infantry to restore law and order at the plant. A largely forgotten chapter in the histories of American labor and aviation, this strike marked the rare times that the army was used as strikebreakers since the Pullman strike of 1894. (Courtesy James Osborne.)

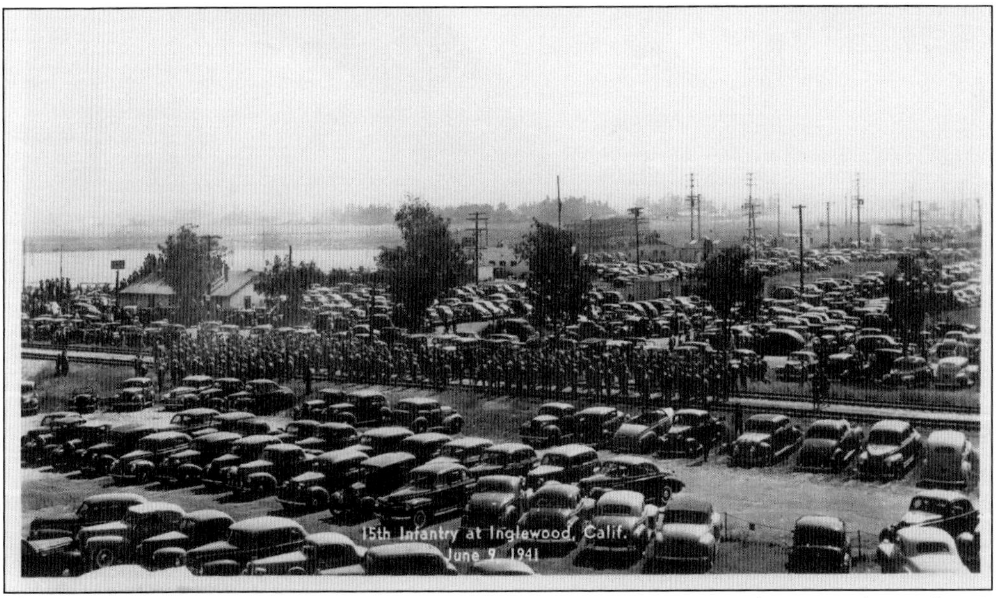

Another RPPC view shows the strike at the North American Aviation plant in Inglewood. U.S. soldiers can be seen lined up along the railroad tracks. After the officer in charge read the federal order to disband, the strikers jeered the soldiers. At the front of the strikers stood the union leader, Walter Reuther, who was later bayoneted in the leg by one of the infantrymen. After he went down screaming, the rest of the strikers broke rank and ran in all directions, ending the strike. (Courtesy James Osborne.)

Four

Palos Verdes Peninsula

"The Hill" in South Bay parlance is the epic promontory dividing Santa Monica and San Pedro Bays. Once owned by Long Beach's Bixby family, who acquired it from the Rancho San Pedro, the undeveloped Palos Verdes Peninsula was bought for $1.5 million in 1913 by a consortium organized by Frank Vanderlip, president of the City National Bank of New York. Nearly a century later, the shrubbery on some "PV" estates was valued at more than that.

The four cities comprising PV—Rancho Palos Verdes, Palos Verdes Estates, Rolling Hills Estates, and Rolling Hills—collectively form one of the most affluent enclaves in America. Maintaining a semirural ambiance and Vanderlip's notion of a community of horse ranches, the Palos Verdes cities form the high ground in the South Bay in more ways than one.

Rancho Palos Verdes is the largest in terms of population (about 41,000) and area (13.7 square miles) in the 21st century of the four PV cities. It was incorporated in 1973 as a way to stem haphazard development in the former Los Angeles County lands. "RPV" has contained the three great attractions of the peninsula: the Lloyd Wright–designed Wayfarers' Chapel (1951), the famous Marineland of the Pacific "oceanarium" (1954 to 1987), and the Point Vicente Lighthouse (1926).

The gated city of Rolling Hills was incorporated in 1957 and maintains a rural atmosphere for less than 1,900 residents, with no traffic lights and many equestrian paths. The striking factoid that emerges from municipal reports about the centrally located Rolling Hills is that while the median family income and median household income are well over $100,000 in the other three PV cities, in Rolling Hills's 3.1 square miles of prime real estate, both numbers exceed $200,000.

Rolling Hills Estates incorporated in 1957 and contains much of the commercial properties on PV, including the upscale Avenue, formerly the Shops at Palos Verdes. In terms of cartography, Rolling Hills is akin to a serpentine-shaped city with a python bulge at the lower elevations around Hawthorne and Crenshaw Boulevards on the Torrance side of the Hill.

Palos Verdes Estates is the westernmost city on PV, a buffer zone between Torrance's Hollywood Riviera and the rest of the Hill, containing the charming Malaga Cove, Lunada Bay, and Palos Verdes Country Club.

Except for the tourism draws of Wayfarers' Chapel, Marineland, and a few other locales, the PV communities have not produced an abundance of postcards. The following are some of those collected by the authors.

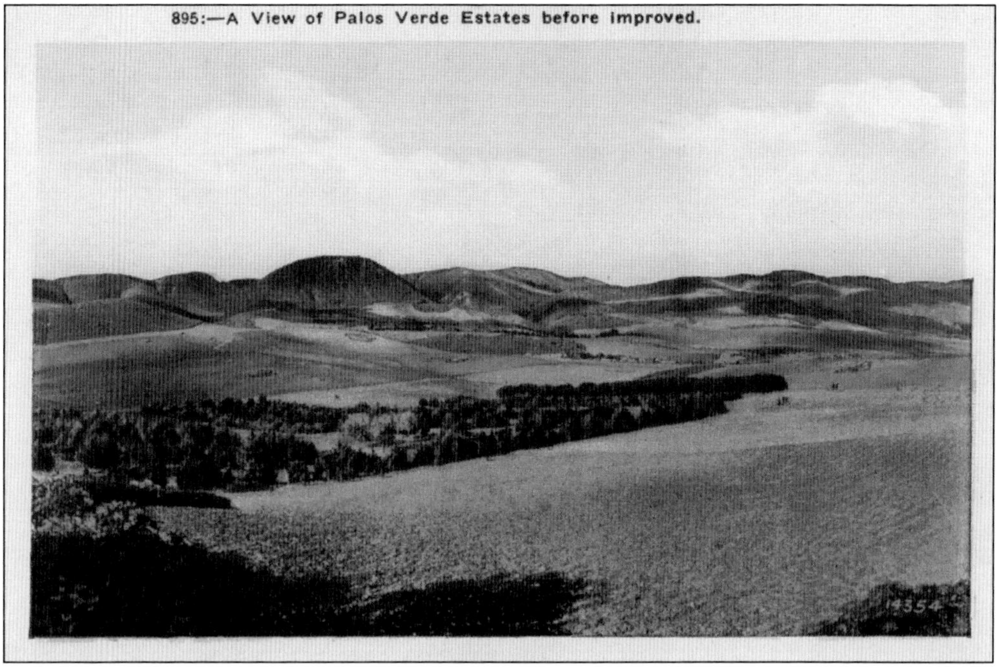

"A view of Palos Verdes Estates before improved" is the title on this postcard. Today these gently rolling hills are covered with homes. (Courtesy James Osborne; published by M. Kashower Company, Los Angeles, California.)

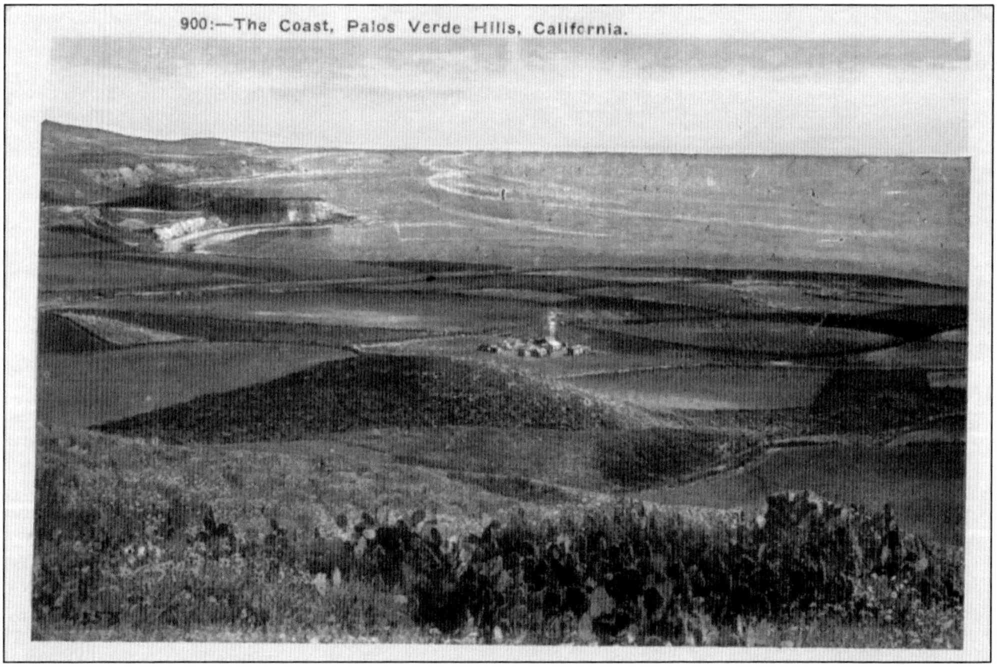

The Pacific Ocean coastline is depicted in this scene, taken from the Palos Verdes hills. This particular area is still known as Portuguese Bend, where a whaling station was once set up in the 19th century. Smuggling also occurred here when California was still under Spanish rule. (Courtesy James Osborne; published by M. Kashower Company, Los Angeles, California.)

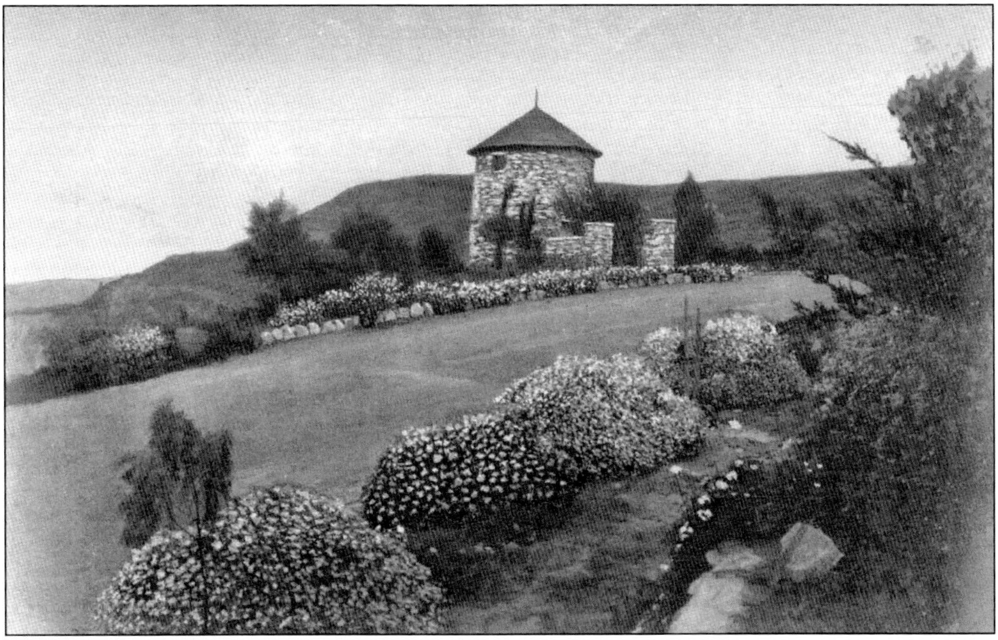

Seen here is the Via Mirlo Gate Lodge, which marked the east entrance to Palos Verdes Estates. The road on which the building still stands is now known as Via Valmonte. The old stone structure still serves as a private residence. (Courtesy James Osborne; published by the Albertype Company, Brooklyn, New York.)

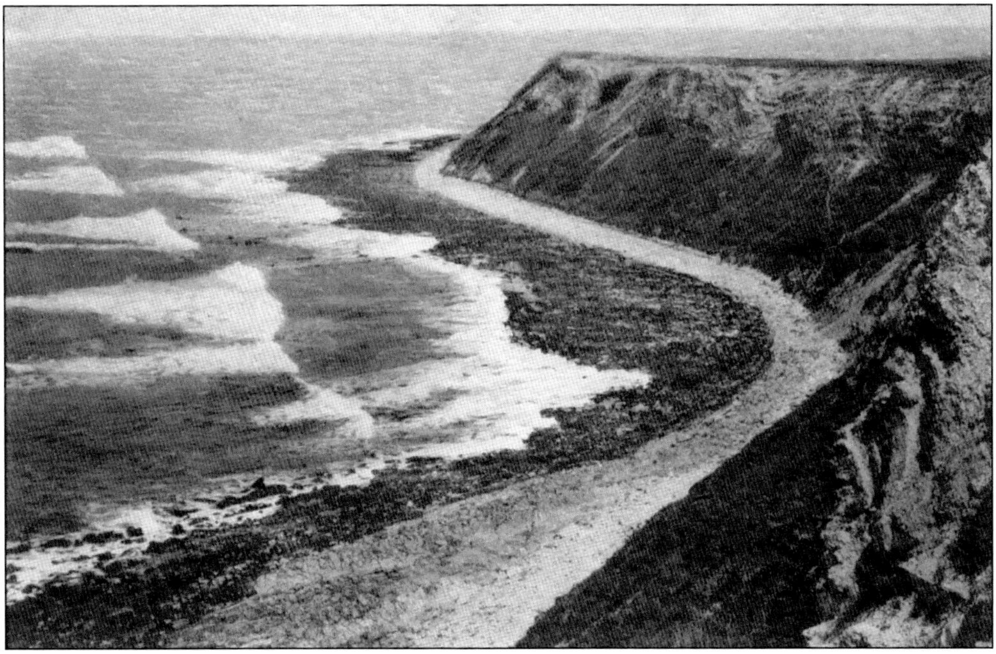

"Bluff Cove—California's 'Little Waikiki,'" reads the opposite side's caption, with the elaboration, "Where the surf boards come in, Palos Verdes Estates, California." Bluff Cove is just around Flat Rock Point from Malaga Cove. (Courtesy Marilyn Ron; published by the Albertype Company, Brooklyn, New York.)

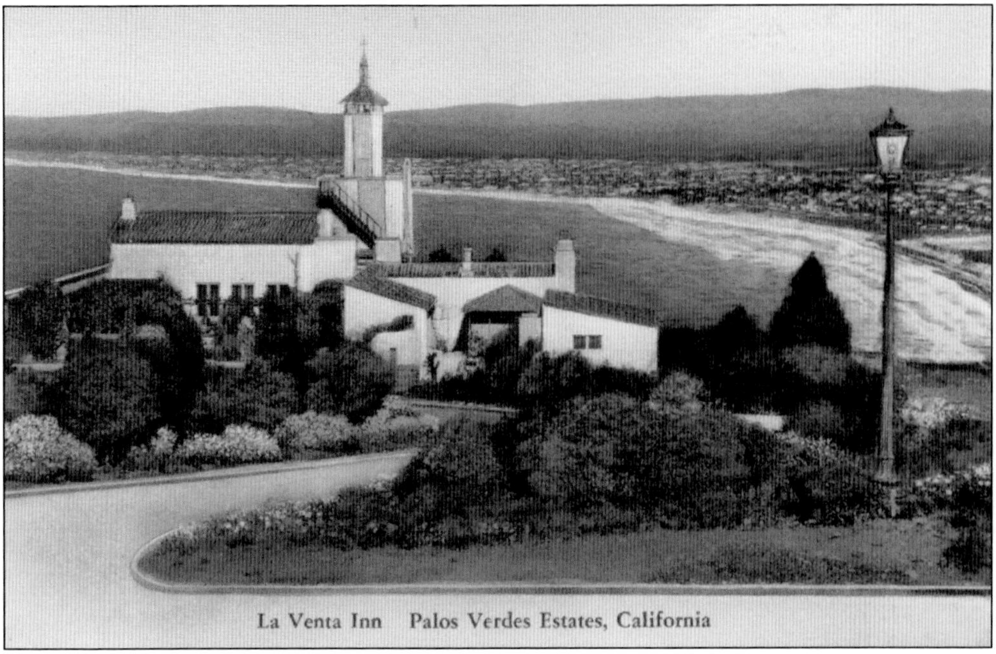

La Venta Inn was built in 1923 and was a popular spot for dining. It was situated high on the Palos Verdes hills and offered spectacular views of the Santa Monica Bay. Tourists and the Hollywood crowd as well as honeymooners and families stayed at La Venta. (Courtesy James Osborne; published by the Albertype Company, Brooklyn, New York.)

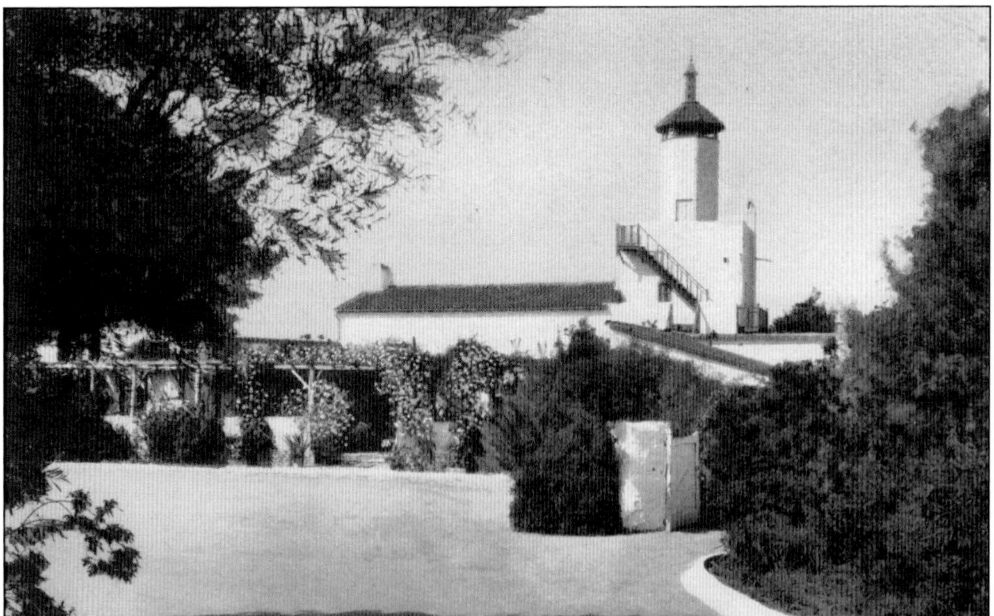

Another view depicts La Venta, a renowned honeymoon and vacation retreat, located just east and above Palos Verdes Drive West on Via Del Monte. (Courtesy Marilyn Ron; published by the Albertype Company, Brooklyn, New York.)

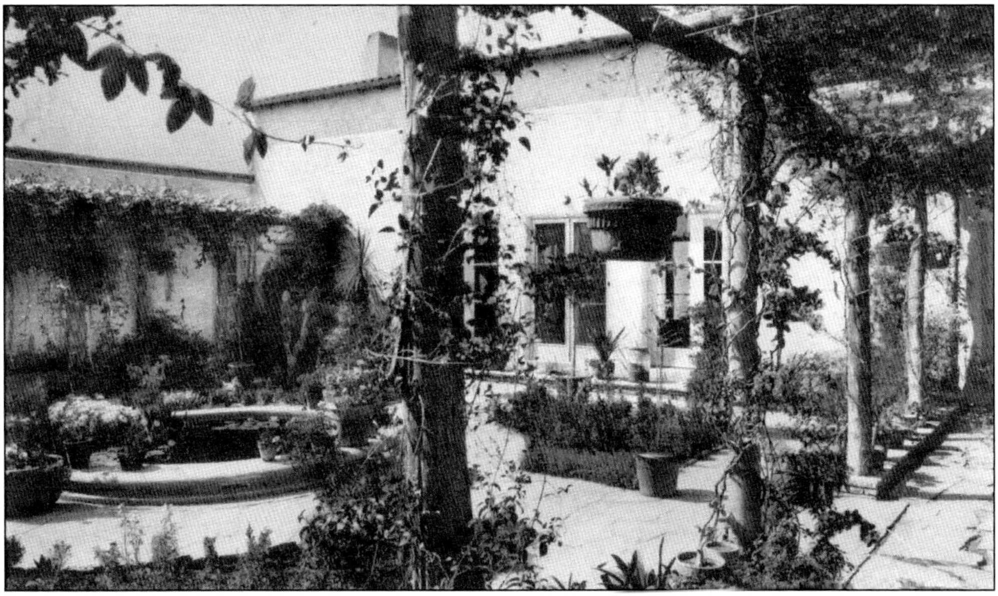

The inner courtyard of La Venta Inn is depicted here. The setting provided a backdrop for various films from the silent period onward, such as *Spanish Sunlight* (1925). La Venta played host to numerous weddings over the years. (Courtesy James Osborne; published by the Albertype Company, Brooklyn, New York.)

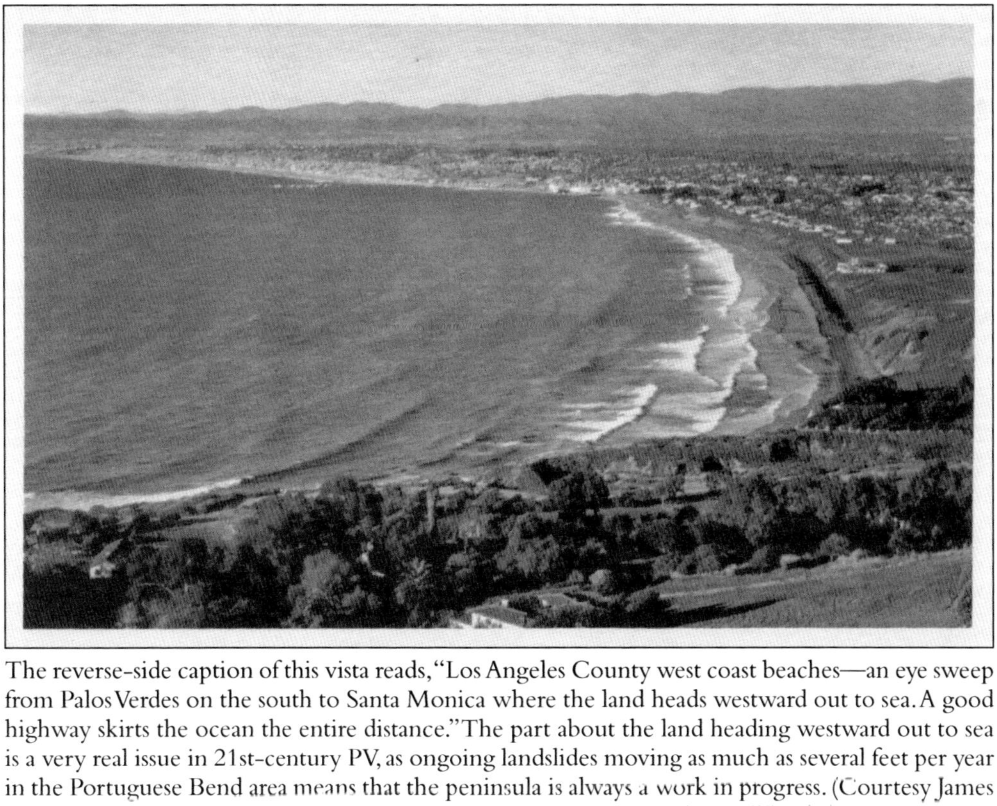

The reverse-side caption of this vista reads, "Los Angeles County west coast beaches—an eye sweep from Palos Verdes on the south to Santa Monica where the land heads westward out to sea. A good highway skirts the ocean the entire distance." The part about the land heading westward out to sea is a very real issue in 21st-century PV, as ongoing landslides moving as much as several feet per year in the Portuguese Bend area means that the peninsula is always a work in progress. (Courtesy James Osborne; published by Fidelity Reproduction Company, Los Angeles, California.)

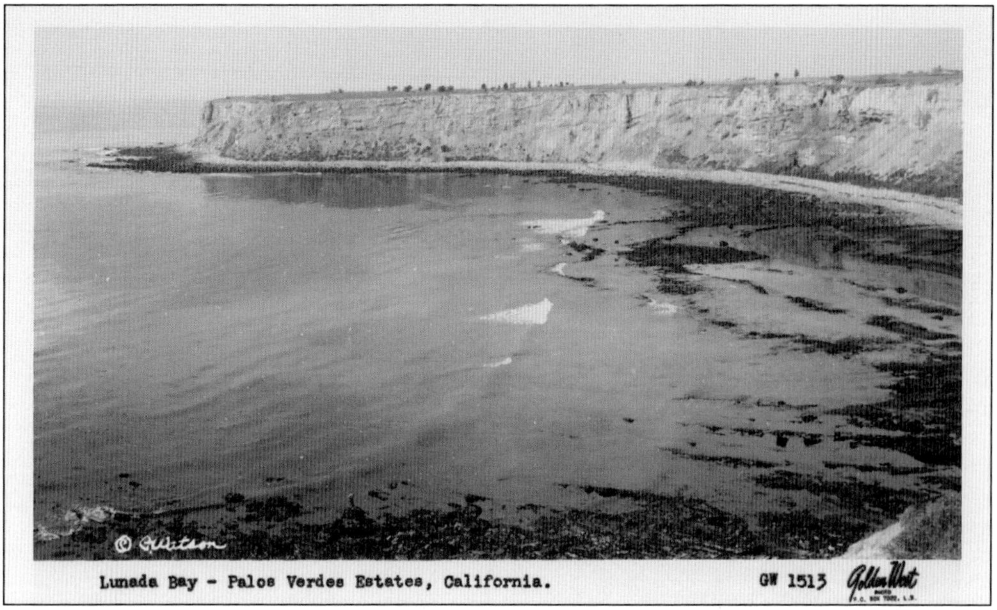

This real-photo postcard offers a view of Lunada Bay in southwestern Palos Verdes Estates. At one time, developers of the Palos Verdes Project proposed constructing a breakwater across this bay to accommodate swimmers. (Courtesy James Osborne; published by Golden West, Long Beach, California.)

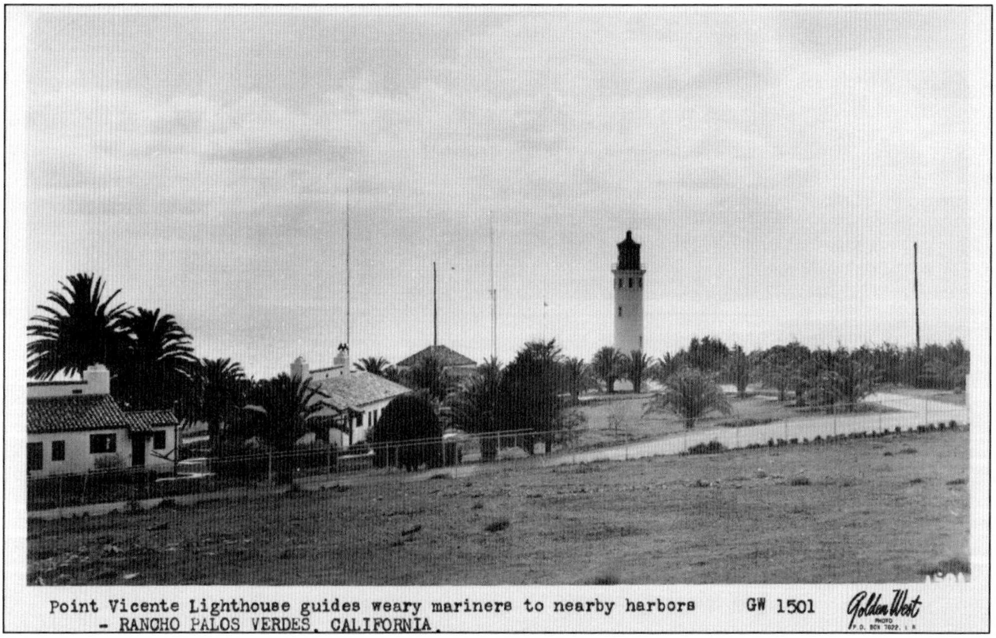

The Point Vicente Lighthouse is depicted here. The location was named in 1790 by explorer George Vancouver to honor his friend Friar Vicente of the Mission Buenaventura. Vancouver was honored by a city and province in Canada bearing his name, and the present-day city and county of Ventura, northwest of Los Angeles, were named after the Mission Buenaventura. The Point Vicente Lighthouse began operation on May 1, 1926. (Courtesy James Osborne; published by Golden West, Long Beach, California.)

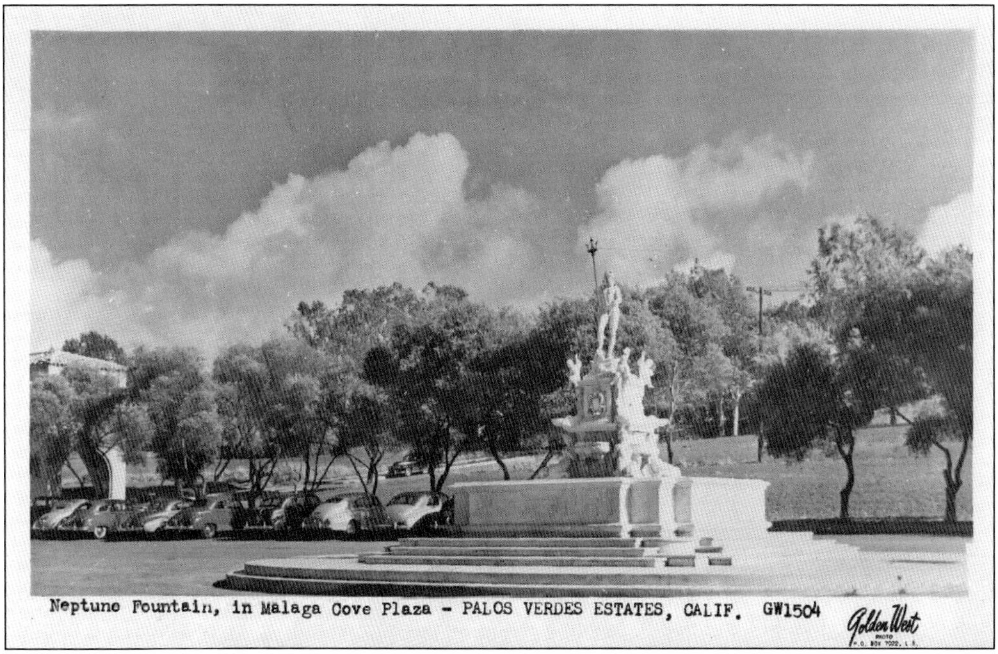

The statue of Neptune in the Malaga Cove Fountain was modeled after one in Bologna, Italy. The *Neptune* shown in this postcard was installed in 1930. But it eventually crumbled and was replaced in 1969 with a slightly smaller replica that included a fig leaf. (Courtesy James Osborne; published by Golden West, Long Beach, California.)

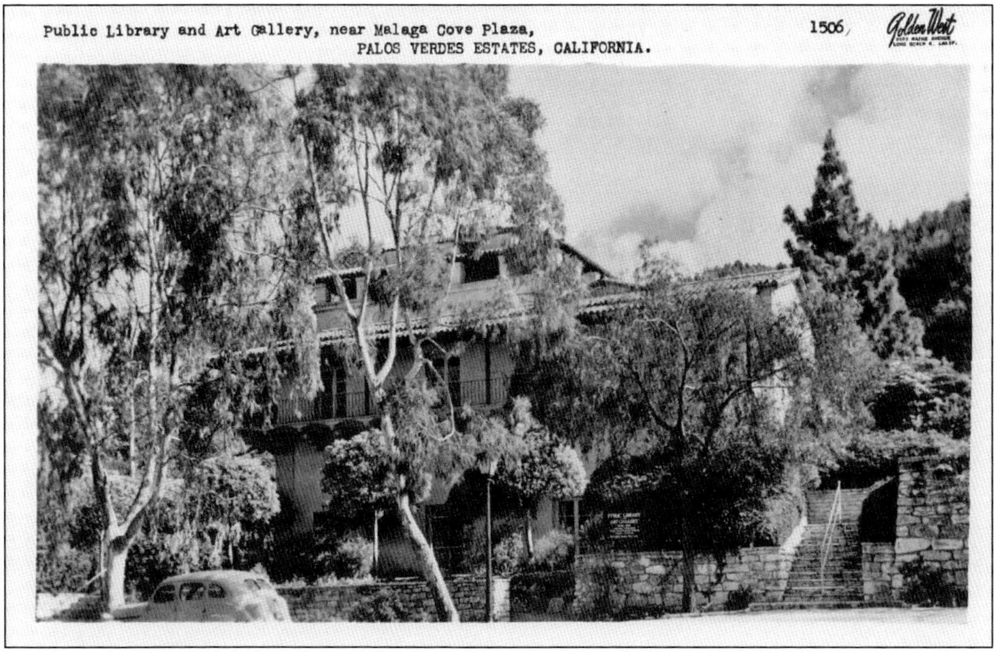

This postcard depicts the Malaga Cove Library and Art Gallery, which opened in June 1930. The building was designed by architect Myron Hunt. (Courtesy James Osborne; published by Golden West, Long Beach, California.)

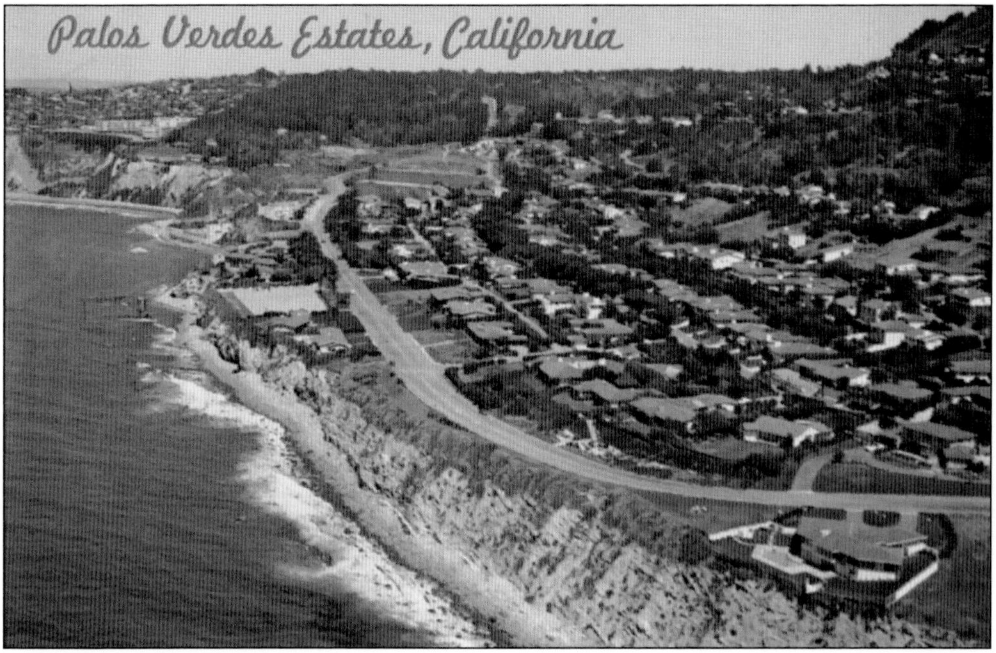

"Homes along Palos Verdes Drive West, Bluff Cove, and Malaga Cove are seen in the distance," relates the caption on the rear of this postcard. (Courtesy Marilyn Ron; published by Golden West, Long Beach, California.)

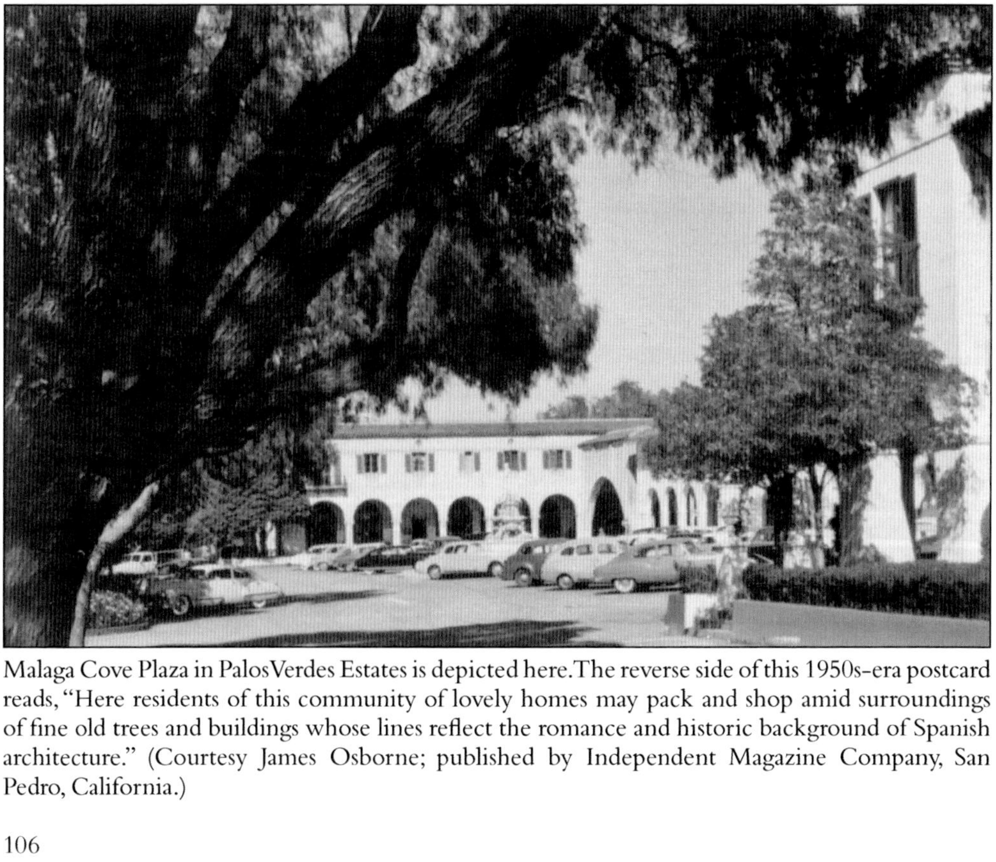

Malaga Cove Plaza in Palos Verdes Estates is depicted here. The reverse side of this 1950s-era postcard reads, "Here residents of this community of lovely homes may pack and shop amid surroundings of fine old trees and buildings whose lines reflect the romance and historic background of Spanish architecture." (Courtesy James Osborne; published by Independent Magazine Company, San Pedro, California.)

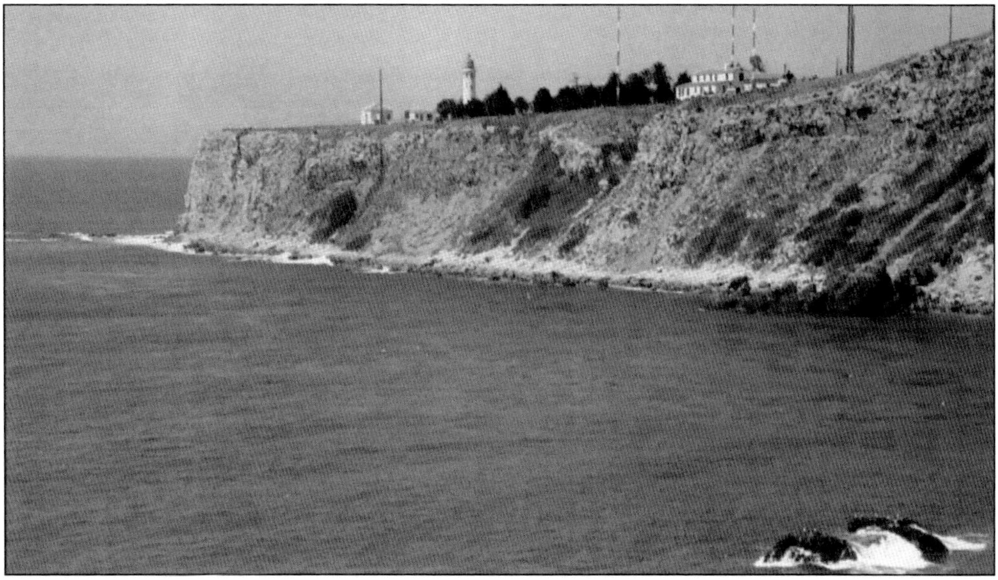

"Historic Point Vicente, Rancho Palos Verdes, California, near Marineland of the Pacific," reads the caption, which elaborates, "Trying to set up Pacific outposts for Britain after the American Revolution, Capt. George Vancouver named this point on April 18, 1793—eight years after Rancho Palos Verdes was founded by the Spanish. A lighthouse and Coast Guard Station now occupy the point. (Courtesy Marilyn Ron; published by Golden West, Long Beach, California.)

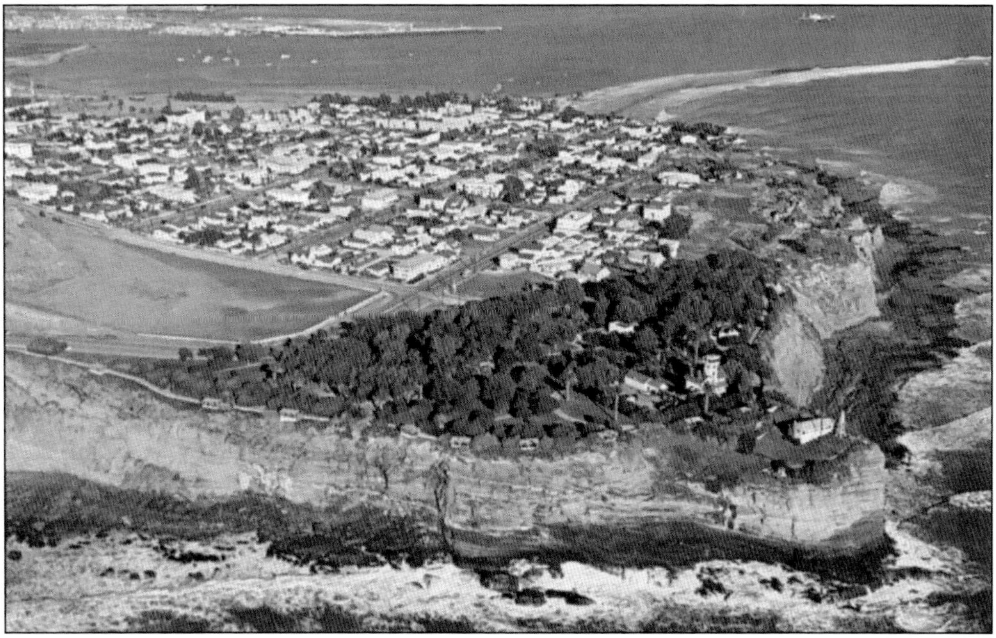

While this easterly-looking aerial overlooks the westernmost extents of San Pedro with the Port of Los Angeles in the upper left and San Pedro Bay and the harbor's epic breakwater in the upper right, this postcard also depicts in the left foreground the southernmost reaches of the Palos Verdes Peninsula in the city of spread-out Rancho Palos Verdes. The promontory at the bottom right is Point Fermin, which, like Point Vicente, was also named by George Vancouver. (Courtesy Marilyn Ron; published by Golden West, Long Beach, California.)

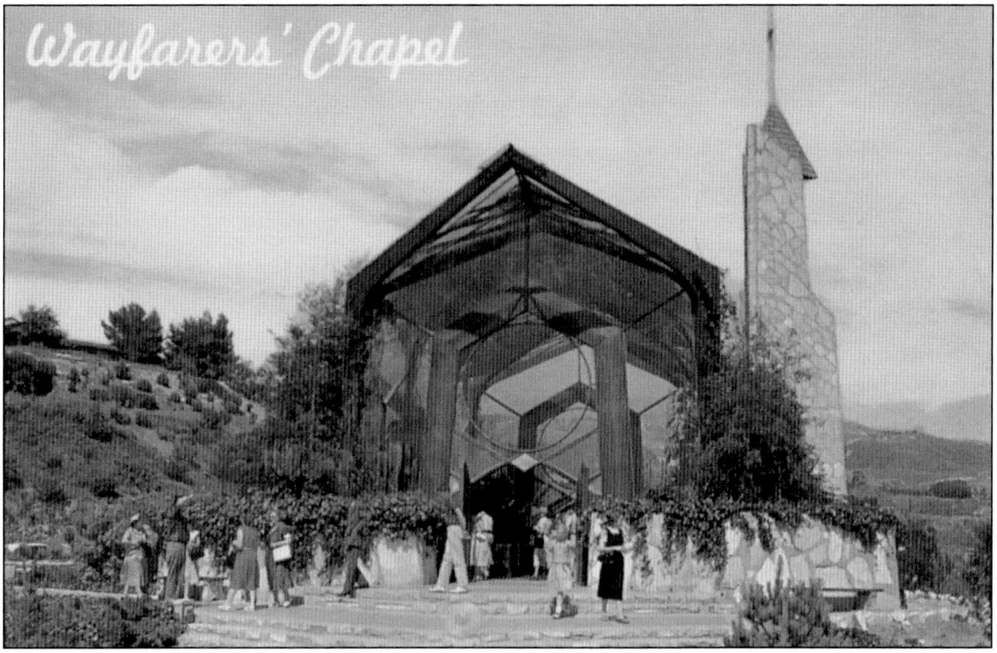

This postcard provides a 1950s view of Wayfarers' Chapel, otherwise known as the "Glass Church," the dominant man-made feature of the Portuguese Bend area. The chapel was completed in 1951, the Campanile in 1954. The architect for this church was Lloyd Wright, the son of the famed Frank Lloyd Wright. (Courtesy Marilyn Ron; published by Golden West, Long Beach, California.)

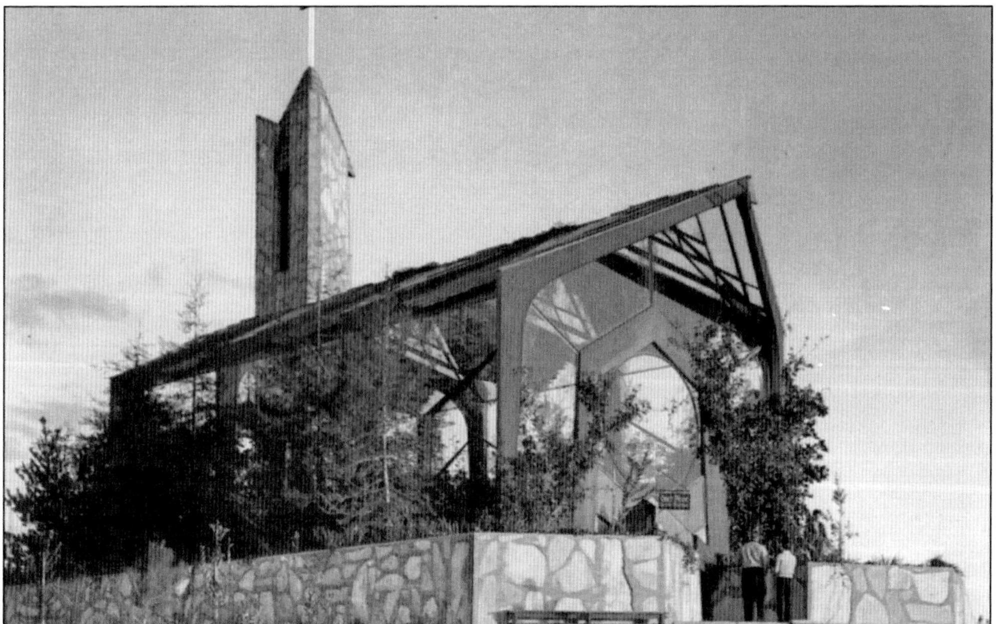

The source idea for Wayfarers' Chapel was to build a memorial to the great Swedish scientist, theologian, mystic, and philosopher Emanuel Swedenborg (1688–1772), who delved into dreams and Christian thought. (Courtesy Marilyn Ron; published by the Union Oil Company.)

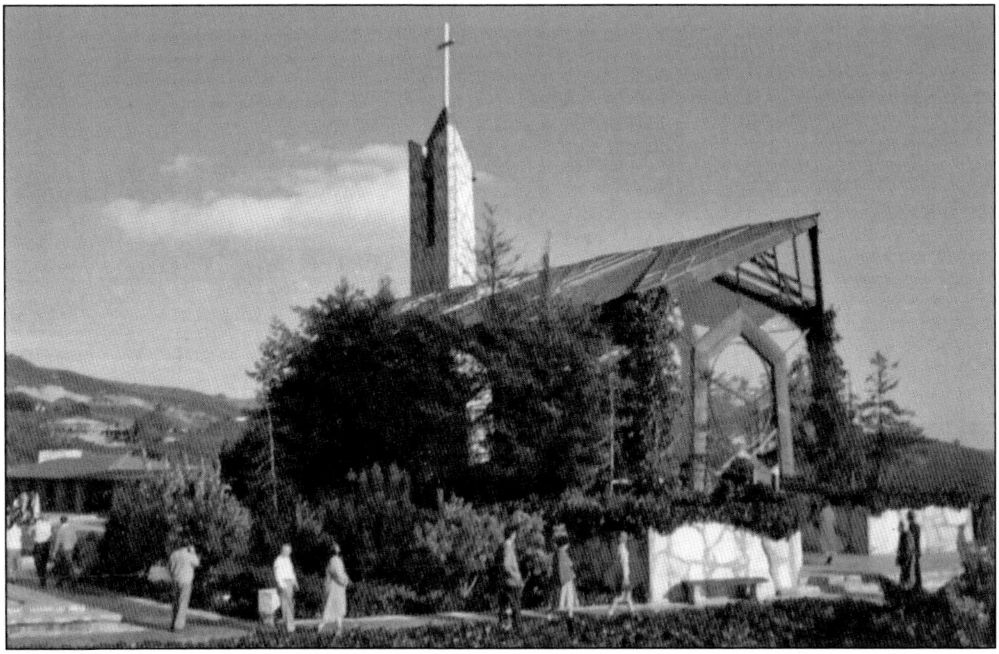

Wayfarers' Chapel inspiration Emanuel Swedenborg is quoted on the reverse side of this postcard: "Heaven is such that all who live well, from whatever religion, have a place there." (Courtesy Marilyn Ron; published by Golden West, Long Beach, California.)

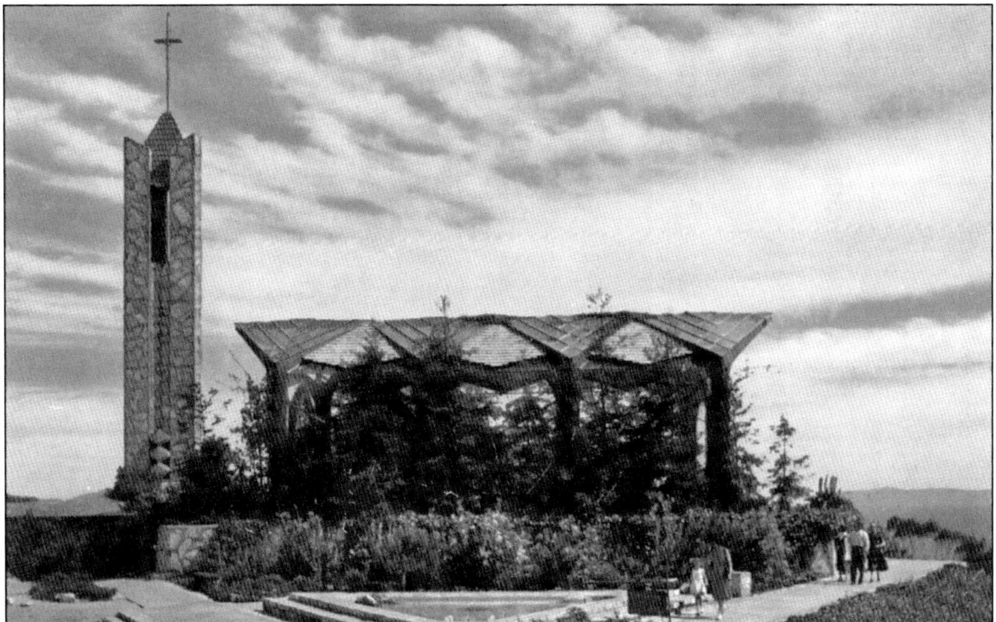

Funding for Wayfarers' Chapel was provided by the Church of the New Jerusalem, which was founded on the teachings of Emanuel Swedenborg. (Courtesy Marilyn Ron; published by Golden West, Long Beach, California.)

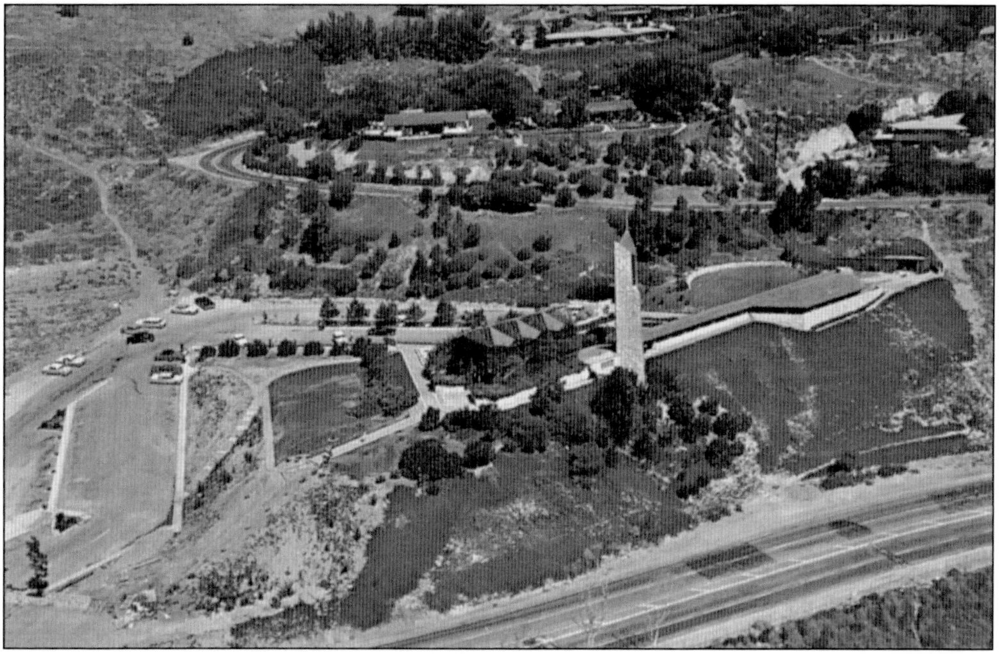

Built almost entirely of glass, Wayfarers' Chapel is surrounded by evergreen trees on both sides. This aerial view depicts the church property and, at the bottom of the image, Palos Verdes Drive South. (Courtesy Marilyn Ron; published by Western Publishing and Novelty Company, Los Angeles, California.)

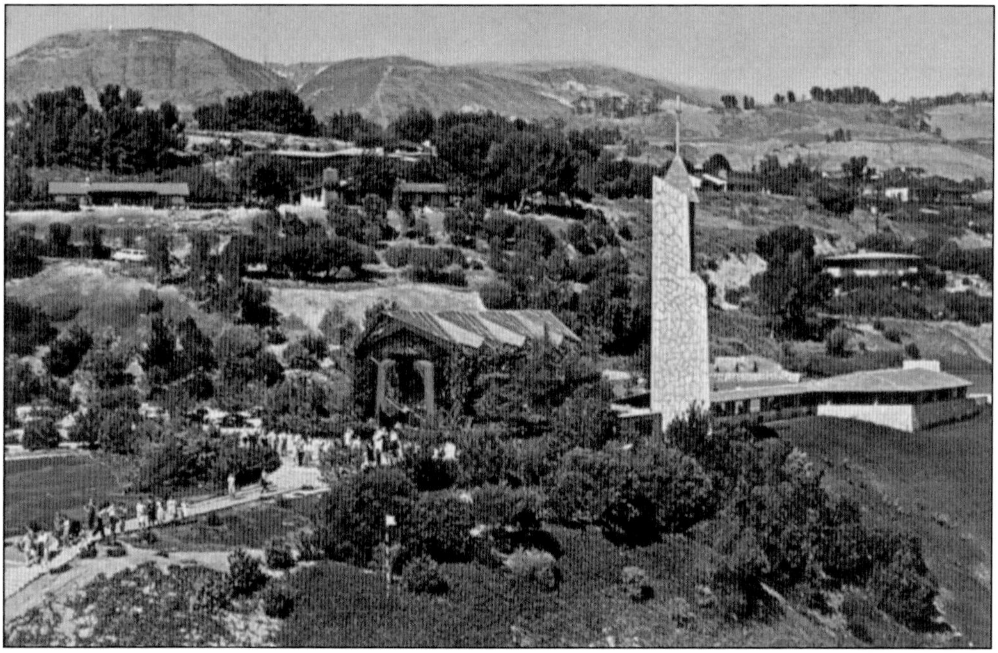

The reverse side of this card carries this partial description: "Standing in dramatic, beautiful simplicity on a knoll above the Pacific Ocean." The chapel has been host to a thousand and one weddings. (Courtesy Marilyn Ron; published by Golden West, Long Beach, California.)

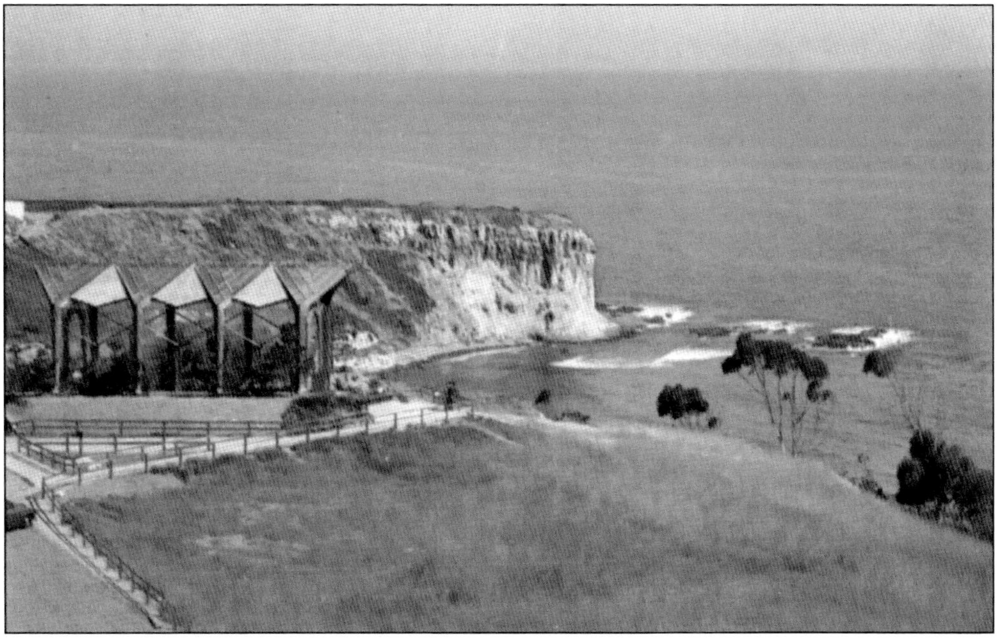

This broadside view shows the chapel in its landscape, with Portuguese Bend curving below. Once a smugglers' cove, Portuguese Bend has been for more than half a century the site of one of America's most famous churches. (Courtesy Marilyn Ron; published by Golden West, Long Beach, California.)

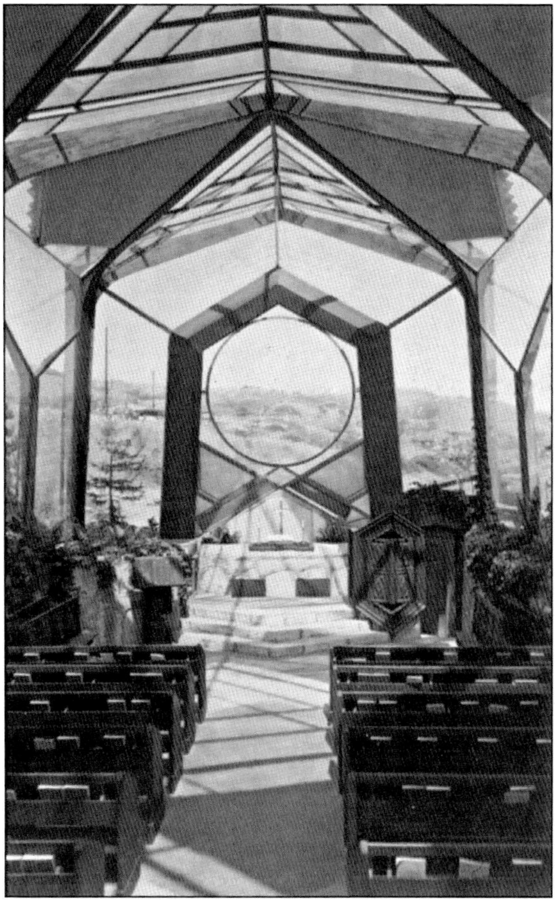

Here is an interior shot of the church. The son of Frank Lloyd Wright, Wayfarers' Chapel architect Lloyd Wright escaped his father's enormous shadow, working for landscape architects Olmsted and Olmsted, who designed the City of Torrance, and Irving Gill, who designed many Southern California public buildings. Lloyd Wright also did a stint at Paramount Pictures in Hollywood. (Courtesy Bill Ron; published by Golden West, Long Beach, California.)

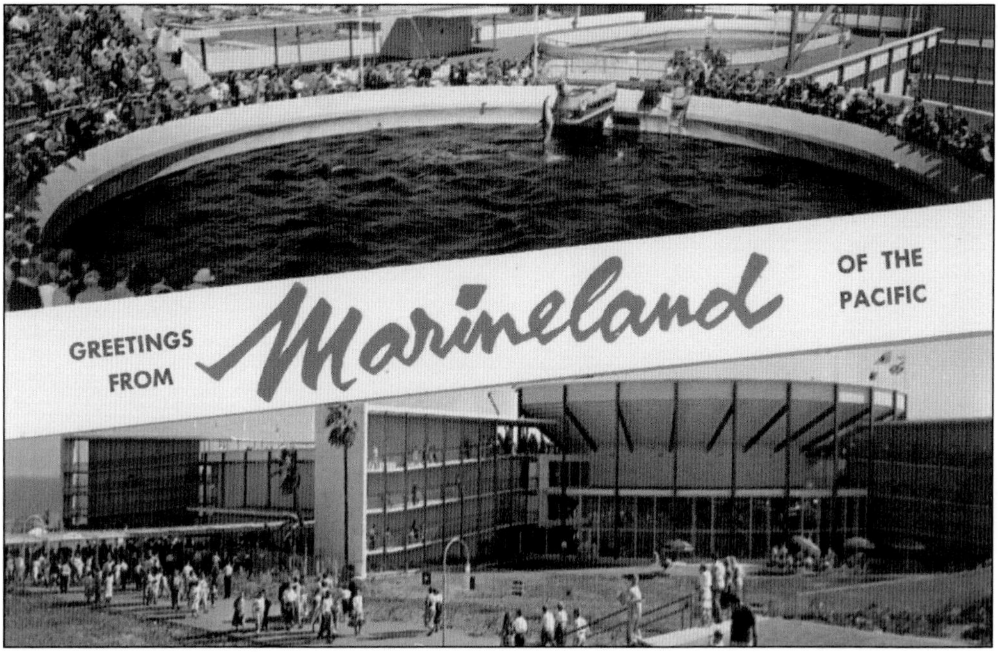

Marineland of the Pacific was once the world's largest oceanarium. Thousands of fish and sea animals lived in two huge 22-foot-deep tanks, which had viewing windows on three levels below the water's surface. Ramps connected each level and led to the amphitheatre on top, where visitors watched the playful porpoises. (Courtesy Marilyn Ron; published by Golden West, Long Beach, California.)

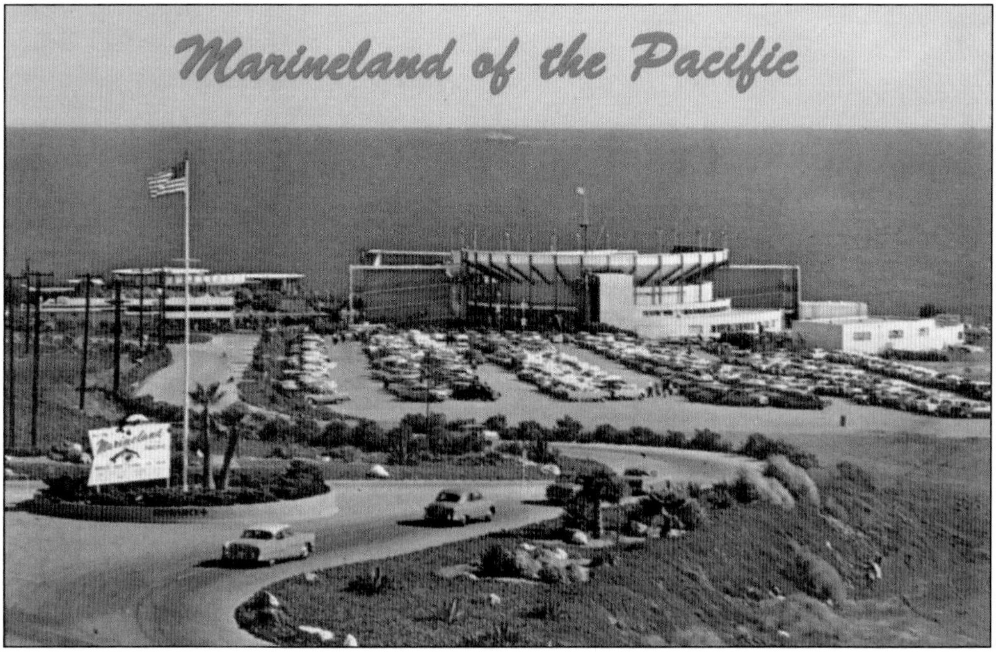

Marineland of the Pacific was located on the Palos Verdes Peninsula near Portuguese Bend between Redondo Beach and San Pedro, California. It was the world's most spectacular three-ring circus of marine life. (Courtesy Marilyn Ron; published by Golden West, Long Beach, California.)

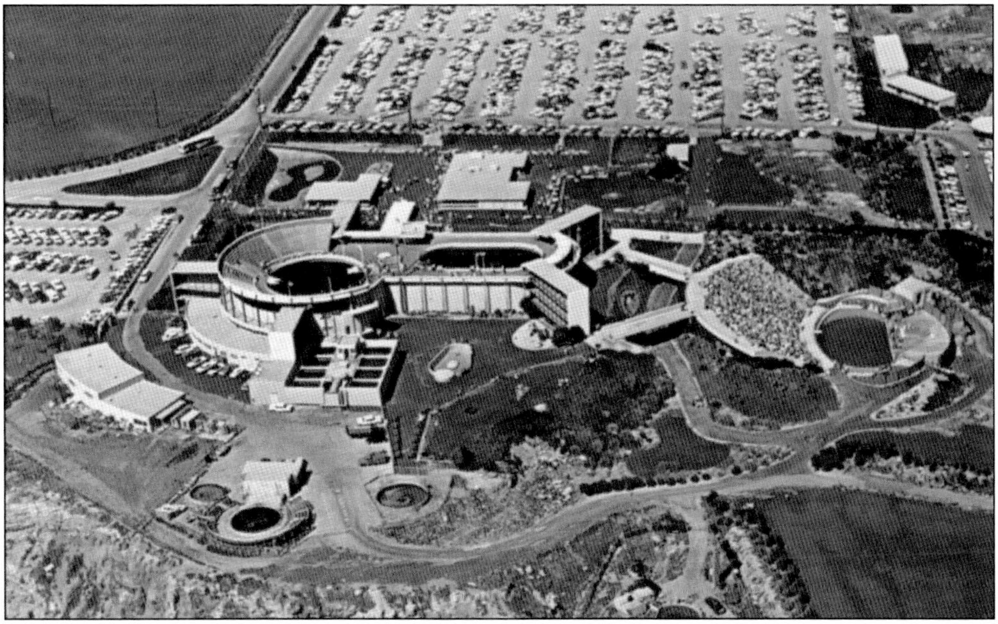

This postcard shows an overview of the Marineland complex, offering an idea of its size. The card reads, "Marineland of the Pacific—World's Largest Oceanarium. Situated on Palos Verdes Drive South between Redondo Beach and San Pedro in Southern California. Marineland is surrounded by spacious well-kept grounds. In its round Whale Amphitheatre, Oval Fish Tank and its Sea Arena, visitors are entertained by performing whales, sea lions, porpoises and thousands of fish and other sea animals." (Courtesy Marilyn Ron; published by Golden West, Long Beach, California.)

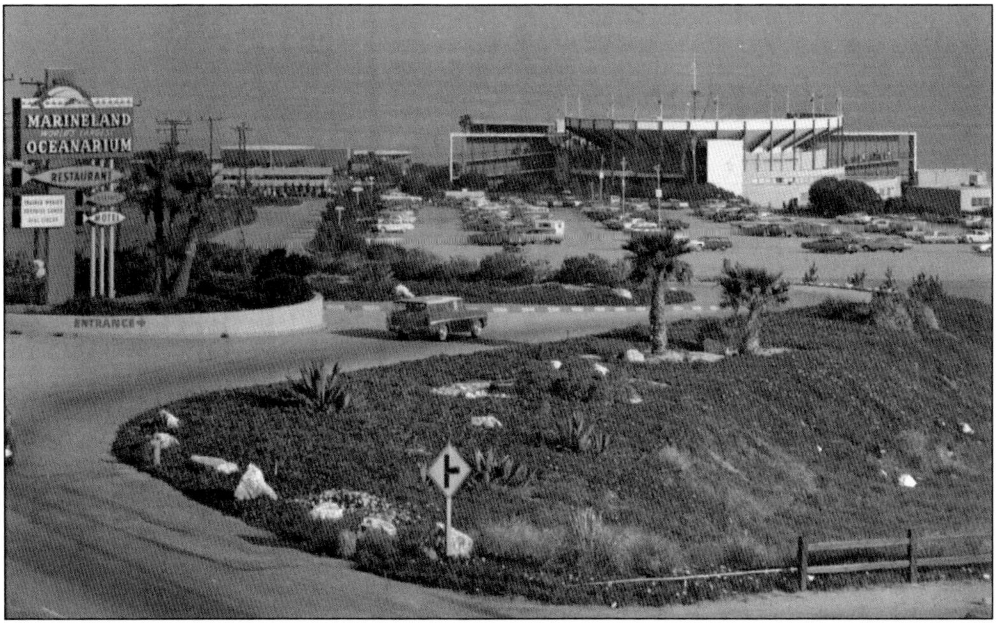

The Oceanarium grounds of Marineland of the Pacific are depicted here as they were seen from Palos Verdes Drive South in the vicinity of Point Vicente. The Oceanarium Building is to the right of center, beyond the spacious parking lot. (Courtesy Bill Ron; published by Golden West, Long Beach, California.)

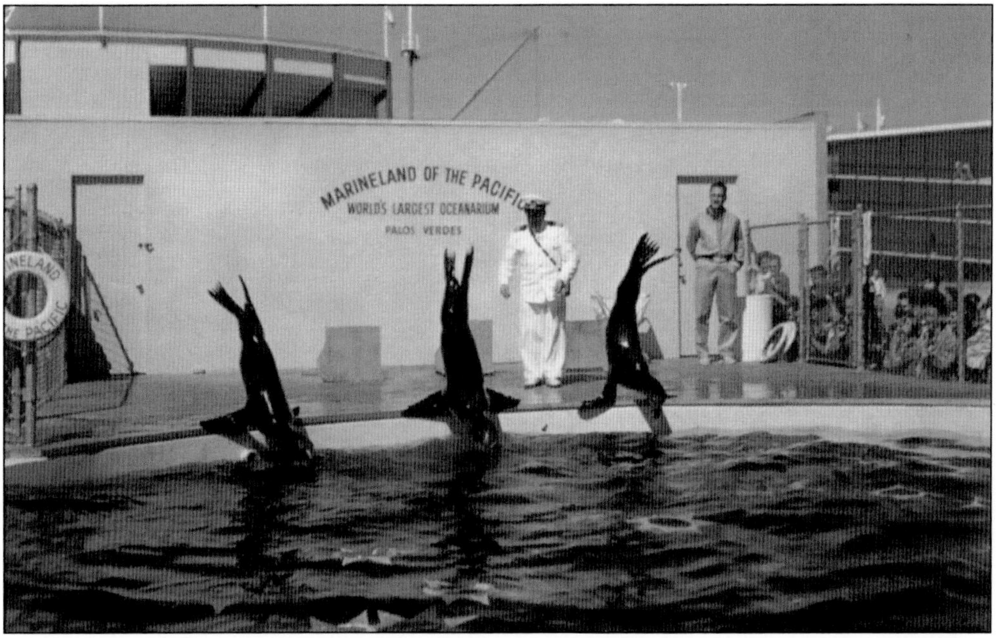

In Marineland Seal Stadium, Capt. Harold Winston's world-famous sea lions gave several shows each day. Seal Stadium was part of Marineland of the Pacific, the world's largest oceanarium. These talented mammals are veterans of numerous Hollywood movies and television shows. (Courtesy Marilyn Ron; published by Golden West, Long Beach, California.)

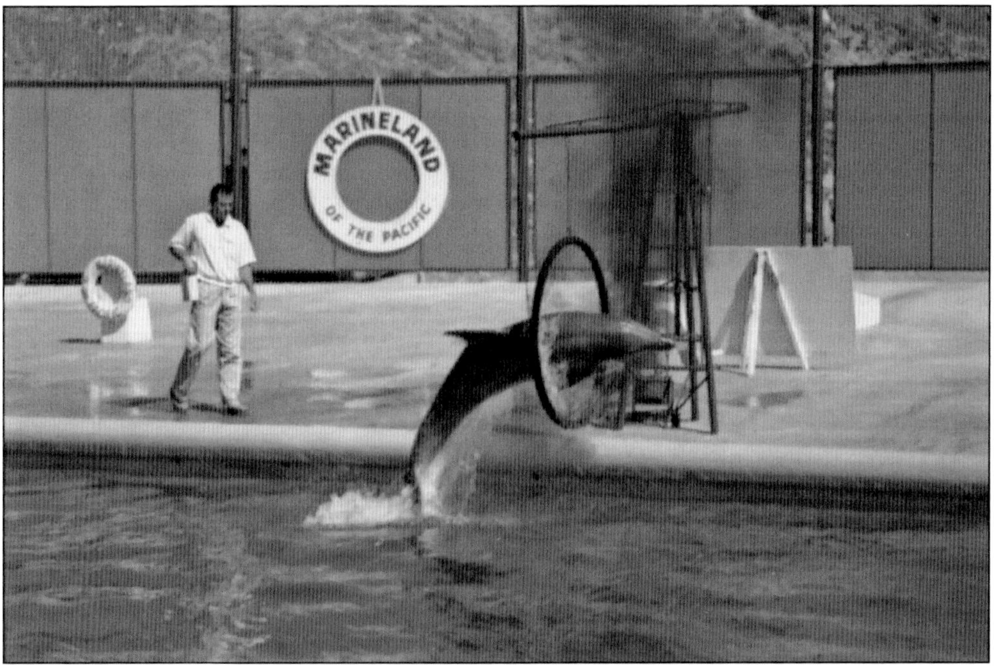

With a watery rush, Zippy the bottle-nosed porpoise jumps through a flaming circle of fire in one of its acts during the spectacular Sea Circus, once held regularly in Marineland's huge Sea Arena. (Courtesy Marilyn Ron; published by Golden West, Long Beach, California.)

Holy mackerel! Zippy, the bottle-nosed porpoise leaps for a mackerel treat. Marineland served as the host for many films and television shows, including *Revenge of the Creature* (1955) and the series *Sea Hunt* starring Lloyd Bridges. (Courtesy James Osborne; published by Colourpictures, Boston, Massachusetts.)

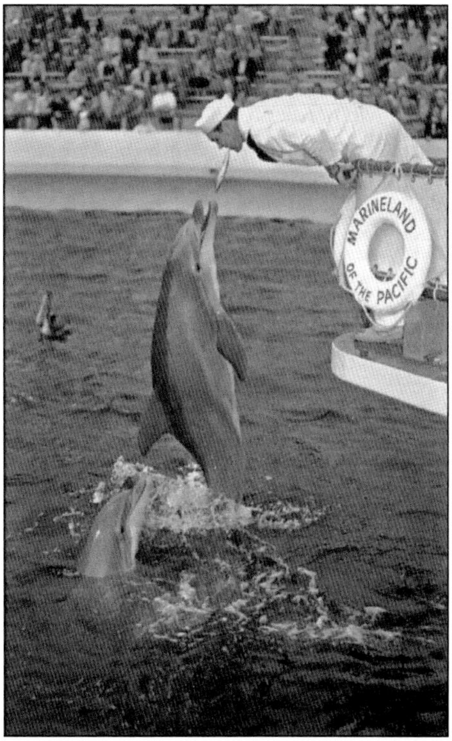

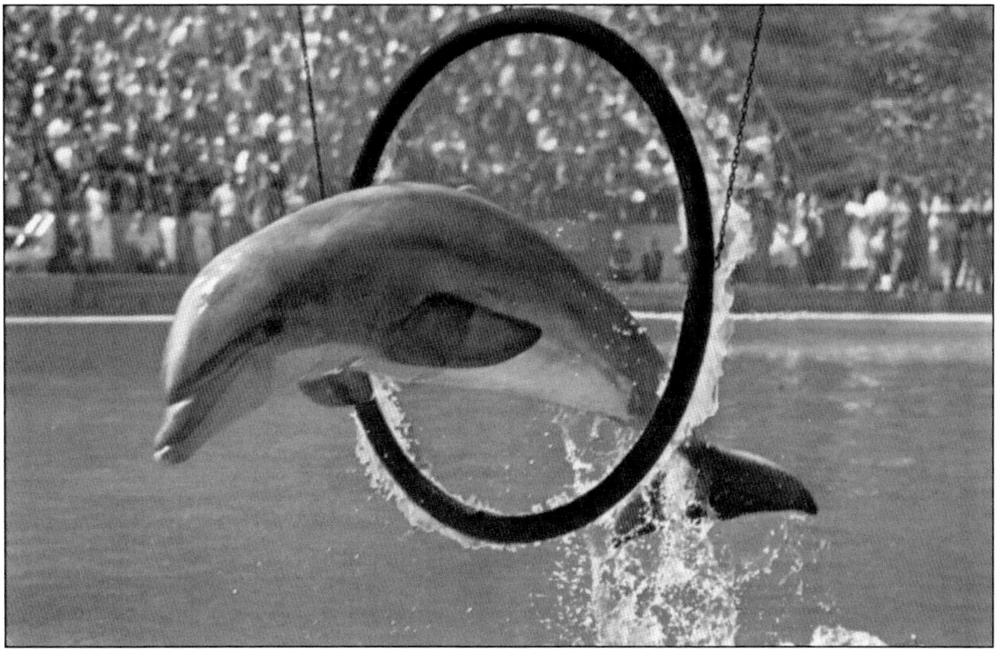

Marineland's huge Sea Arena was the showplace for trained bottle-nosed porpoises, such as this one. Marineland operated from 1954 to 1987. It was bought in that final year by Busch Entertainment, Inc., a subsidiary of Anheuser-Busch, Inc., which owned Sea World in San Diego. The new operator moved the wildlife to Sea World and closed the Palos Verdes facility. (Courtesy Marilyn Ron; published by Golden West, Long Beach, California.)

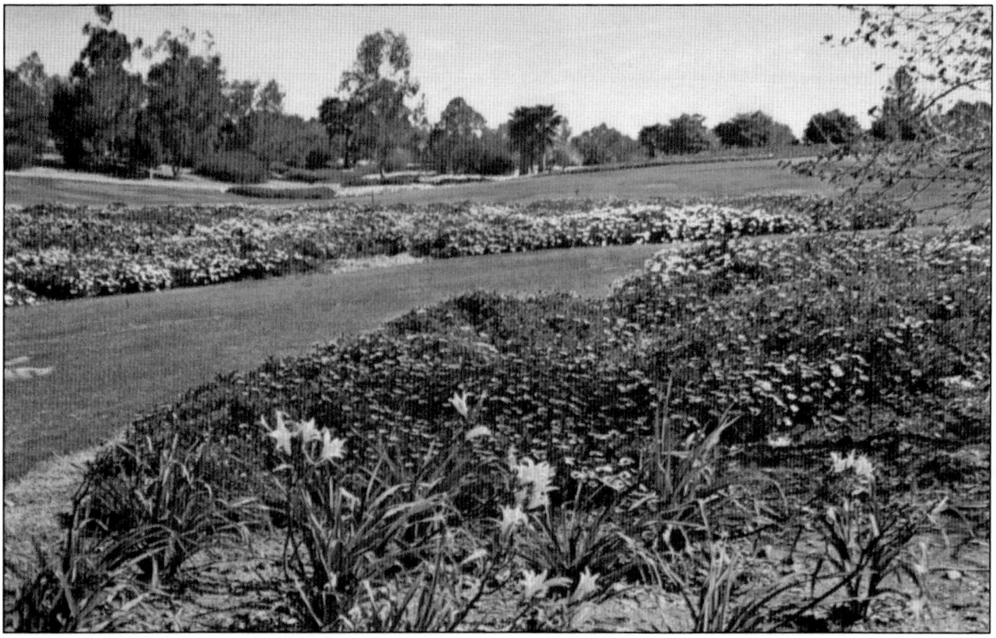

The South Coast Botanic Garden was founded by Francis Young in 1961. The 87-acre site contains more than 2,500 different species of plants from various places across the globe. The reverse-side caption reads, "South Coast Botanic Garden, Palos Verdes Peninsula, CA. Rolling hills of African daisies. The beautiful garden is situated on a sanitary landfill." (Courtesy James Osborne; published by Mike Roberts, Berkeley, California.)

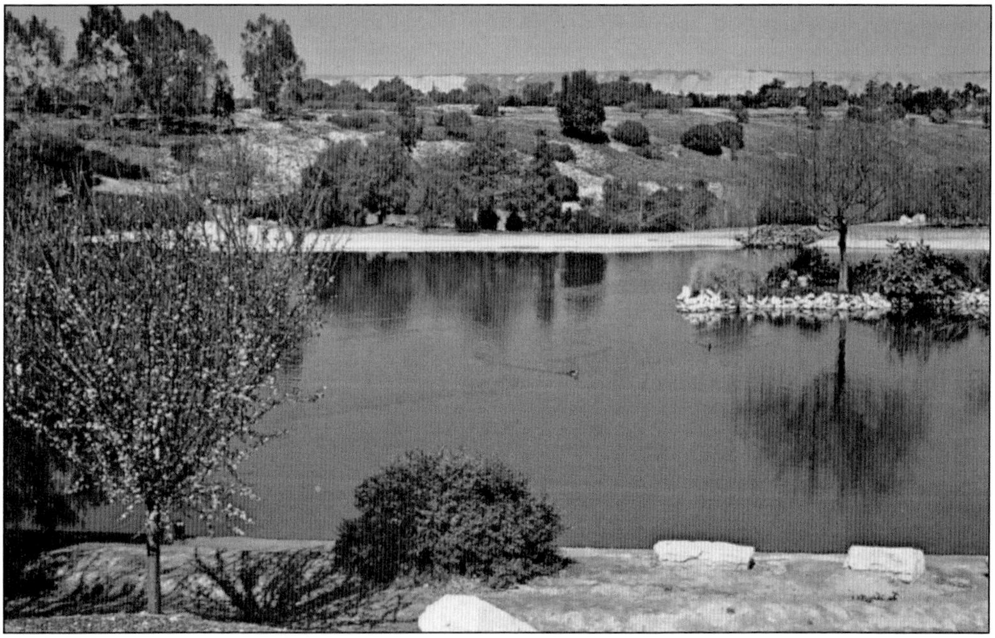

"Lake and bird refuge at South Coast Botanic Garden, Palos Verdes Peninsula, CA," reads this postcard's opposite side. The South Coast Botanic Garden is located off Crenshaw Boulevard and surrounded by the city of Rolling Hills Estates. (Courtesy James Osborne; published by Mike Roberts, Berkeley, California.)

Five

Harbor Area

San Pedro won the political war over Santa Monica and Redondo Beach in the early years of the 20th century to become the port for growing Los Angeles. San Pedro and neighboring Wilmington were annexed in 1909 by Los Angeles, precipitating an umbilical-like geographical oddity connecting the main portion of the big city to its port. This north-south strip of city of Los Angeles land is the Harbor Gateway, only blocks wide in some places and 8 miles long, extending from Watts to Harbor City along today's Harbor Freeway (I-110) corridor.

Traditionally blue-collar neighborhoods with strong ties to maritime traditions and American labor unions, San Pedro, Harbor City, Wilmington, and the industrialized Terminal Island form the southernmost extents of L.A. proper. They also form the southeast corner of the South Bay and, with the contiguous city of Carson, one of the most ethnically diverse areas in America.

As the Port of Los Angeles bustles in its second century as a vital deepwater nexus of worldwide shipping, the people in the shadow of the harbor-spanning Vincent Thomas Bridge, surrounded by enormous gantry cranes off-loading cargo containers night and day, continue to carry on the old-country traditions of Italy, Croatia, Mexico, Greece, Portugal, Japan, the Philippines, and African and Latin American and other cultures—as they have for more than a century.

Actually situated on San Pedro Bay, the coastal arc of the Los Angeles River estuary, the harbor area has generally been accepted as an integral portion of the South Bay, even as the "South Bay" nomenclature represents Santa Monica Bay, located just over the Palos Verdes Peninsula to the west. As one of the most industrialized of harbors after a century-plus of wharf ravages, L.A. harbor has maintained a striking photogenic quality.

San Pedro has been used hundreds of times by Hollywood as settings and backdrops, and the waterfront as much as anywhere, in *The Long Voyage Home* (1940), *Chinatown* (1974), *To Live and Die in L.A.* (1985), *The Usual Suspects* (1995), *Gone in Sixty Seconds* (2000), and many others.

The authors have been cognizant of Arcadia Publishing's previous volumes in its Postcard History Series by Joe McKenzie, *San Pedro* and *San Pedro Bay*. The images on the following pages are just a smattering of the other existing postcards of the harbor area that have not before been featured in book form.

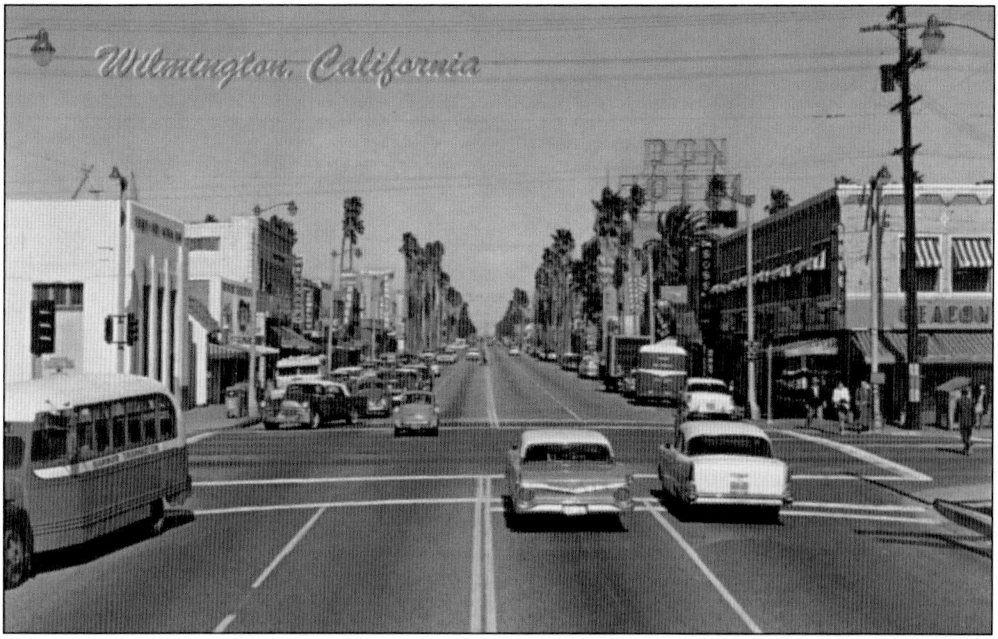

"Greetings from Wilmington, California," declares the caption on the back side of this card. "Looking north on Avalon Boulevard, from Anaheim Street in the downtown shopping district. The town was named by Phineas Banning, its founder, in 1858." (Courtesy James Osborne; published by Golden West, Long Beach, California.)

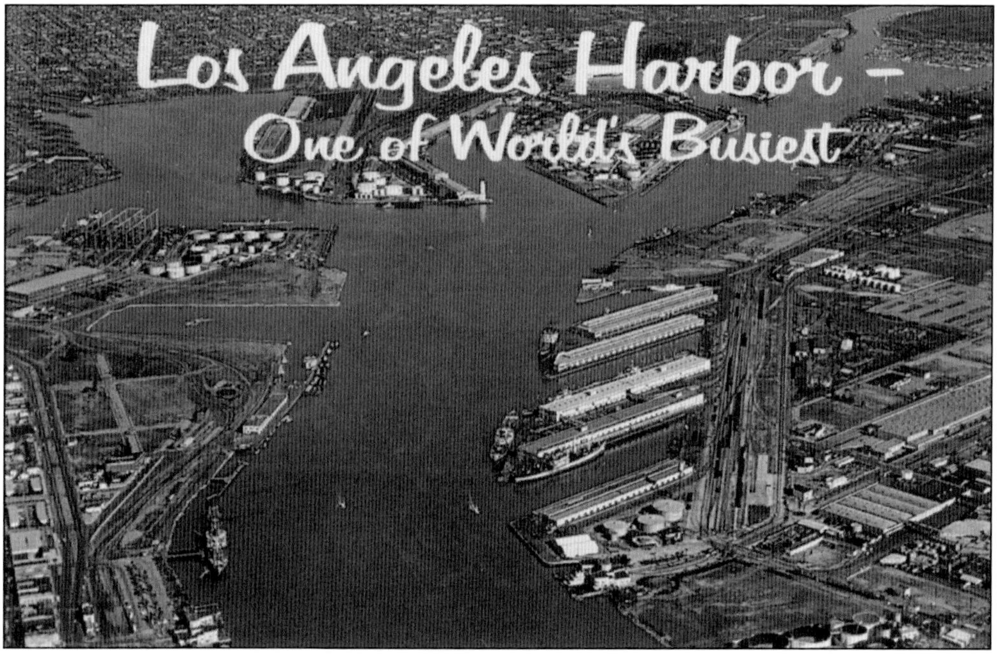

The Port of Los Angeles is depicted in this aerial view looking north, with San Pedro to the left and west and Harbor City and Wilmington in the upper portions. (Courtesy James Osborne; published by Mitock and Sons, Sherman Oaks, California.)

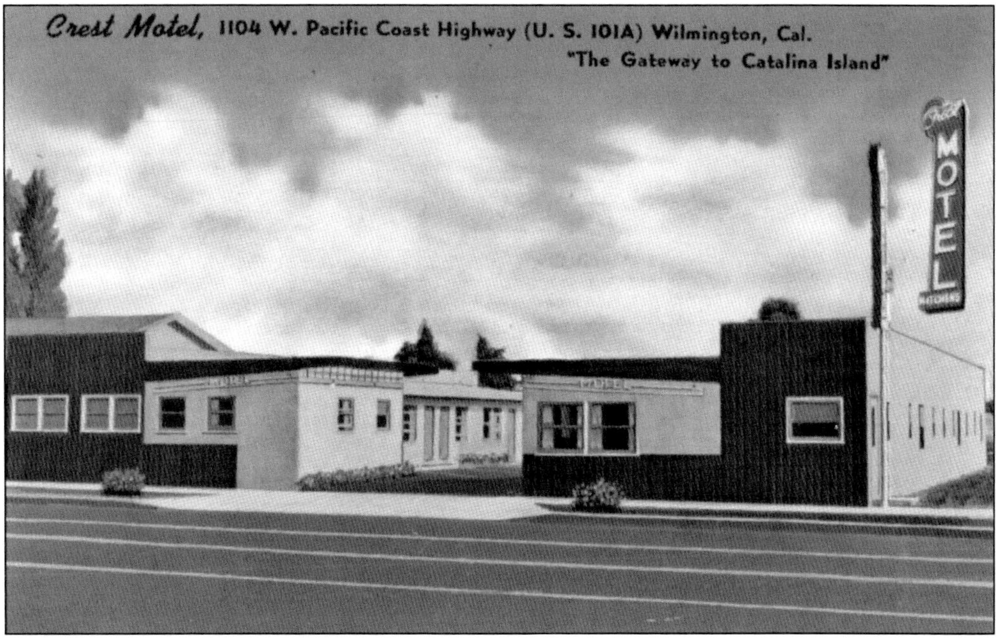

The Crest Motel, located at 1104 West Pacific Coast Highway in Wilmington, is depicted here. The back caption reads, "A new, nicely furnished, 14 unit, carpeted motel with full-tile showers, panel-ray heat and electric clocks. Youngstown kitchenettes, Beautyrests, radio, rooms with television." (Courtesy James Osborne; published by Colourpicture, Boston, Massachusetts.)

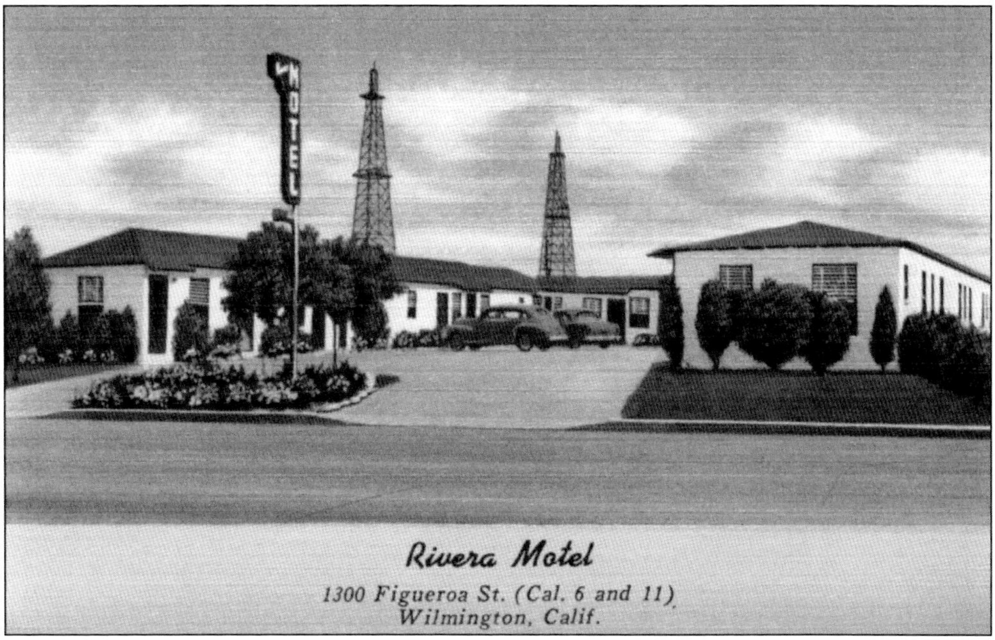

The Riviera Motel, located at 1300 Figueroa Street in Wilmington, is seen here. The digs were described on the flip side: "A new, fully modern 14 unit carpeted motel with or without kitchenettes. Radios. Close to good restaurants. At the Gateway to Santa Catalina and the Hawaiian Islands." (Courtesy James Osborne; published by Elmo M. Sellers, Los Angeles, California.)

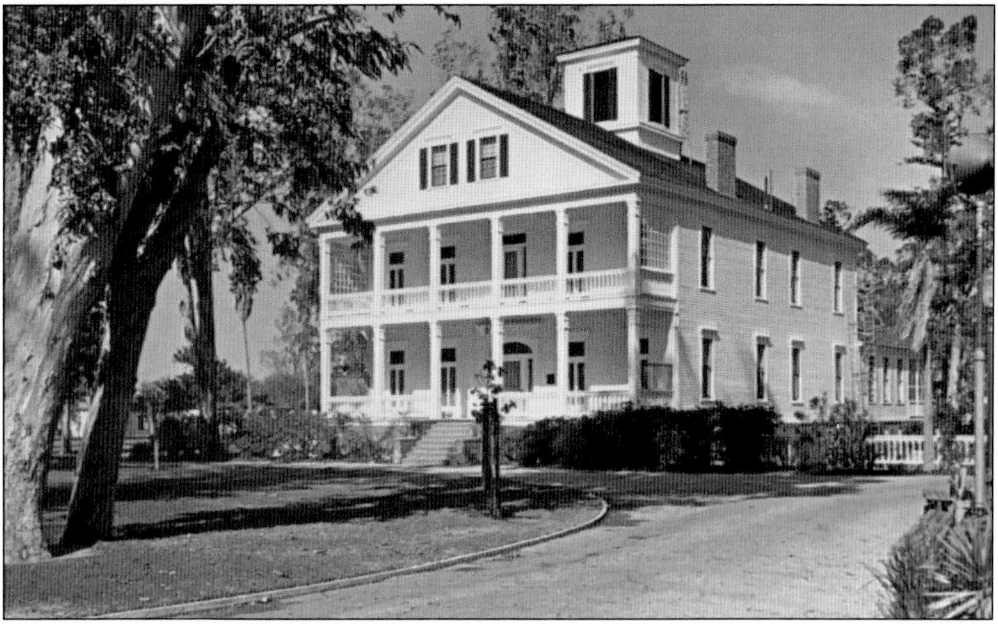

Seen here is the mansion built in 1864 by Wilmington founder Phineas Banning. The reverse-side caption of this 1960 card reads, "Built nearly one hundred years ago of lumber cut and seasoned in the east and carried to Southern California in sailing ships around the Horn, this fine early California home stands in Banning Park, a monument to Phineas Banning, who built it. It contains many memories of the early days." (Courtesy James Osborne; published by Golden West, Long Beach, California.)

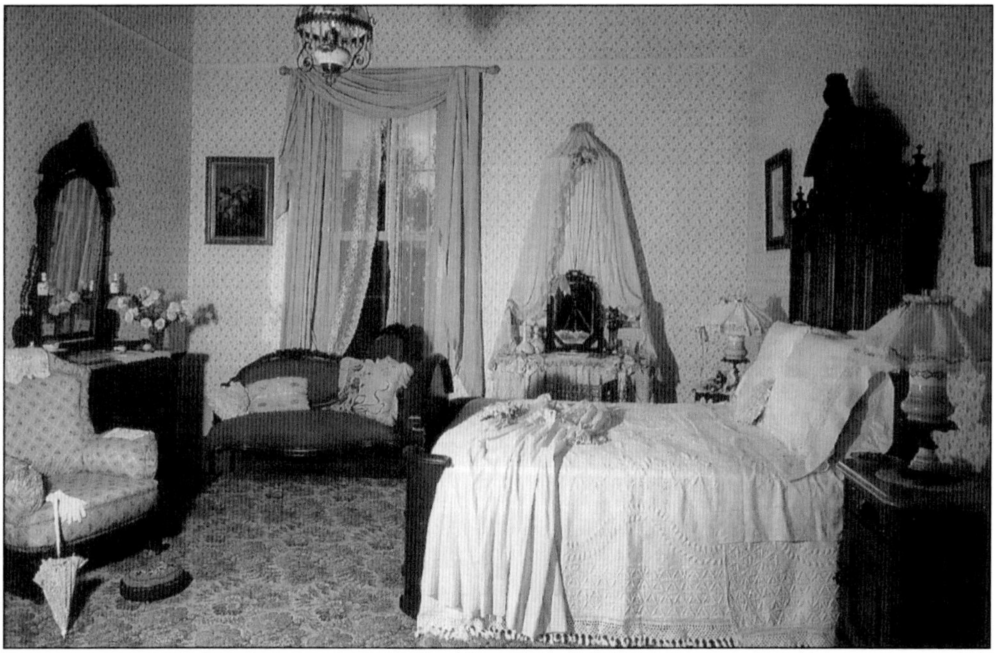

This postcard shows the bedroom in the Phineas Banning Museum, one of the harbor area's biggest tourism draws. It is furnished in the Eastlake style, which was popular in the Victorian era. (Courtesy Marilyn Ron; published by Kolor View Press, Hawthorne, California.)

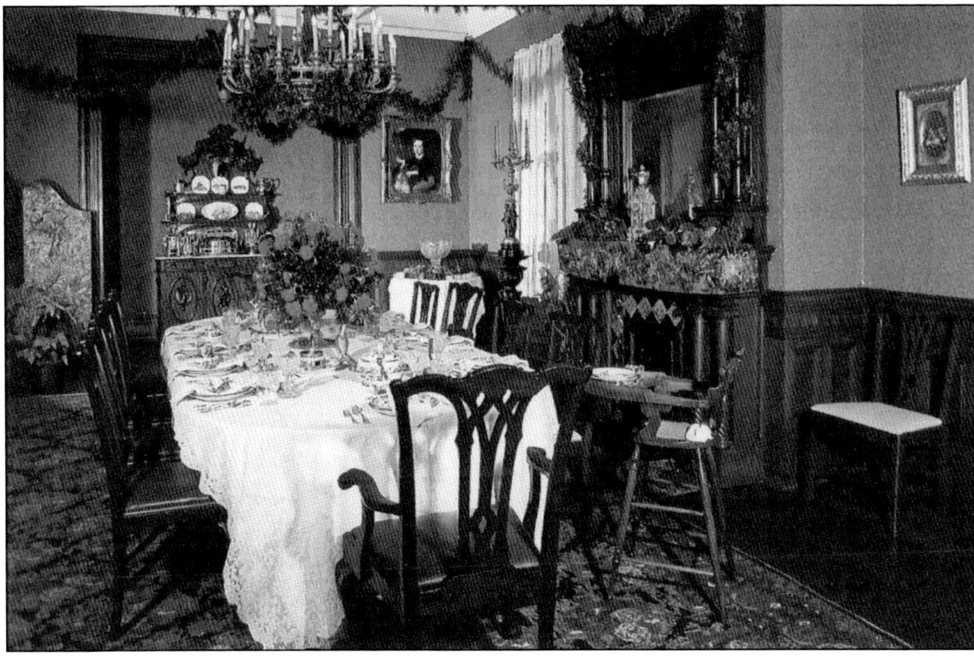

This postcard shows the dining room at the museum decorated for the Christmas holiday. Note the beautiful Victorian sideboard, fireplace, and baby's highchair. (Courtesy Marilyn Ron; published by Kolor View Press, Hawthorne, California.)

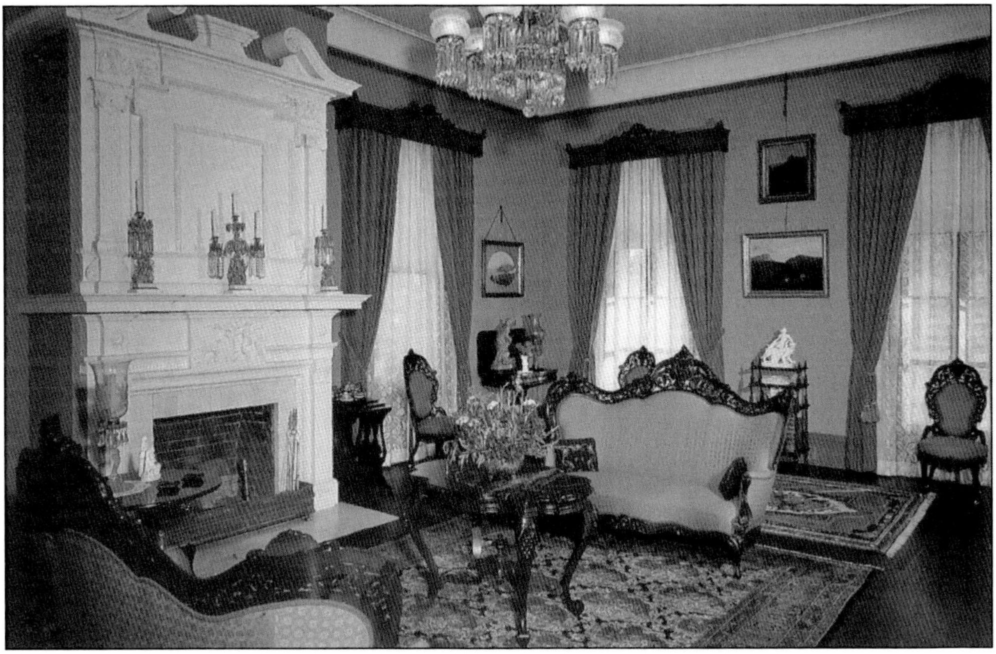

This postcard shows the tastefully appointed living room of the museum. Note the crystal chandelier and candlesticks on the fireplace mantle. (Courtesy Marilyn Ron; published by Kolor View Press, Hawthorne, California.)

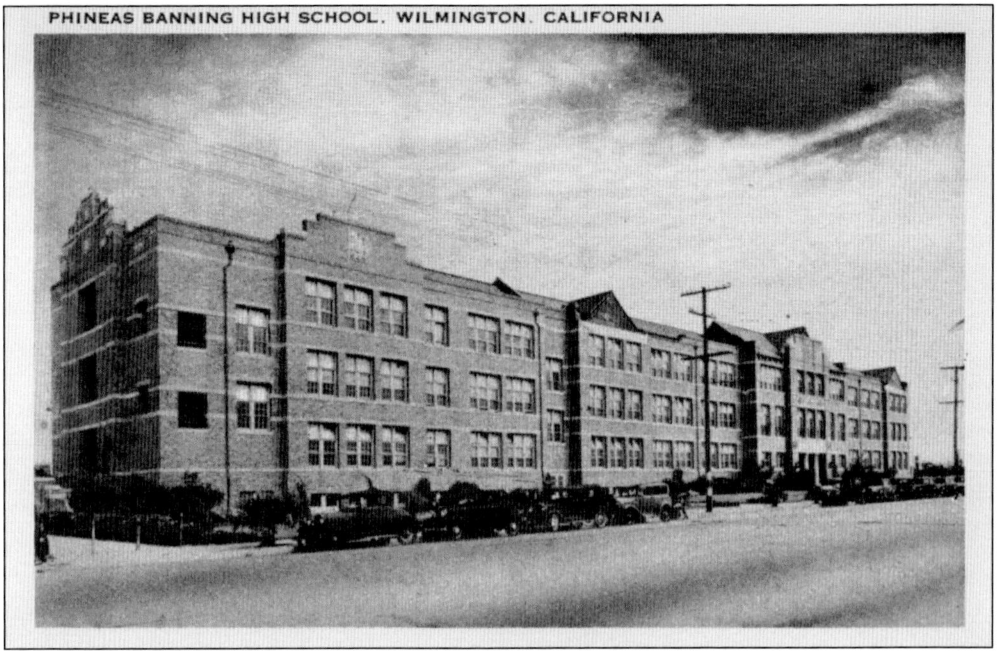

Phineas Banning High School was originally named Wilmington High School. It was renamed in honor of General Banning after a newer school building at Avalon Boulevard and Pacific Coast Highway opened in 1926. After the new building suffered damage in the 1971 Sylmar earthquake, it was demolished in 1973. (Courtesy James Osborne; published by M. Kashower Company, Los Angeles, California.)

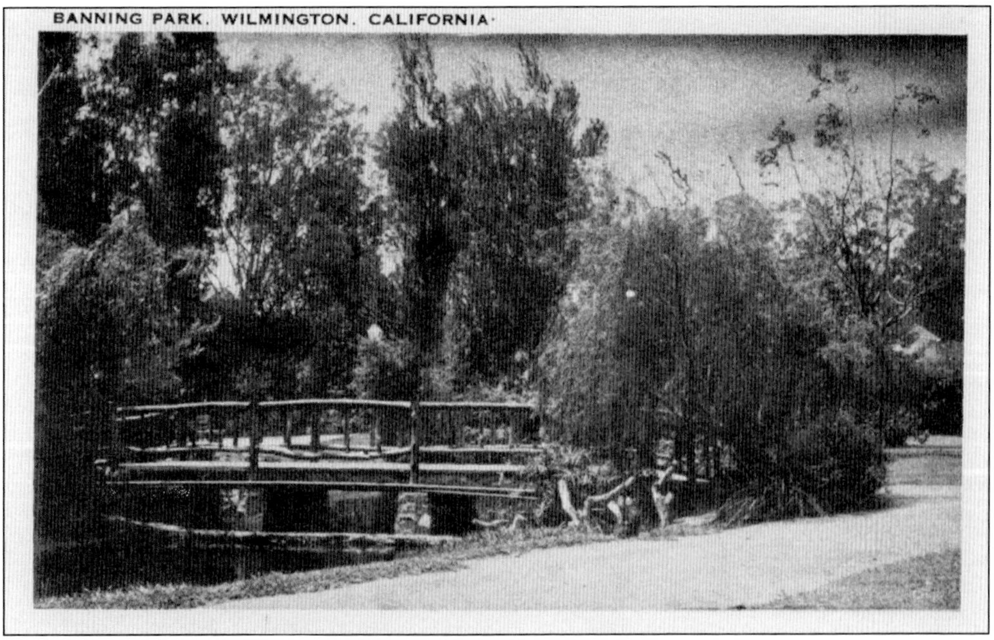

This postcard depicts a scene including the bridge in Banning Park. The Banning Mansion and Museum is an attraction in the park today. (Courtesy James Osborne; published by M. Kashower Company, Los Angeles, California.)

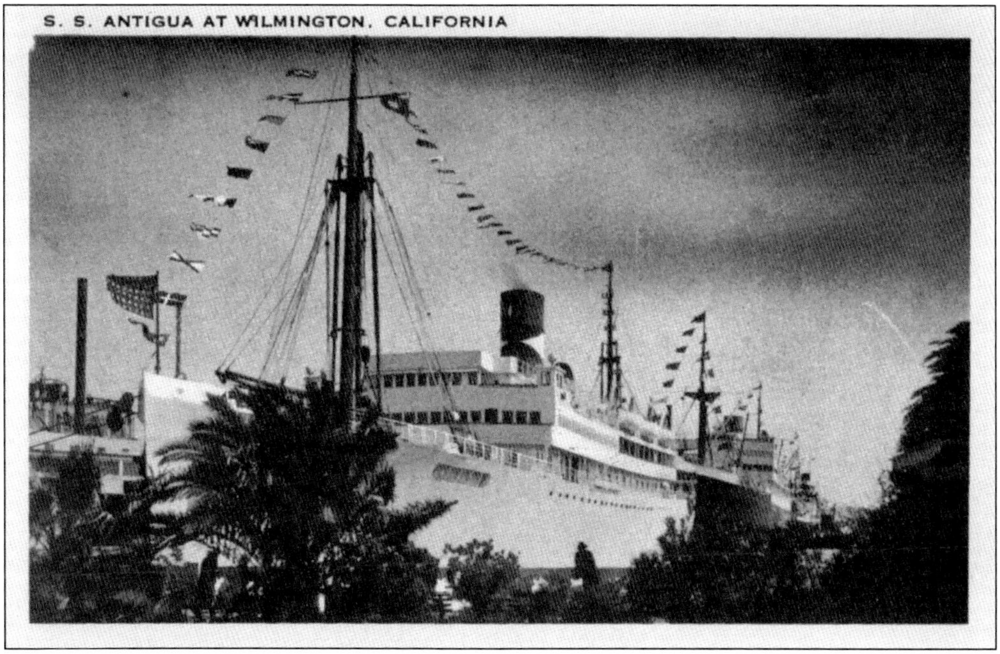

The SS *Antigua* is shown coming into the Wilmington Port. This ship was owned by the United Fruit Company and at one time was used to bring in scrap from Pearl Harbor in the Hawaiian Islands. (Courtesy James Osborne; published by M. Kashower Company, Los Angeles, California.)

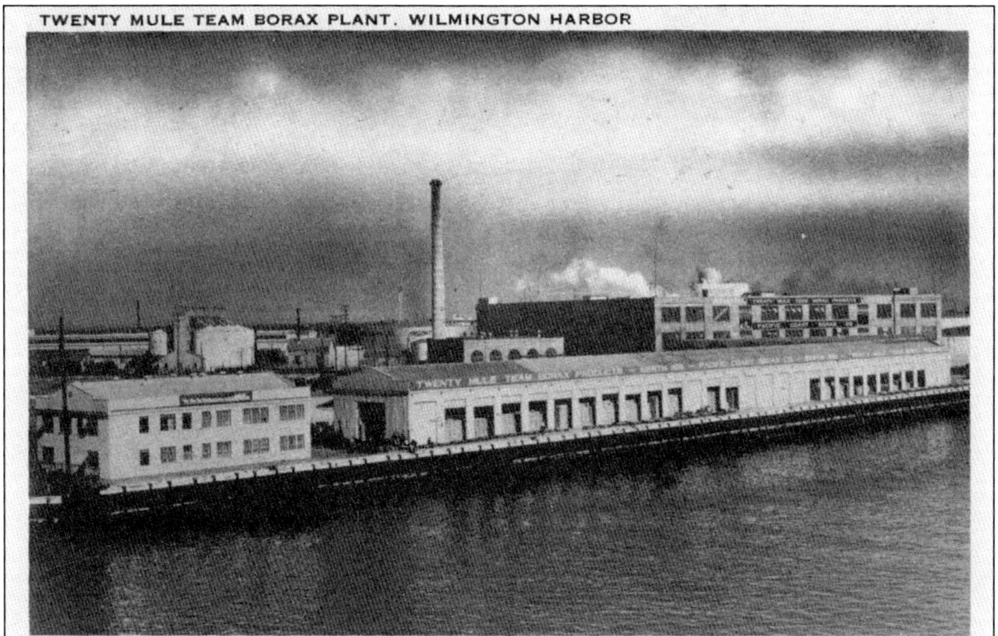

The Twenty Mule Team Borax Plant can be seen is this postcard, which is postmarked September 26, 1943. The handwritten message on the reverse reads, "Dear Bro. Received your letter. Will write soon. Your bro. P.F.C. Neaden, U.S. Army, 229th M.P. Company, Wilmington, Calif." (Courtesy James Osborne.)

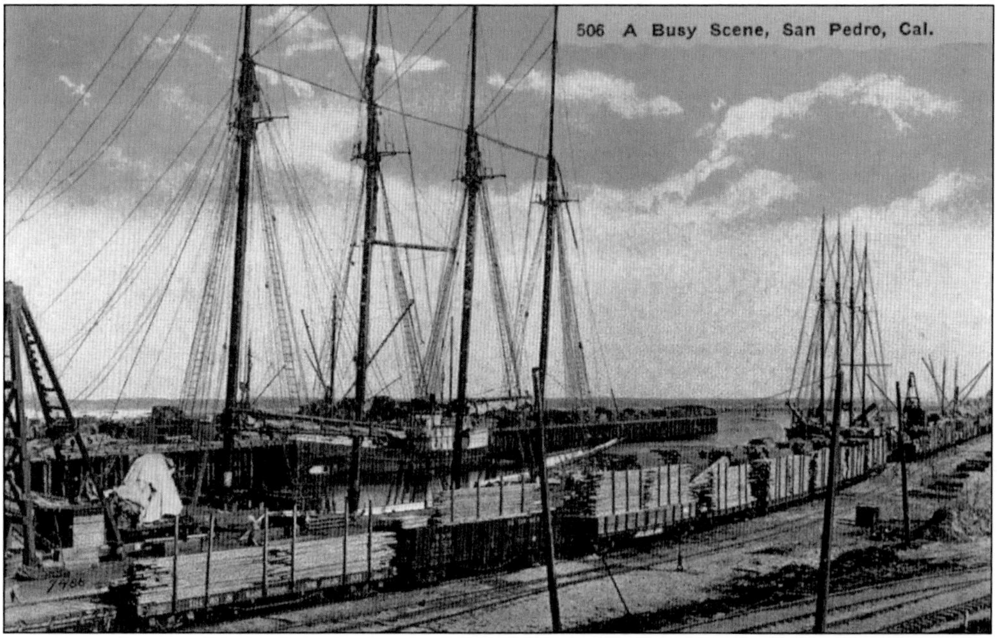

Labeled "A Busy Scene, San Pedro, Cal.," this postcard depicts the days when the Port of Los Angeles was a huge lumber delivery point. Aboard lumber ships, "random lengths" were the odds and ends, boards of various lengths stacked in around the large-cut planks. A longshoreman's term, it lives on in San Pedro's enduring community newspaper, ***Random Lengths***. (Courtesy James Osborne; published by M. Kashower Company, Los Angeles, California.)

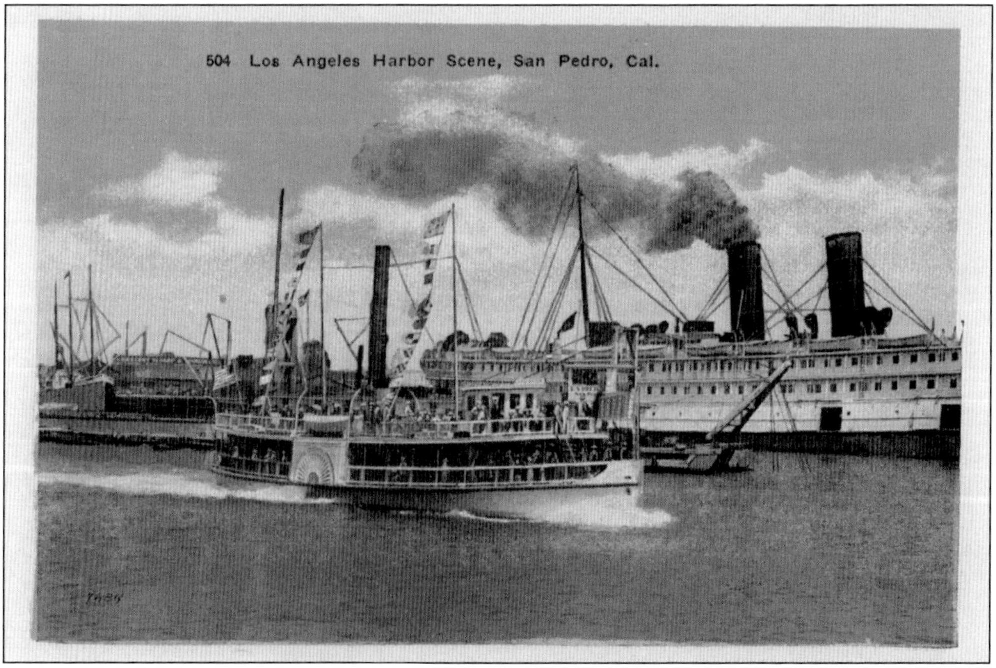

The size, shape, orientation, nationality, and seaworthiness of the various vessels that have called at the Port of Los Angeles have run the gamut for more than a century and a half. (Courtesy James Osborne; published by M. Kashower Company, Los Angeles, California.)

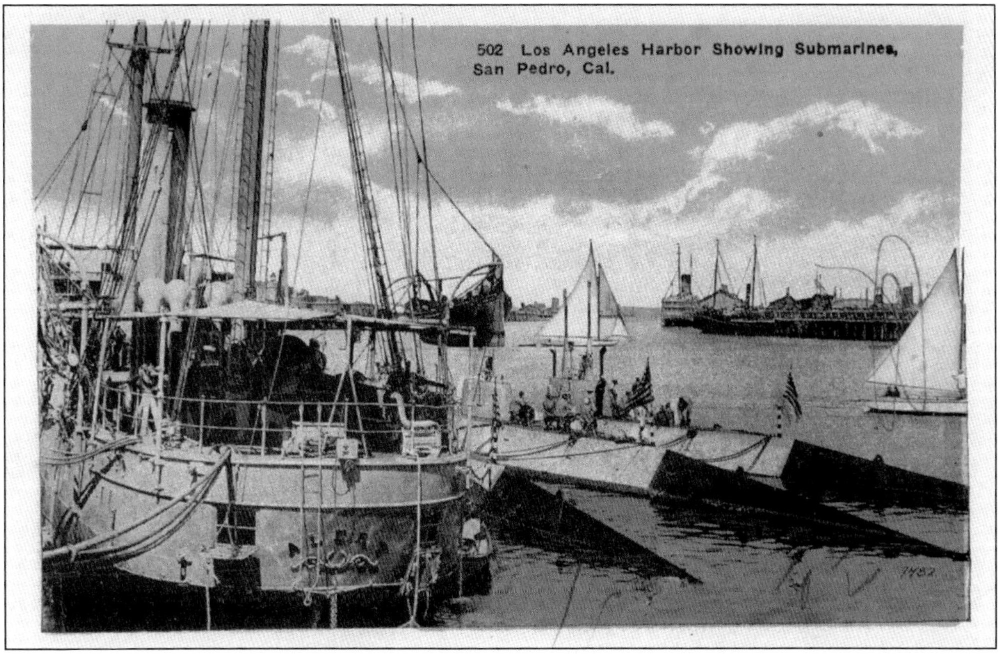

"Los Angeles Harbor Showing Submarines, San Pedro, Cal.," reads the label on this card. Los Angeles was the main Pacific Ocean port for the U.S. Navy prior to 1940, when it moved to the Hawaiian Islands for maneuvers and stayed there, moored at Pearl Harbor. (Courtesy James Osborne; published by M. Kashower Company, Los Angeles, California.)

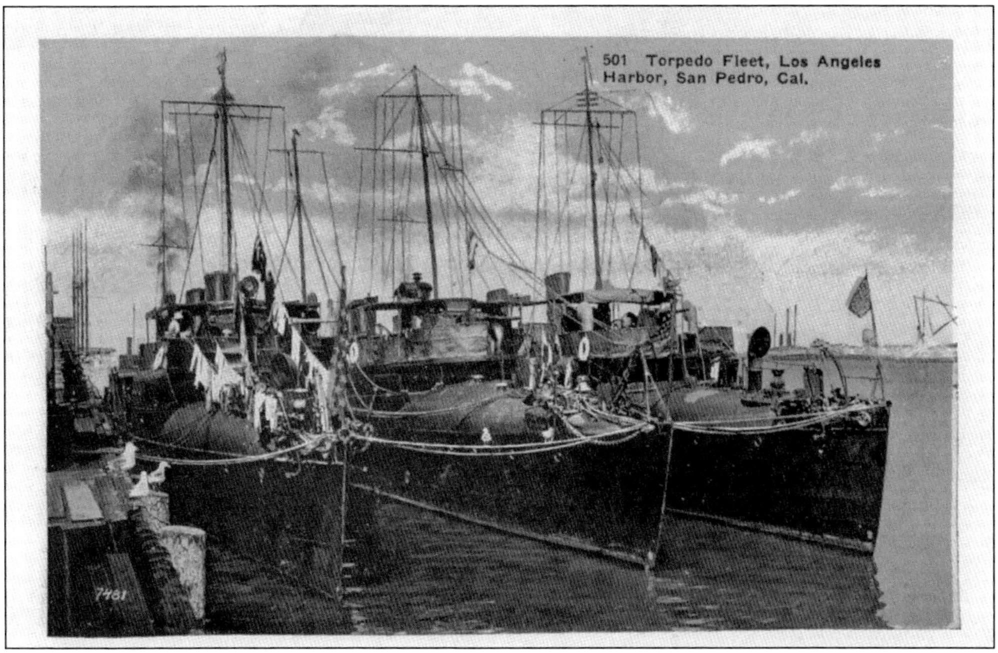

This postcard depicts the "Torpedo Fleet" at San Pedro. After the fleet was infamously bombed by the Japanese on December 7, 1941, to draw the United States into World War II, the navy reorganized into Pacific and Atlantic Fleets. The Pacific Fleet then stayed on at Pearl Harbor. (Courtesy James Osborne; published by M. Kashower Company, Los Angeles, California.)

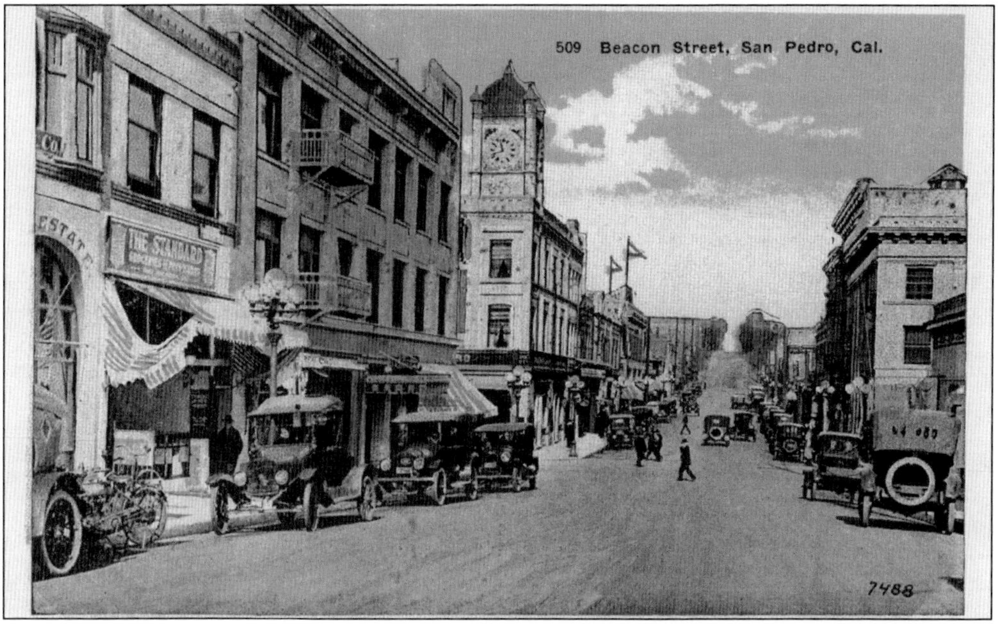

This is a view of Beacon Street in San Pedro. Today Beacon Street parallels Harbor Boulevard, which is located down the hill and just east along various berths, maritime facilities, and museums, including the SS *Lane Victory* and Los Angeles Maritime Museum. (Courtesy James Osborne; published by M. Kashower Company, Los Angeles, California.)

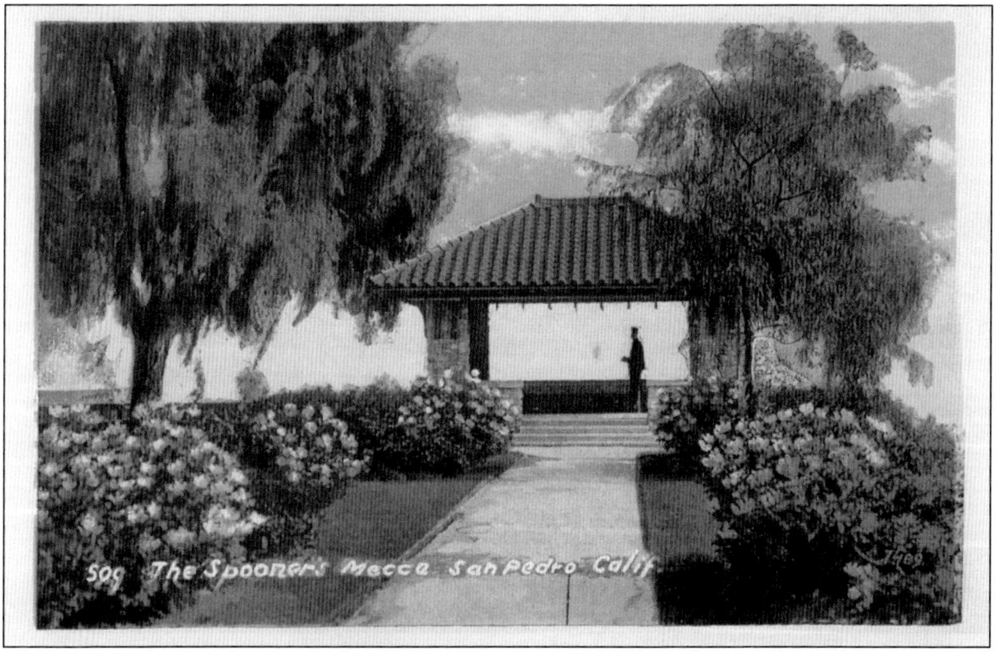

San Pedro is home to a great many idiosyncratic and historical locales and features, including Cabrillo State Beach, Cabrillo Marine Aquarium, Point Fermin Lighthouse, White's Point, World Cruise Center, Vincent Thomas Bridge, Angels Gate Cultural Center, Fort MacArthur Museum, Maritime Research Institute, Harry Bridges Institute, and others. (Courtesy James Osborne; published by M. Kashower Company, Los Angeles, California.)

Bibliography

Areyan, Alex Moreno. *Mexican Americans of Redondo Beach and Hermosa Beach*. Charleston, SC: Arcadia Publishing, 2007.
Barnard, Bonnie Mae, and Save Historic Old Torrance. *Old Torrance: Olmstead Districts*. Charleston, SC: Arcadia Publishing, 2005.
Dennis, Jan. *Manhattan Beach*. Charleston, SC: Arcadia Publishing, 2001.
Dixon, Walt, and Jerry Roberts. *Hawthorne*. Charleston, SC: Arcadia Publishing, 2005.
Gardena Heritage Committee. *Gardena*. Charleston, SC: Arcadia Publishing, 2006.
Gerber, Judith. *Farming in Torrance and the South Bay*. Charleston, SC: Arcadia Publishing, 2008.
Historical Commission of Redondo Beach. *Redondo Beach*. Charleston, SC: Arcadia Publishing, 2005.
McKinzie, Joe. *San Pedro*. Charleston, SC: Arcadia Publishing, 2007.
———. *San Pedro Bay*. Charleston, SC: Arcadia Publishing, 2005.
Miller, Chris, Jerry Roberts, and the Hermosa Beach Historical Society. *Hermosa Beach*. Charleston, SC: Arcadia Publishing, 2005.
———. *Hermosa Beach*. Charleston, SC: Arcadia Publishing, 2007.
Osborne, James. *Lawndale*. Charleston, SC: Arcadia Publishing, 2005.
Tino-Sandoval, Cindy. *Carson*. Charleston, SC: Arcadia Publishing, 2006.
Schaadt, Mike, Ed Mastro, and Cabrillo Marine Aquarium. *San Pedro's Cabrillo Beach*. Charleston, SC: Arcadia Publishing, 2008.
Wilmington Historical Society. *Wilmington*. Charleston, SC: Arcadia Publishing, 2008.